The Socialist Debate

The Socialist Debate

BEYOND RED AND GREEN

Bogdan Denitch

Introduction by
Michael Harrington

London · Winchester, Mass.

First published by Pluto Press
345 Archway Road, London N6 5AA
and 8 Winchester Place, Winchester
MA 01890, USA

British Library Cataloguing in Publication Data

Denitch, Bogdan
The socialist debate: beyond red and green
1. Socialism
I. Title
335

ISBN 0–7453–0381–1

Library of Congress Cataloging-in-Publication Data

Denitch, Bogdan Denis.
The socialist debate: beyond red and green

Includes bibliographical references.
1. Communism 2. Socialism. 3. Capitalism.
I. Title
HX44.D415 1990 335.43'09'048 89–8751
ISBN 0–7453–0381–1

Typesetting by Opus, Oxford
Printed and bound by Billing and Sons Ltd, Worcester

Contents

Preface and Acknowledgements

This book has been influenced by the comments, criticisms and suggestions from a number of friends, colleagues and comrades who read the manuscript in whole or in part. The manuscript was turned in to be published in April 1989. It is important to date a book which deals with contemporary political developments if for no other reason than to make clear what are archaisms and what are plain mistakes in analysis or prediction. Most of the first chapter on the crisis of socialism has appeared in *Nase Teme*, a political journal published in Zagreb. Versions of Chapter 3 on the crisis of Yugoslav socialismhave appeared in *Dissent*, Winter 1989, and *Praxis International*, Spring–Summer 1989.

This is not a collection of essays written over time but an attempt to reach an overall assessment of the crisis and prospects of socialism in our time. Further, as I make explicitly clear from the first chapter on, this book does not pretend to be a dispassionate academic work, 'from the outside'. I have written it as an attempt to work out my own thinking about the prospects of a movement and a set of ideas which have been central to my own life since I arrived in North America at the age of 17 in 1946. Since that time I have been an active member of what there was, at that time, of a democratic socialist movement and milieu in the United States, first as a student and youth leader, later as a full-timer and a trade union activist and much later, from the late 1960s on, as an organized socialist academic and publicist. In that sense I am an exception to Russell Jacoby's generalizations in his *The Last Intellectuals*. That is, my work is not directed to specialized academic audiences but rather to an educated and political public. This is not because of any special virtues of my own but because I have remained an active participant in a socialist organization, the *Democratic Socialists of America* (DSA) and a socialist institution, the journal *Dissent*. The book therefore avoids the magisterial and academic we, or the impersonal, and speaks in the first person singular. The reason for this apparent digression is to explain that the first and most obvious acknowledgement for this book is to the organized democratic socialist milieu in the US.

The second collective acknowledgement must be to two international conferences which have been around for enough time to have become institutions in their own right. The annual conference in Cavtat, Yugoslavia, which brings together thinkers, publicists and intellectuals from the world socialist and communist movements and journals to a remarkable open forum, and the Socialist Scholars Conference, which takes place at my City University of New York, have both been invaluable as a source of ideas, arguments and above all questions without which this book could not have been written.

Individuals who have helped with criticism, polemic, suggestion and comments are many but a few have to be mentioned as a matter of intellectual honesty as well as gratitude. My good friend Val Moghadam, at that time at New York University, read the early drafts, particularly of the first chapter and the chapters on real socialism, Yugoslavia and above all the chapter on the Third World. I have clearly benefited from her trenchant criticism. Frances Fox Piven, a valued comrade and colleague from the City University, read the first draft and made many detailed and valuable criticisms and suggestions, as did Arthur Lipow from Birkbeck College and my old friends and comrades, Ellen Willis and Stanley Aronowitz, who all had sharp and pointed criticisms and suggestions to make. Danmir Grubisa, the Director of the Yugoslav Cultural Center in New York, was also an early reader and critic of this book. It was he who recommended it for publication in Yugoslavia. I should also acknowledge the criticisms and suggestions of my younger colleagues and assistants, particularly John Mason, Kimberly Adams and Neil McLaughlin. Typically I accepted some criticisms fully, and yet others influenced the reformulation of some of my views. After all, the subject matter of this book bears directly on contemporary, passion-invoking controversies on the broad contemporary intellectual left. My colleagues, comrades and I by no means agree on those questions of controversy, but what I believe we do agree on is that this controversy is indispensable if there is to be any kind of revival of any socialist movement worth its name.

Lastly I should acknowledge the support of the City University of New York. Both the Queens College and the Graduate School Departments of Sociology have been supportive and helpful. A generous grant from the CUNY-PSC Foundation helped with some of the research expenses, particularly for Chapters 5, 6 and 9. Naturally the persons and institutions whose help is acknowledged here bear no responsibility whatsoever for my views and errors. Those remain my very own.

Bogdan Denitch
New York, November 1989

Introduction

MICHAEL HARRINGTON

At first glance, the central thesis and authorship of this important new book by Bogdan Denitch seem preposterous. Can it be seriously argued that democratic socialism, which has suffered nothing but disappointments and defeat in or out of power during the past decade and a half in Europe, is the wave of the future? And isn't it strange that this far-fetched argument should be made by an American – albeit a Yugoslav American – which is to say a citizen of the country of pre-eminent socialist failure?

After all, the shrewd British analyst, Peter Jenkins, was obviously addressing reality when he wrote, in *Mrs Thatcher's Revolution: The End of the Socialist Era*, that already in the 1970s,

> The Socialist Age was coming to an end. What was happening in Britain was part of a world-wide phenomenon: everywhere in the industrialised democratic world the old manual working class was in decline, trade union membership was falling, old class loyalties were crumbling . . . In part democratic socialism was the victim of its own suggestion. The welfare societies it had helped to build had opened other and less-collectivist avenues of advance. Affluence had eaten into old class loyalties. Education had provided ladders of escape from the working class.[1]

This obituary for socialism is utterly compelling if, *and only if*, one identifies welfare-state capitalism under social democratic administration as 'socialism', something that was often and thoughtlessly done by socialists in their heyday during the Great Prosperity after the Second World War. But if one understands that that accomplishment – and it was very real, transforming the conditions of life of tens of millions of working people – was a *stage* in the history of the socialist movement, then the sweep of Jenkins' critique loses much of its force. Denitch, the reader will discover, is utterly aware of the negatives which led to the crisis of the welfare state and of some of the social-democratic illusions to which it gave rise.

But, and this is one of the singular merits of this book, he is also conscious of *counter-tendencies*, of new socialist possibilities opened up by the very changes in class structure which Jenkins cites as causes of the death of socialism itself. The rise of a 'Green' political tendency – taken in the broadest sense of the term as the social movements led by college-educated feminists, anti-racists, ecologists, peace and development advocates – was often counterposed to the politics of the traditionally socialist, blue-collar working class of Europe. In West Germany that took the form of an actual political party which took votes away from the social-democrats; in Britain and other countries, including the United States, it was a mood which split the historical left along new lines. But, Denitch argues, shrewdly I think, this very same development now holds out the possibility of a new socialism.

Still, the second question remains: Why listen to an American, to an inhabitant of the only advanced western society *without* a mass socialist movement, on such issues?

Part of the answer has to do with a paradox identified by Marx and Engels in the first 'Marxist' work ever published, *The German Ideology*.[2] The English, they argued, were the most economically advanced of the Europeans, the French were the political vanguard, and the Germans, from the most backward of the major Continental societies – not even a unified nation in the 1840s when Marx and Engels were writing, much less a capitalistist nation – were in some ways the most developed theorists. One reason was that they had the time to develop the intellectual consequences of what the French and British were doing in fact. Kant, living a sedentary life in sleepy Königsberg, developed the German theory of the French Revolution and did it with a *philosophical* brilliance no French revolutionary could match.

In part – but only in part – the American socialists have been sentenced to a similar vantage point. Without any present, or foreseeable, possibilities of actually exercising political power, they have had a chance to sharpen their theoretical insights to a degree that is denied their more activist comrades in Europe. This has resulted in whole libraries of Talmudic exegesis by 'armchair socialists' in the United States, a country with more Marxist books than politically active Marxists; it also and occasionally leads to works of genuine value, to a realism imposed upon those whose national fate does not permit too many illusions about the inevitable and rosy future of socialism.

But that is only a part-truth. If the United States has been backward in terms of its class movements and economic programs – the welfarism of Bismarck in the 1880s, and of Lloyd George in the first decade of this century, was only attained in the US by Roosevelt in the 1930s – it has often been *avant-garde* on social and cultural issues. The 'new left' of the 1960s was not invented in the United States – the term, after all, was imported from France and the movement had roots in the Aldermaston peace marches in England and the Japanese student organization, Zenguarkuren – but there is no doubt that its American variant seized the imagination of politically conscious youth in many countries. 'Berkeley' – where Denitch spent part of the 1960s – became an international symbol and incitement to action.

More broadly, as Gertrude Stein once remarked somewhere, Americans have lived in the future longer than anyone else (that trend might just be coming to an end; it is too early to say). The social movements of the 1960s in this country – against the war in Vietnam, for civil rights, ecology and women's rights – were massive and often well in advance of their European counterparts. Indeed, the more traditional left in France used to refer, somewhat contemptuously, to 'La Gauche Americaine' as being a left defined primarily by social, rather than economic, issues. And since, as Denitch persuasively argues in this book, the coming together of the 'Red' and 'Green' currents of the left is one of the critical characteristics of the new socialism, this American experience is particularly relevant to the future of the socialist ideal.

But this is enough of socialist and American defensiveness. What are some of the positive trends analysed in this book which justify Denitch's optimism?

First, I can testify from personal experience that the shift in religious attitudes toward socialism – and of the Catholic attitude in particular – is of enormous political importance. When Denitch and I first met in 1951, I was a young militant in the Catholic worker movement of Dorothy Day involved in a tiny section opposed to the Korean War. Denitch was a secular socialist who nevertheless reached out to recruit me into the socialist party. At that time of McCarthyism and the dominance of a right-wing cardinal, Francis Spellman, the Catholic left was a marginalized irrelevance. We lived primarily on the books and reports of our European counterparts, above all in France and we did not even dream of Pope John XXIII or of the Second Vatican Council.

But, *mirabile dictu*, John became Pope, convened the Council and – I suspect to the later sorrow of Pope John Paul II – irreversibly changed the Church, a process which had implications, via the growing ecumenical movement, for Protestants and Jews as well as Catholics. Some years later, in the mid-1970s, when the Spanish socialist leader (and later Prime Minister) Felipe Gonzalez made his first visit to the United States, he met with a small group of socialists at the Graduate Center of the City University of New York. What, he was asked, is the greatest change that has taken place in Spain since the Civil War? He answered without hesitation that it was the fact that the immemorial *Kulturkampf* between the Catholics and the secularists had come to an end, that even priests and nuns could now work for the Spanish socialist workers party.

There have been counter-trends since then, not the least John Paul II's attack on clerical activism and liberation theology, but the basic shift from the anti-socialist (and anti-democratic) Catholicism of Pio Nono to the political ecumenicism of John XXIII persists and Denitch is right to see this trend, and the associated tendencies in other religions, as a genuinely new factor in the political equation.

In another area, the internationalization of the world economy through multi-national corporations, one does not have to speculate on the future impact upon the socialists because there is a present effect at work. As early as 1976, when Willy Brandt became President of the Socialist International, it had become clear to the socialists that their only hope of continued relevance was to break out of the white, European ghetto in which they were mainly confined (with exceptions in Australia, Canada, New Zealand, Israel and Japan). In the years since then the International has become, for the first time in history, an organization with a majority of non-European affiliates, including about thirty parties in Latin America and the Caribbean. At the same time, Brandt, the late Olof Palme and Michael Manley developed an international economic program for helping to solve the problems of *both* north and south through a global reflation initiated by the leftist parties of the north.

In a related development, the approach of the 1992 deadline for the closer integration of the European Economic Community has forced both the socialist parties and the trade unions of every ideological stripe to join in work. There have been common socialist manifestos in the European elections and trade union cooperation against national lines. In the debates and struggles which will counterpose a Europe of the corporations against a social Europe these tendencies will, as Denitch rightly argues, be intensified. Thus the international dimension, both as it relates to the Third World and European unification, is an extremely dynamic factor in the perspective for a new socialism.

So is the coming together of the Reds and Greens, a possibility which I have already noted. Actually, recent research has emphasized the degree to which feminism and a multi-class republicanism played a major role in the very origins of the socialist movement.[3] The problem in more recent times has been that the college-educated activists of the women's and environmentalist movements have sometimes ignored the needs of far-from-affluent male workers, or of workers in hazardous factories, which has been reciprocated by a hostility on part of the blue-collar militants to the very important claims of feminists, ecologists and minorities. But, as Denitch stresses, there are signs that both sides may be learning that, if they continue to fight one another, that will simply guarantee the unchallenged dominance of the corporations.

In another international area, Soviet *glasnost* and *perestroika* and their impact upon Eastern Europe and the world Communist movement, I will not even try to summarize Denitch's analysis, in part because his knowledge and expertise in this area is so clearly superior to my own. Clearly, though, he establishes the tremendous importance of these developments for the future of socialism, the way in which they represent, not simply an opening in the societies immediately concerned, but a major shift in ideological structures which were first created in the aftermath of the October revolution. Ironically, the first impact of this trend may well be to discredit socialism – by identifying it with the Soviet and other Communist failures and repression – but in the long run it means the possibility of a much more united international democratic socialist movement.

Finally, Denitch rightly stresses the importance of a certain recovery of the utopian vision which is partly a reaction to the excessive pragmatism of the years of Keynesian social-democracy and partly a consequence of the influence of the social movements. If one defines utopia, not as No Place (from the Greek root, *a-topos*), but as the Good Place (*eu-topos*), then its basic meaning, as Martin Buber rightly defined it, is the triumph of the society over the state.[4] That was unquestionably a central goal of the original, modern socialist movement and it was very much a part of the value system of the mature Karl Marx. As Marx wrote in *The Critique of the Gotha Program* (1875), 'Freedom is the transformation of the state from an organ which dominates society into an organ subordinate to society . . .'[5]

It was the technological development of the mass production factory – and of the transformation of entrepreneurial capitalism into corporate, managed and imperial capitalism – which convinced the socialists that their dreams of cooperatives and the direct rule of the associated producers had to be given up. It was then, in the Erfurt Program of the German social-democracy in 1891, that the equation of socialism and statist nationalization was made. But now, the new technology of computers and robots no longer needs huge plants. It is much more compatible with a small-scale production and it even ideally requires trained and conscious workers rather than human automatons. Which is to say, the utopian possibility of economic and industrial democracy, of a society ruled from below, has become much more of a practical possibility in recent years.

Bogdan Denitch is not an isolated intellectual analysing these developments from the quiet of his study. He is an engaged and political intellectual, a part of the rethinking of the socialist idea that is taking place in the German social-democratic debates over a new basic program, in the Swedish experimentation with wage-earner funds, in the new stirrings in Eastern Europe. His book is an academic achievement of great merit – but even more to the point, it is a contribution to a discussion in a movement which is likely to play a major role in the transformations of the next half century. It is, in short, a political as well as an intellectual event.

Notes

1. *Mrs Thatcher's Revolution: The Ending of the Socialist Era* (Cambridge, Mass.: Harvard University Press, 1988), p.335.
2. *Marx-Engels Werke* (Berlin: Dietz Verlag, 1957–67), vol. III, passim.
3. See, for instance, George Lichtheim, *The Origins of Socialism* (New York: Frederick Praeger, 1969) on Flora Tristan, and *A Short History of Socialism* (New York: Frederick Praeger, 1961) on Saint-Simonian feminism; Barbara Taylor, *Eve and the New Jerusalem: Socialism and Feminism in the Nineteenth Century* (New York: Pantheon Books, 1983) on the Owenite views on marriage as well as E.P. Thompson's description of the Owenites in *The Making of the English Working Class* (New York: Vintage Books, 1963); and *The Utopian Vision of Charles Fourier*, Jonathan Beecher and Richard Bienvenu (eds) (London: Jonathan Cape, 1971).
4. *Paths in Utopia* (Boston: Beacon Press, 1958), p.80.
5. *MEW*, vol. XIX, p.27.

Chapter 1

The Roots of the Crisis

Socialism, as an idea, as a movement and as a practical program is said to be in a crisis.[1] This crisis is hailed or deplored depending on the point of view of the person involved but there is little argument that something of profound importance is happening to what has been the most important secular faith and movement of our century. There are many aspects of the political malaise which pass under the name of the crisis of socialism today. For one thing it is not at all clear that it is socialism which is in a more fundamental crisis than are either contemporary liberalism or conservativism. What is clear is that the major shifts in the societies and economies of the advanced industrial countries, combined with the prolonged stagnation since the oil shock of the early 1970s, have fundamentally shaken both the post-Second World War optimism about the capacity for economic management of national economies and the relative social consensus which characterized the years of stable growth between 1950 and the mid-1970s.

Above all this is a crisis of the post-Second World War class compromises and welfare state settlements and a crisis of faith in the continued possibility of Keynesian economic management of advanced capitalist industrial societies, not necessarily the crisis of socialism and socialist movements. It is more accurate to talk of the crisis of a socially liberal capitalism or even, and more accurately, a crisis of the neo-corporatism which seemed to be the all but invincible wave of the future during the 1960s and 1970s. For that matter the whole Atlanticist Cold War consensus is going through a profound and possibly terminal crisis today; so is the decades-long faith in the efficacy or the exportability of the Soviet and state 'socialist' models of political and economic development.

Despite all these valid caveats, however, it would be disingenuous to try to ignore the obvious crisis of morale and programmatic disorientation within most, if not all, of the mass democratic socialist and social-democratic parties of the advanced industrial world. In this we must include the Euro-Communist parties such as those in Italy, Britain and Sweden.

Further, and unfortunately, a crisis of confidence of a movement committed to a fundamental change of the *status quo* is evidently a more serious problem than similar crises for those who support the existing social, economic and political order. After all, the most elementary of the claims of the defenders of the *status quo* is that basic change, as such, is dangerous, undesirable, or quite simply impossible. On the other hand, historically the most fundamental of the claims by the left in general, and therefore also of the socialists, has been that it is possible for ordinary men and women to make effective transformation of the societies they live in and to make those changes democratically. That it is possible, in other words, in the old Marxist and somewhat woolly language of the socialist movement, for the objects of history to become its subjects. It is this belief, rather than belief in state or social ownership of the means of production, or confidence in the ability to plan national economies, or achieve high industrial growth rates, which is fundamental to even the possibility of a democratic socialism.

It is that belief in the *possibility of democratic and equalitarian social economic and political transformation* which is today under systematic attack not only by the neo-conservatives but also, although in a very different way, by the various brands of post-modernists, academic 'armchair' ultra-leftists and post-structuralists. It is also that idea which has been repeatedly violated or postponed into the ever receding future by the state socialist and Third World socialist countries and ruling parties. With less violence this same ideal was frittered away and pushed into the far distant and vague future by the socialist and social-democratic governments of the advanced capitalist democracies.

However, one should immediately add here that it is also, and perhaps even more fundamentally, the moral and ideological dimension of the present demoralization which is so difficult to confront within the socialist parties and movements. Given the mistakes, crimes and horrors committed in the name of socialism and defended with the vocabulary of Marxism and socialism, democratic socialists have lost or *should have lost* their innocence. One now has to specify what previously did not have to be specified, what could be taken for granted can no longer with any confidence be taken for granted.[2]

A Central Problem – Socialism, 'Socialism' or Socialisms

The socialism one is trying to imagine here is not the one which has produced the Gulags, or the cold impersonal and manipulative bureaucracies, or the ruthless social engineers like Pol Pot or the late Mao or even the socialism of those who had voted to maintain the French military presence in Algeria or for that matter endlessly continued Israeli presence in the occupied territories. Nor is it the socialism of the decent but tired social-democratic politicians. Nor is it, on the other hand, the socialism of the instant revolutionaries who were prepared to give, as one of them put it to me, three or even four years to the working class, and have been let down, disappointed by that class's failure to produce a revolution.

Writing a book on contemporary socialism, one is in a continual dilemma of how to escape the tyranny of inverted commas which Foucault tried to deal with. That is, one is in a permanently tense state about the use of the very word socialist. Is it socialism when we speak of the unsullied ideal and goal and 'socialism' usually modified by an adjective when we speak about the currently existing political systems and parties calling themselves by that name? Is it all or only some of the parties and movements and governments which require the inverted commas and modifying adjective? How is one to justify the use of a term if one insists that the vast majority of those using that term have no right to it? But the same can be said for democracy and Christianity and yet we do not use either modifiers or inverted commas as a rule.

Marx and Engels tried to deal with this issue in their time by calling their manifesto the *Communist Manifesto* to differentiate themselves from the various other existing and in many cases better-known strands of socialism. I and those who have similar views use the term socialist almost always in the modified form of *democratic* socialist. That is of course begging the question since, on one hand, I believe that there cannot be an undemocratic form of socialism, that would be an oxymoron, i.e. a term which is a contradiction in itself. This is because I belong to that intellectual tradition which identifies socialism with the extension of democracy from the political into the economic and social fields. I am not willing to accept the present state 'socialist' politocracies,[3] even with all the present reforms, as being either in any legitimate line of descent from the Marxist tradition, or even, for that matter, from the Bolshevik revolution led by Lenin and Trotsky.

Then that raises a whole host of additional issues which can only be lightly hinted at. For example, I do consider the Bolshevik revolution to have been a part, a flawed part, flawed by desperate hope and subjectivism, but still a part, of the mainline tradition of world socialism. For all its flaws, that revolution, in the words of Rosa Luxemburg, herself an unflinching democrat and revolutionary socialist, saved the honour of the international workers' movement which had been sullied by the fact that most of the mass socialist parties had tamely backed their own governments in entering the First World War. Whatever criticism one has of the early years of Soviet rule it seems to me reasonably clear that the second Russian revolution or counter-revolution launched by Stalin in 1929/30 represented a fundamental departure from the common socialist and Marxist tradition and culture to which the Bolsheviks belonged. That tradition was pluralistic and contentious and though the Bolsheviks represented a sharply embattled confrontational faction on the radical fringes of the movement, they were still flesh of the flesh of the historical socialist movement and operated within its basic paradigms. Stalin and his heirs, at least to me, represent the gravediggers of that tradition.

But cannot this just as reasonably be claimed for the millions who joined the Communist movements, above all in underdeveloped countries, to fight for the same ideals and goals of socialism which the movement had historically fought for? I believe that the answer is no, it cannot, since these people do not wield state power nor is it at all clear what they would do if they gained and held that power independently. They are mistaken in their understanding of the history of the workers' movement and the Soviet experience, perhaps doomed to be betrayed by the parties and movements they give their allegiance to, but comrades of what there is of an international socialist movement nevertheless. The political reforms now taking place in the Soviet Union, from top down, under the leadership of the Party Secretary Gorbachev may well, and this would be the most optimistic scenario, lead to a healing of the historical rupture between the two branches of the world movement using the name of socialist. The fact that this optimism can be even imagined today represents a break – the long overdue and slowly unfolding break with the bloody past of Stalinism.

One minor straw in the wind was the presence of delegations of observers from the parties of the Socialist International at the last Congress of the Soviet Communist Party for the first time in many decades. That would have been unimaginable in the old days, and is at least a symbolic step. At least two independent Communist Parties, that of Italy which is by far the largest Communist Party in the capitalist world and the Yugoslav Party[4] are slowly but surely evolving to an observer status in the Socialist International as are Third World parties and movements which seem almost equidistant from the two world currents in the workers' movement.

When leaving the realm of futuristic hope and turning to the realities of the Soviet and Eastern European state 'socialism' I am reminded of a fragment of the the terrible and moving *Poem for Adults* by the Polish poet Adam Wazyk from the Polish intellectual and democratic ferment of 1956:

> We must educate.
> They have changed people into preachers.
> I have heard a wise lecture:
> 'Without properly distributed economic incentives,
> we'll not make economic progress.'
> These are the words of a Marxist.
> This is the knowledge of real laws,
> the end of utopia.

This is almost but not quite counterposed to Leszek Kolakowski's lengthy bitter prose poem *What is Socialism* written in those same magic committed days, when he was still a socialist and a revolutionary democrat and believed those to be possible even if difficult goals worth engaging for. He begins: 'We will tell you what socialism is. But first we must tell you what socialism is not. It is a matter about which we once had a quite different opinion than we have today.'

After listing all that socialism is not, for endless lines like:

> Well then, socialism is not: . . .
> A society in which one person is unhappy because he says what he thinks, and another happy because he does not say what is in his mind . . .
> A state whose neigbours curse geography . . .
> A state in which there is private ownership of the means of production . . .
> A state which produces excellent jet planes and bad shoes . . .
> A nation which oppresses other nations . . .
> A nation which is oppressed by other nations . . .
> Any system of government toward which most of the governed are hostile . . .
> A state which determines who may criticize it and how . . .
> A state which considers itself solidly socialist because it has liquidated private ownership of the means of production . . .[5]

he finally ends, 'That was the first part. But now listen attentively, we will tell you what socialism is: Well, then, socialism is a good thing.'

That is all wonderful, intelligent and painful irony but it will not do. After all it was the Poland of the *Poem for Adults* and Kolakowski which has produced wave after wave of struggles for democracy and equalitarianism, and that for decades afterwards. That is to say the hope that a society can be achieved which is minimally decent and democratic and which in all essentials remains socialist. And for decades that same Poland did produce massive numbers of people who found *that something* worth fighting for. This did occur after all despite all the irony and world-weariness of its intellectuals and despite the fact of the countless democratic activists being ground down by years of petty repression and small defeats. This occurred despite the even more damning fact that Leszek Kolakowski did, after many years, drift to the right, or at least to the center, and has essentially abandoned that hope.

Socialists in advanced industrial societies cannot begin to resolve the present crisis of confidence in the socialist movement and above all the crisis about the goals of socialism without some sharper image or at least the outlines of an image of what a socialist society would look like anymore. Or more to the point, they have to be able to point to a sufficiently commonly agreed upon goal which both inspires some passion and has sufficient realism to inspire respect. The even more complicated and difficult problem is to re-create a common political culture out of a socialist movement. That culture can be heterogeneous and pluralistic as was the broad left culture before the First World War. But it cannot be quite as broad and wonderfully, optimistically naive and certain that history itself is on the side of progress and therefore democracy and socialism. Too much history has taken place since then.

This Crisis is Not New: It is an Old Acquaintance

This is by no means the first time in history that socialism has been in a 'crisis' and the fact that the crisis of socialism is a recurrent phenomenon permits at least some mild optimism about the current one. Merely naming the major past crises of socialism can help place the current one in perspective: the collapse of the First International, the defeat of the Paris Commune, the social patriotic betrayal by the major parties of the Socialist International during the First World War, the rise of fascism and the defeat of the workers' parties in Italy, Austria and Germany. Even more deadly in the long run was the rise of Stalinism in the Soviet Union and post-Second World War spread of authoritarian 'socialisms' throughout much of the world.

The final crisis of western socialist movements and projects was announced during the 'end of ideology' debate in the advanced industrial democracies in the 1950s, followed two decades later by the demise of the orthodox mass Communist parties and, finally, by the fizzling out of Euro-Communism. The youth revolt in the 1960s and the rise of social movements and the rage for post-modernism and post-Marxism among intellectuals of the left in Western Europe and the United States have all in turn been seen as evidence of the crisis or even the end of socialism.

It was at the end of a decade of such continual crises and premature announcements of their demise that the labor-based social-democratic and labor parties achieved their widest electoral gains only to be turned back by the economic crisis following the oil shock of 1973. It is after all during the present crisis of the late 1980s that the socialists, with the Italian Communists, have come to constitute the plurality in the European Parliament.

But let us not cheat. There are facts and figures which can be pulled out to show that things are not all that bad, that here and there the movement is doing well. The elections in both France and Sweden in 1988 went very well indeed for socialists. For that matter so did those of Equador. There are new hopes developing even in the Soviet Union for better days.

There is a worldwide crisis of socialist movements which is about both goals and strategy. What has not happened as yet is a crisis of organizations, that is to say the parties and trade unions. Outside of Great Britain, the socialist and social-democratic parties are not doing badly: their death notices are much too premature.

The Need for New Strategies and Vision

However, the present class stalemate, political paralysis and electoral stand-off for the mass democratic socialist left in Western Europe will continue unless there is a revival of vital, confident, inspiring socialist politics and culture in those parties and movements. Otherwise the reality of the crisis will catch up with the political institutions. These have always suffered from a cultural time lag.

I focus on Western Europe primarily because that is where the roots of the crisis are to be found and it is there that solutions will also have to be found. It is the failure, if it was ever possible for it not to have been a failure, of the revolutions or even successful reformist socialist projects in the west in the 1920s and 1930s which doomed the Soviet Union to the decades of Stalinism. It was also the failure to move beyond social-democratic managed welfare states in the post-Second World War period which leaves the socialist ideas and the mass movement programmatically exhausted at this time. It was the failure of the far left and generational movements of the 1960s and 1970s – and that failure was or should have been predicted – to do more than shake the stodgy and boring cultures of the advanced industrial societies (a very good thing in its own right but hardly storming the heavens), which leaves a whole generation depoliticized and cynical about the possibility of a politics at all. And yet, it is in Europe, and in the first place in Western Europe, that the best prospects for a renewal of socialism can be found.

One could add to the usual list of the causes of the crisis of socialism the surprising and depressing persistence of nationalism even in the advanced industrial societies and the revolt against modernity often taking the form of fundamentalist and sectarian religious revival. For that matter in many ways the revival of dormant nationalisms and the rise of nationalisms in those groups which have had a recognized nationality can very well be understood as a revolt against modernity and the destruction of the traditional communities.

The savage nativism and racism which has developed in Western Europe and most visibly in Great Britain and France in response to the large and growing immigrant worker population from non-European and non-white countries and societies is a part of the same perverse reaction by those who see the traditional communities and way of life threatened. In the absence of active and vital workers' movements to defend those communities in an affirmative way, there develops a sour racism informed by a primitive view that society is a zero-sum game. This is one of the consequences of the wholesale assault on the welfare state in Britain and the US and of the faltering of employment and growth in all western capitalist societies.

But nationalism can be, as the recent developments in the Soviet Union and Yugoslavia show, the result of a prolonged repression of normal democratic debate and the right to organize on other lines, the lines of class, political beliefs or social movements around passionately supported issues. For that matter nationalism often becomes the language of those oppressed who can find no other way of expressing their alienation of the official norms and values of the society. It can also be the response to national oppression.

Another and quite separate factor is the dismal record and defeats of the left-wing regimes calling themselves socialist in the Third World, with the ravages that the very term socialism has suffered as a consequence. Not the least consequence has been the cynical withdrawal of the waves of disillusioned solidarity activists who were repeatedly drawn to Third World revolutionary experiments not only out of a misplaced romanticism but also out of those generous instincts and hope without which one cannot expect to renew socialist movements. Movements are after all not built by burned-out cynics, and therefore these defeats of the optimistic hopes in the Third World socialist experiments impoverished the entire social and political milieux in which the left in the advanced countries lives.

But a movement whose often-announced crises and demise repeatedly appear to have been premature, which seems to rise as a phoenix from its many funeral pyres, must surely be resilient. What follows is an attempt to examine some aspects of this crisis and to speculate about some possible outcomes. The most immediately and obviously visible aspect of the crisis of socialism today is the strategic, programmatic and ideological crisis of organizations which call themselves socialist. Much more serious, however, is the fundamental and difficult crisis of the socialist project itself. The shape of it has become too amorphous in popular consciousness and the word covers far too many sins.

There must surely be problems with a concept which is today used to describe such an array of polities as: half the regimes in Africa, state 'socialist' politocracies of Eastern Europe and the Soviet Union, social-democratic egalitarian welfare states, 'Marxist-Leninist' fantasies of instant revolutions and the left-socialist and libertarian projects for direct workers' control of production. Unless one defines one's socialist project in terms which are clear and refer to the problems of contemporary societies, it is impossible even to talk of the possibility of a revival of socialism as a movement and a program.

Revival of Marxist Studies in the Academy: 'Armchair' Marxism

There has been a massive development of Marxist academic studies from the early 1970s on, interestingly and depressingly enough, above all in the United States and Great Britain, rather than in countries where some version of the Marxist tradition had taken root within the mass workers' movements. What also gives pause when examining this revival, is its location in the universities with the consequent academization, one could almost add castration, of Marxism as an engaged theory of a movement if not a class.

There is today a substantial amount of quite impressive Marxist or Marxist-inspired work in social sciences and aesthetics. Of course there is also a great deal of jargon-ridden, trendy and shallow nonsense that passes for Marxist scholarship. It is an open question whether there can be such a thing as an academic Marxism as distinct from the academic studies of Marxism or Marxology.

Marxism was never meant to be merely academic or just a theory, it was always primarily a matter of praxis.[6] In any case today this traditional juncture between theory and the movement, theory and the project is nearly fatally flawed. This can be easily illustrated by the existence of 'Marxists' who are indifferent to radically democratic demands of popular empowerment and who prattle, usually in democratic capitalist states to be sure, about the unimportance of 'bourgeois' democracy and 'bourgeois' individual civil liberties. With friends like that, Marxism and socialism hardly need enemies.

Soviet and Other State Socialisms

For the past 40 years the major monkey on the back of the socialist project, at least in the advanced industrial countries as well as among the Eastern European and other citizens of 'currently existing socialisms', has been the reality of the Eastern European and Soviet experience. But one should also add that there are two basically authoritarian models of 'socialism' existing today: the Eastern European and Soviet one, on the one hand, and the derivatives of a bastard Fabianism (in Africa and some of the other modernizing states) where bureaucratic planning *per se*, order, and modernization from the top down had begun to be things unto themselves.

China, while of enormous significance for the developing countries and the Third World, has not been a meaningful current general model of socialism or an ideological influence since the brief Maoist and Maoisant flash in the 1960s and early 1970s. This is not to underestimate the enormous significance of the changes now taking place in China and the very real possibility that China – a much reformed China – will assume an even more important role in the future. Today the Chinese experience with the devolution of centralized control over the agricultural communes and increased decentralization of the economy in general certainly represents a more daring experiment than the one now being undertaken by Gorbachev in the Soviet Union. While the results in agriculture are promising, the jury must debate for some considerable time on the rest of the experience. That is why China does not play much of a role in the contemporary discussions of the crises or prospects of socialism.

Third World: Imperialism and Neo-Colonialism

The two authoritarian models which do retain some general relevance for the current debate on the prospects of socialism remain the Soviet and the

Third World authoritarian models. In fairness it should be added that it is as at least lesser evils that they are generally considered today. Except for the very young, the naive or the very calloused these societies are no longer the near-utopias which they used to be. But then even lesser evils are no small thing in the present world. Numerous observers contrast the visible absence of searing poverty and hunger in Cuba and China with the neighbouring Caribbean countries in the first case and India in the second. That is hardly irrelevant, all criticism of those regimes notwithstanding. It is also important to add that both of these authoritarian models have become the dominant images of socialism in the contemporary world mainly because of the repeated failures of the mass labor and social-democratic parties of the advanced industrialized countries to produce more than advanced welfare states. That is, they have failed to produce a vibrant and attractive model of a socialism which is both democratic and effective and which meets the social, economic and spiritual needs of modern society.

The Western European and North American workers' and socialist movements and parties have in the past been far less effective and generous than they could have been in offering support to the struggles against colonialism and imperialism in the Third World. In few rare cases this was because of a direct complicity with that colonialism or imperialism but the much more common problem was the Euro-centrism of the Western European movements and the general insularism of the North American movements.

Again in the interests of accuracy one should add that the Communists and the smaller radical groups did often practice a much-flawed internationalism or even 'Sovieto-centrism' to be replaced in turn by fascination with all things Chinese, Algerian, Cuban and Nicaraguan. Whatever the value of that 'internationalism' for the groups in question, it did little to help the movements in the Third World with the problems of building socialism.

The possible minor exception to this was the undoubted aid which the broad anti-war movement in the US gave to the Vietnamese Communists in helping to end that war through massive protests against continued aggression of their own government.[7] There is no evidence at all that this had any political effect on the Vietnamese Communists, such as possibly broadening their view of how a victorious regime should proceed. Of course the economy and society of Vietnam were devastated by years of murderous warfare and the United States is responsible for the damages to that society. But given this, even criminal, responsibility of the United States, it is also reasonably clear from reports by Scandinavian and other relief agencies that the policies of the Vietnamese Communists have contributed heavily to the miseries of their people after their victory. Generous reparation and aid in rebuilding Vietnam would have undoubtedly eased the rebuilding of what is one of the world's poorest societies. This could have been a beginning of a two-way communication between movements. But of course the western leftists in the anti-war movements were too guilt-ridden on one hand and too optimistic about the prospects of yet another beloved community developing in Vietnam after the war.

The Vietnamese Communists were too certain that they had the scientific answer as to how to proceed to build socialism. To be sure, forcing into exile close to 2 million people, mostly Chinese, who are notoriously the most entrepreneurial in that region, did not help. Equally clearly, that at least cannot be blamed on the United States. But then, while repressive rigid centralization may be explained by the circumstances, it certainly is not, and has been historically proven not to be, a more effective way to develop. To put it briefly, *it is not a shortcut,* even if one is willing to pay the price.

The prolonged Euro-centrism of the mass democratic socialist parties and movements has also left a vacuum as far as strategies and tactics of struggle and development in the Third World were concerned. That vacuum was filled by various 'short-cut' strategies which have for the most part ended up creating over-centralized, authoritarian and above all inefficient and corrupt states. All too often these newly independent states have assaulted their own nascent civil societies in ways at least as brutal as colonialism was in its later stages. However, if one views the Third World radical regimes both as responsible actors, not mere pawns of an impersonal and all-powers world system or market, and victims of centuries of imperialism *and* of neglect and ignorance by the socialist movements in the advanced industrial countries, one can begin dealing with the depressing realities of these societies without useless guilt or excessive scapegoating.

These Third World regimes are the way they are, among other reasons, because of the decades of Cold War and the failure of the socialist movements in the west to transform their own societies. Conversely the best way to help those seeking a democratic and just social order in the Third World is by creating an effective and decent democratic socialist movement in the advanced industrial societies. That is the most effective form which genuine internationalist solidarity can take today.

But while that may be true, it is scant comfort to those who need help now, who are under the gun of imperialism and neo-colonialism today, or to those who have been stuck with power in societies which are not ripe for socialism because all other alternatives seemed worse and who are now trying to build decent democratic societies. It will not do here to preach what should have been: history is after all made by human beings of flesh and blood and subject to enthusiasms and errors and an eternal willingness to take chances. In such cases, and I believe that the Sandinistas in Nicaragua are such a case, they deserve the aid and support and solidarity of decent democratic individuals and parties and movements around the world. For democrats and leftists in the United States, however, that solidarity and help are transformed into moral and political imperatives because it is above all the United States which most grossly distorts and limits the possibilities of decent outcomes in Nicaragua today. The most effective way to express that solidarity, although not always most emotionally fulfilling, is to change those US policies to at least non-intervention.

The contemporary generations of socialists and Marxists live in the shadow of great flawed transformational upheavals. One could even call these the failed Promethean efforts where the failures have dwarfed that which remains possible. The Bolshevik revolution of 1917, the rise of Stalinism, the Chinese revolution and the anti-colonial revolutions in the Third World all in turn shaped, fascinated and scarred generations of socialist activists and intellectuals. They still represent the key, inspiring and traumatic events of our epoch with which some kind of a historical settling of accounts is essential to make possible any grappling with the present crisis of socialism.

I will therefore begin this examination of the crises of socialism and 'socialism' with the present situation in the Soviet Union and Eastern Europe, then discuss the relationship of the Soviet experiences and power to the Third World revolutions and regimes, after which a discussion of the advanced industrial societies and the prospects for a new socialist strategy and renewal can be logically addressed. To prevent this effort from becoming unbearably long I will try to keep the historical details as brief as possible and concentrate on contemporary events and debates. The notes will all be found at the end of the book.

A Brief Personal Note

In writing about matters as politically charged as the prospects of a movement and idea which has been at the center of political conflict and controversy for the past century, it is less than honest not to specify from which vantage point the author writes. What is his or her intellectual and political location? One can even perhaps ask in a whisper, what are their politics? This seems to be the closest to an indecent question we can get to ask nowadays in the academic world.

In my own case, I make no claim to any analytic distance and impartiality from the subject under discussion – the situation and the probable fate of modern socialism in advanced industrial societies. I would consider such claims to be doubtful or at best naive in most cases when dealing with highly emotionally charged controversial political questions. Such claims are really the form of poetic 'conceit' which academic writing has made almost mandatory and which helps make so much of it so lifeless and irrelevant.

Of course such claims of academic impartiality or balance are also a statement of political values, the values of a professional distance from the messy and often bloody subjects of contemporary social struggles and politics. But these claims to objective and yes of course judiciously balanced social scientific analysis also underpin a world view and a politics which accepts the present reality, the present, objective, *status quo* reality as inherently rational and legitimate.

The more cynical journalists in Eastern Europe today at least describe their profession a little more objectively. Jug Grizelj, one of the leading journalists in Yugoslavia, writes that journalists at their best are like musicians in a brothel. Their work when it is good does no harm and at least it entertains – something which can hardly be said for most of the work of academic social scientists, or for that matter academic Marxists nowadays.

It is more honest to specify the nature of one's own approach and interest. On one hand, I use such training in history and social sciences (if there really are such things) as I have. On the other hand, I would be less than honest not to point out that I also – note well, *also* not instead – write as a person who has spent four decades as an activist and participant in the socialist and workers' movement in the United States and abroad. It has been the major commitment which has informed my entire adult life and has been the intellectual and moral framework within which I have operated since I tentatively entered into what were the fragments of a socialist movement in the United States in 1947.

The date may be of some significance since that was the period of what can be best described as high Stalinism in the Soviet bloc and within the world Communist movement. It was also the period of extreme isolation for left-socialist activists and intellectuals characterized both by apocalyptic fears of the approach of a Third World War and the consequences of the evident rise of McCarthyism and the general anti-left witch-hunt in the United States. To become a socialist in the United States at that time, in the shadows of Auschwitz and Buchenwald and knowing about the Gulag archipelago decades long before it became widely known, required some optimism. To do so at the beginning of what was being widely hailed or denounced as the beginning of the American Century did require stubbornness or possibly poor judgement or even masochism. It also required the ability to live and remain actively committed to left politics with a tragic view of history and of the prospects for an effective democratic socialist movement.

In those days, in the late 1940s, I would have much preferred the adjective libertarian or revolutionary to modify my use of the term socialist rather than democratic – after all, I was young. But looking back over all those years, language aside, the small movement which existed and which I joined was crystal clear then that its socialism would be democratic. In the later years when I spent a good decade as an industrial worker 'implanted' by my political movement into my trade as a machinist, and later a tool and die maker, and a trade union activist, it turned out that if there was any consistency to what one did as a socialist inside the trade unions, it was to fight relentlessly for union democracy and the ability of the rank and file to run their own unions. *That was the essential way we left-wing socialists 'raised consciousness'*.

It was not much, perhaps, but it did help put some of the abstract ideological disputes in the then scattered remnants of the organized Marxist left in the United States in some perspective. It helped also to be reassured by living experience that workers, living real workers in trade unions, were at least as attached to the idea of democracy and grass-roots power as leftist activists. In fact they very often proved to have healthier instincts than many self-selected vanguardists. It is also true that, like all people made of flesh and blood, they were subject to all the temptations and pressures of the society we lived in and the United States of the 1950s was not a society which rewarded or appreciated either civic consciousness or rank-and-file activism on the part of workers. To sustain that one needs a mass movement.

It was clear to us then what mattered. Democracy, genuine messy turbulent democracy, was central to what we tried to do and it was more important than our endless ideological debates. In the eternal almost talmudic arguments between leftist grouplets we, that is my little band of comrades living on the intellectual fringes of the then also almost unknown New York Intellectuals, were for the sailors at Kronstadt and the anarcho-syndicalists and POUMists in Barcelona in 1937[8] and the left opposition in Russia in the late 1920s and 1930s. We had opposed the deportation of Japanese Americans during the Second World War, the imposition of a no-strike policy on the labor movement during the war. We opposed the dropping of the nuclear bombs on Hiroshima and Nagasaki. For that matter we had opposed the mass bombing of the cities of Germany during the war and the return of the colonies to France, Britain and Holland at the end of the war. We certainly opposed the forcible extension of Soviet power throughout Eastern Europe and the imperialist agreements of Yalta and Teheran which legalized the new division of the world. Our journal choice was Dwight McDonald's wonderful *Politics* and I for one was heartbroken when he stopped publishing in 1949 with a gut-wrenching issue entitled *Dilemma*. The title was well chosen since the dilemma in question was: could one continue a journal which was opposed to the two imperialist superpowers if no perspective for an effective opposition was in sight and the West had become a lesser evil. At that time I agreed that no mass effective political alternative to the two superpowers was even in sight, but I did not agree that the West was the lesser evil. This view made me appear obviously wrong at the time; my position was 'impossibilist' since I argued that one had to oppose both imperialist superpowers, not exactly a popular position during the height of the Cold War. By the by, that impossibilism became very much less obvious in the later years. In the years of the Vietnamese war my until-then-instinctive gut opposition to US imperialism and militarism no longer appeared so naive.

In short, we had been on the losing side of every major issue involving democracy, workers' rights and empowerment through most of the recent history. Even our humor in that period was a sort of gallows humor, quoting Dwight McDonald, that we should be called the 'glass wall brigade' since a glass wall would be needed for our executions so that both sides in the Cold War could see to shoot us simultaneously. That was romantic nonsense of course. But it was hardly the same romantic optimistic nonsense which the young newcomers to the movement had at other times, at the times of the great hopes aroused by the Bolshevik revolution or for the later generations by the Chinas, Cubas and Nicaraguas.

I must say that I have often envied this virginal faith and regretted its inevitable aftermath of disillusion. If you have no illusions you cannot lose any. What you can do is burn out in frustration in an activism and commitment for a seemingly unachievable and therefore hopeless ideal. One of the first and cruellest temptations for leftists, particularly in the United States, is to try to discover a reasonable facsimile of an existing utopia or at least to suspend one's judgement long enough to have more than mere hope – to have an image of one's very own socialist state somewhere. For western intellectuals and leftists that 'somewhere' kept shifting from country to country, from movement to movement. That is not an unreasonable thing to hope for but we have not been living in reasonable times.

We, on the other hand, never lived with the immanent hope for the victory of socialism in our own country, and were quite sceptical of that prospect in most of the world. On the contrary, socialists of my generation in the United States joined the movement when pessimism was a sign of intelligence and sophistication. The problem was how to keep a militant commitment *and* a sophisticated, unflinching and realistic assessment of the prospects. For many if not most of my generation it turned out to be a choice of *either/or*. And most eventually chose pessimism and inactivity. The others burned out as activists or became embittered. We had not yet heard of Gramsci's phrase, 'pessimism of the mind and optimism of the will' which expresses what was then needed and what is still needed by a sane socialist movement.

Chapter 2

Currently Existing 'Real Socialism' in Eastern Europe and the Soviet Union[1]

The debate on the political and economic reforms which have been launched in the Soviet Union by Gorbachev has pushed the prolonged low-level crisis in the Eastern European state socialist systems temporarily into the background. However, it is important to consider the Eastern European Communist state systems, with all their differences and similarities, since they can permit us to begin to speculate within limits about the future of at least some of the proposed Soviet reforms. They also permit us to speculate about a more general question: what are the limits and possibilities of change in the Communist single-party states? A number of the proposed Soviet reforms, or others essentially similar in conception, have been experimented with willy-nilly for over two decades on the much smaller scale which individual Eastern European countries afford.

Comparisons have to be made with caution, since the Eastern European Communist regimes have been imposed on these states from the outside and are in any case more recent than the Soviet one. The order of scale itself is also important. However, there are sufficient similarities in the types of regimes involved for Eastern Europe to be a cracked mirror of the Soviet Union's possible future, or at least the most probable future. I do not accept the notion that the social, economic and above all political system of the Soviet Union is *sui generis*. That is why we should look at a range of these systems if we want to be able to speculate about the direction in which they may be evolving as we approach the twenty-first century.

The fate of these societies and political systems has a direct bearing on any prospects of a socialist revival in the rest of the world since it was in good part the flawed and perverted experiences of the Soviet and Eastern European societies which have helped put the very idea of socialism in question. Whatever democratic socialists and various native intellectual dissidents say about these societies not being genuine socialist societies and therefore no valid test of the possibility of socialism, and I share that view, for the vast majority of the world those experiences do bear on the validity of at least some major assumption which had been shared by socialists in general. They cast a very negative light on the performance of highly centralized command economies at other than early industrialization stages of development.[2] There is also some distorted family resemblance and of course there is the common vocabulary.

The possibility of a Communism with a human face during the Prague Spring in 1968 was greeted with joy and relief by activists and leaders in the mass Communist parties in the industrial capitalist democracies – it showed, or seemed to show until the brutal crackdown by the Warsaw Pact armies, that Communism in power had the possibility of regenerating itself. Two decades later the Gorbachev reforms raise hopes again and among a far wider political public, although – or perhaps *because* – they occur under conditions of a general and evident moral and ideological crisis of *both* Communist politocratic regimes *and* the general socialist project.

The hope for internal redeeming reform and transformation of the Communist politocracies remains a powerful expression of a hope that all the sacrifices and brutalities under these regimes shall not have been in vain. More mundanely major reforms in the bloc will speed up the possibility of moving to an end of the Cold War as we now know it. Not to mention that a substantial improvement in the lives of a large part of the world population is no small thing in itself.

The term Eastern Europe as used here is not a geographic concept. For my purposes, Greece is not in Eastern Europe, while East Germany is. What we are really talking about are the state socialist politocratic systems which have developed since the Second World War in the area awarded to the Soviets by the Yalta and Teheran Agreements. Two of the countries, Albania and Yugoslavia, have managed to leave the bloc. Therefore, for my purposes, Eastern Europe essentially consists of the Warsaw Pact countries: East Germany, Poland, Czechoslovakia, Hungary, Romania and Bulgaria.

All are in trouble, none have lights at the end of any tunnels. Probably none have any tunnels, that is, a generally agreed-upon path of development, no matter how long range or unpleasant, which would solve these societies' economic and social crises. Most proposals for political and economic reforms put forward by the more liberal wing of the Communist parties in the region have one thing in common: the continued rule or at least domination over these societies by their ruling Communist parties. On the other hand, it is precisely the continued political monopoly of the Communist parties that is increasingly unacceptable to a growing majority of the population. Thus the reforms from above are sharply self-limiting in range and only encourage demands for more concessions.

If there is a lesson to be drawn from the defeats of the Hungarian revolution, the East Berlin uprising, Prague Spring, the numerous Polish upheavals and the stand-off and compromise between Solidarity and the present military regime in Poland, it is that, while the *legitimacy of the Yalta and Teheran Agreements is increasingly questioned, the reality of the power relations which those agreements imply is not.* At least not as yet. Or to put it more simply, *no change unacceptable to the Soviet Union will occur within the systems of Eastern Europe,* and although the Soviets' acceptance levels have changed considerably over time, two essentials appear to be undebatable. One is the continued rule or at least political hegemony, of the Communist party, and the other, subordination to the Soviet Union's policies in international affairs. Either of those two constraints can be modified individually within narrow limits, provided the other remains.

Long-Range Crises of Eastern European Communist Systems

Politically, Soviet-dominated Eastern Europe has stabilized with a series of unlovable and unloved, increasingly nationally specific, regimes which show that they are capable of ruling but not of obtaining any legitimacy and popular acceptance. The degree of popular resentment varies from regime to regime but today, with the possible exception of Hungary, it is doubtful if one of them would survive the withdrawal of Soviet sponsorship and support for any length of time. The crisis of Eastern Europe, however, is if anything more fundamental than the bankruptcy of its political institutions.

There are three separate loci of the crisis:

1) the complete collapse of the official 'Marxist' ideology as a mobilizing instrument useful to the ruling elites;
2) the demoralization of the in-system reformers and the present startling absence of any reform currents within a recognizably Marxist or socialist framework among the intelligentsia or the other opinion-forming groups;
3) the increasing and increasingly visible and obvious gap in technology, productivity, living standards and social standards between Eastern Europe and the Western European industrial states.[3]

While it was possible to write learned books about the onset of a technochronic Communism in East Germany and the convergence of

US and USSR in the late 1960s, it is clear today that *the real issue is: will Eastern Europe be doomed to be a backwater of Europe or will it slide into the Third World?*

I use the image of sliding into the Third World because, while there are sectors in the fields of culture and science which are world class, as in many Third World countries, it is the *overall* performance of the economy and society which is dreary and discouraging in Eastern Europe and the Soviet Union. Thus the decade of the relative normalization of personal existence in most of these states has been followed by more than a decade and a half of deterioration in living standards, very sharp in some cases, accompanied by a general drop in productivity and technological innovation. They have not even entered into the race where the information revolution is concerned and are backward as examples of smoke-stack economies. This increasingly evident backwardness is particularly painful for regimes which, being unloved, had based their claims to legitimacy on economic performance. Even the genuine achievements of these regimes, the creation of crude and all-but-universal welfare states which did raise the living standards of wide sectors of the population, particularly in the years of growth, i.e., the late 1950s and through the 1960s, no longer produce regime support. The second and third generations of industrial workers and urban dwellers do not find the welfare state a novelty but, on the contrary, take it for granted and therefore focus on its many inadequacies.

The economic, social and political problems are exacerbated by the increasing porousness of what used to be known as the Iron Curtain and the fact that at least the young are completely taken with western and more often American cultural forms. It must gnaw at the regime 'culture workers' of Poland, East Germany and Czechoslovakia, or the Soviet Union for that matter, to know that the young prefer punk and New Wave to anything that is written in their own countries – unless perhaps it is the Polish and East German versions of punk and New Wave. While the youth are attracted to the western youth culture, the rest of the population is mostly mesmerized by an attraction to western mass consumerist values and a consequent exaggerated attraction for 'western', that is to say, consumerist, materialist and sometime even petty-capitalist values. This is particularly widespread among the educated middle classes, including sections of the political elite, as can be seen by both the mythification of the market as the solution for the economic problems of these societies and the increasing differences in lifestyles and access to goods between the more privileged strata and the working class. Forty years of politocratic 'socialism' has all but destroyed any fabric of social solidarity in these societies. That is not the least important criticism of Communist parties in power.

In the field of mass culture and mass media the regimes have long lost the battle – the official ideology is quite simply seen as boring. The parties are perceived simply as channels for careerists and, while they *are* channels for careerism, anybody who pretends to take the parties in the least bit seriously in terms of program or ideology is held in utter contempt by the younger generation and careerists in those societies. More painfully, the ruling elite itself is increasingly cynical and obviously instrumental about 'Partinost' (party loyalty).

It is grim to live in a society which seems to be walking backwards into its own future.[4] But more, Marxism – particularly official Marxism – itself emphasized the link between technology of production and political organization. Capitalism was progressive vis-a-vis feudalism because it released enormous creative energies: it was evidently technologically superior or, to put it more precisely, capitalist class domination was most congruent with breakthroughs in technology and the organization of production then made possible by these scientific and technological innovations and discoveries.

Marx and certainly most of his mainline successors thought of socialism as having an analogous relationship to capitalism, that is, of capitalism beginning to act as a restraint on the creative productive forces of society and breaking down and being finally overthrown by a more advanced form of society which would be superior not merely in terms of moral and egalitarian values but also in terms of the ability to organize society more rationally and more effectively. That is what presumably made Marxist socialism 'scientific' as distinct from various, much-scorned, forms of 'true or utopian socialism'. For western Marxists who choose to remain Marxists, one way out is simply to assert that these societies are not socialist. But whatever one's views about the Eastern European and Soviet states, whether one even extends the name socialist to them at all, it is clear that these societies are not technologically more efficient than capitalism, particularly the capitalism of the Pacific Rim states, and certainly not more efficient than the welfare states of Western Europe today. Even growth is not much of an argument for the Eastern European states, since a whole range of societies, some of which are in their own ways as unlovely as the Eastern European states, and which also had to deal with the problems of industrialization and modernization, like Korea, Taiwan and Hong Kong, are far more productive and efficient at introducing new technologies and scientific breakthroughs than either the Soviets or Eastern Europeans.

But official Soviet and Eastern European Marxism has always been scientistic and therefore to give up the claim to inherent scientific superiority is to give up the very essence of the elite ideology. To be sure, one can have other Marxisms – democratic and humanist Marxisms which stress non-productivistic aspects of Marx, and which rest on the theories of alienation and the need for empowerment of the previous unempowered strata in society. But *that* Marxism was the Marxism of the opposition, that was the Marxism developed by the internal exiles, in the jails, among the ghettoized academic intellectuals and in the little samizdat publications.

That humanist Marxism is also in a crisis today, although for different reasons more having to do with a relentless, grinding litany of defeats. Nevertheless, it is a fact that oppositional Marxism exists primarily outside the Warsaw Pact countries in Eastern Europe, that is, it exists in Yugoslavia where, almost alone in Eastern Europe, both the opposition and the defenders of the regime still use Marxist language. But then, even the US State Department has stopped treating Yugoslavia as a part of Eastern Europe.

Repression does not permeate these societies any more and the bulk of the population, especially the young, are no longer frightened. To say that they are not frightened does not mean that they are straining at the leash to attack the regimes. There has been an effective widespread depoliticization and massive demobilization of the population over the years. Much of the official mobilization of the young and of the urban workers in the 1940s and 1950s had been of a fraudulent character, but some did have the effect of mobilizing the ever-latent idealism of the young. By the 1960s whatever capital had been there had been long spent through years of dull repressive manipulation of the liberating symbols of socialism in the interests of the new politocratic ruling class.

Younger workers have never experienced terror and take whatever social and economic gains exist as their right and are rightly cynical about any official version of a work ethic since it is clear that work, official work which you are paid to perform, is not the way to advance. This is made evident by seeing who does well economically in these societies: political hacks and those who work the legal or the not-so-legal boundaries of the gray or alternative economy. Thus neither the carrot nor its stick are particularly effective with younger workers. The possibility of effective, progressive, political and social change is generally treated with cynicism. It is a cynicism which is reinforced by the increasing tolerance of petty corruption and individual advancement which exists within all of these societies. Hungary is a superb example of this cynicism as an effective instrument for maintaining social peace. You do not work very hard, you can take a trip to Austria for black market goods, a little dealing in black market currency is taken for normal, as is working 'off the books' for private cash payment which affects an ever-wider sector of the skilled workers.

The grotesquely inefficient organization of services and repairs has given birth to an entire Black Economy which is no longer even underground and which the regime largely ignores as it obviously does not pose a threat. It would be a mistake to assume that the informal economy is a feature of the marginal private sector alone: it permeates the official institutions and economy as well – from the petty 'gifts' one is expected to bring to one's doctor or dentist, to the 'informal incentives' one gives to the storekeepers when one needs auto parts or building material, to outright bribery.

When all is said and done, the absence of active repression in most of the Eastern European states today has led to a grudging *modus vivendi* where the regimes recognize that they are doomed to continued unpopularity and are now content to be obeyed if not loved. The population, in turn, recognizes that, short of a major breakdown, they are stuck with the present regimes. There is the sneaking fear in the back of the minds of most Eastern Europeans that a major breakdown or upheaval would probably be accompanied by Soviet intervention or social chaos which would only worsen the situation. It is *that* realization which makes these societies so depressing.

Breakdown of the Social Pact with the Working Class

The problem is that this state of affairs – the stand-off between inefficient regimes and a surly and indifferent working class – rested on a tacit social pact which had developed by the 1960s and which is now increasingly being challenged by forces outside of the control of the regimes. Those forces reflect the growing integration of Eastern Europe into the world market under circumstances where the technological and productivity gap between Eastern Europe and the rest of the world becomes unbearable. Poland, Hungary, Romania and Yugoslavia all owe money to the World Bank as well as to private banks and all are under pressure to increase their exports to meet the payments. It does not help that all, except Romania, have far more efficient and advanced economies and economic organization than the Soviet Union. That is no yardstick for comparison and in any case they do not have the Soviet Union's vast natural resources.

To attempt to resolve the economic problems of these regimes the Soviets have encouraged, even pushed, the Eastern European economies into the world market and *there* the rules of the game have an unfortunately universalist character which measures the Eastern European regimes by very different yardsticks to the ones they had been accustomed to. They would now be obliged to produce adequate goods of decent design and quality at reasonable cost if they were to have a chance to export.

This is taking place at a point when Western Europe is increasingly protectionist and the competition from the Pacific Rim nations and rising Third World economies, like that of Brazil, increasingly savage. The solution was two-fold: to modernize the industrial plant (thereby increasing the indebtedness to the western banks for the purchase of the machinery) and to get better productivity, i.e., to speed up the workers. This speed-up, however, if debts were to be repaid, had to be accompanied not by pay increases but if anything by pay decreases. Increases in living standards, to be sure, are promised in the future, once the economies have been reformed.

However, far too many promises have already been made over the years to the Soviet and Eastern European populations for much credibility and trust to remain. To make things even worse, the features of the economic reforms which are almost universal and which people *do* believe would be delivered are greater economic inequality and unemployment. In politocratic systems that inequality would obviously benefit the political ruling stratum, not necessarily the more economically productive. In either case greater economic inequality will hardly encourage workers to accept unemployment and speed-up which are necessary features of the proposed economic reforms.

The brutal period of industrialization of the first decades of Communist rule has created a large and increasingly homogeneous working class. The process which took place in Western Europe over many generations was compressed into two short decades in Eastern Europe. Several not-so-obvious consequences followed. The first is that the regimes favored the industrial working class and the cities against the rural sector and the peasantry. It was in the cities where the almost universal crude welfare state first developed, where education became massively accessible to the working class and where the rapid upward social mobility of workers and peasants into the new layers of state, party, economic and mass organizational bureaucratic hierarchy took place.

Secondly, the industrial workers who had belonged to the traditional proletariat were 'compensated' for the destruction of their independent trade unions, parties and institutions by historically unprecedented mobility into the new social and economic elites. To be sure, much of this mobility was the result of the structural changes in the economy. As a consequence the 'rewards' were distributed often as a result of mere chance and the good fortune to have been in the right place when the party cadres desperately searched for promotable bodies. An entire existing old political class of the pre-war bourgeoisie and its parties had been eliminated and now needed to be replaced.

The new Stalinist regimes were heavy on administration and therefore needed many, many more persons to fill the slots that had previously been occupied by the old ruling class. That after all is the hallmark of an administrative society. It was top heavy with bureaucracy from day one. Short of reliable party cadres, the regimes had three sources of recruits: the new party members who could at least be assumed to be faithful out of gratitude if nothing else, a handful of previous bourgeois experts and technicians who were willing to adapt to the new regime, and the workers. It goes without saying that all the party cadres within the working class, few as they were, had meteoric careers and, until the new universities began to produce politically correct experts and technicians, the most reliable managerial types were workers who had been promoted through the party.

While not necessarily competent, they were loyal (but then the pre-war bourgeoisie was not necessarily competent either). The unanticipated effect of this rapid social mobility was to remove the reliable party cadres from the working class and to increase the distance between the actual manual workers and the Communist party, which was increasingly based on white-collar employees, technicians and managers. To put the above proposition more succinctly, by the mid-1950s a worker could be reasonably sure that the person working next to him or her on the assembly line or in the mines was not a police or party agent if they had been there for any length of time. If they had been party agents they would long ago have been promoted. With a whole second generation of workers beginning to enter the workplace in the 1960s, the chasm between the party and the working class increased and the informal lines of solidarity and mutual support against the bosses, the managers, the state and all things external to the working class began to develop.

But then Eastern European blue-collar workers had other special characteristics which were bound to create trouble. Not only were the workers now increasingly abandoned by the party in the workplace, but throughout the 1950s and 1960s were housed in massive quasi-slums, almost homogeneously working class. Not only did you not work next to a party cadre, or informer, you were unlikely to live next to one, since, if party membership was good for anything at all, it was good for obtaining better housing and other perks. Thus in many ways the blue-collar workers of Eastern Europe resembled the industrial proletariat in smoke-stack industries of an earlier period in Western Europe, a period of great industrial militancy and self-assertion in Western Europe.

Continued labor turbulence is part of the future forecast for Eastern Europe, and it is affected by three factors:

1) the Soviet Union itself is going through a series of wide-ranging technological and administrative reforms which are an implicit critique of some of the Eastern European elites (for example, both the Czech and East German regimes are notably cool to the Gorbachev reforms in the USSR and the Czechs have even on occasions simply failed to report some of the measures taken in the administrative liberalization);

2) it is difficult to repress the bulk of the working class. Regimes, to be sure, have had difficulties repressing intellectuals as well but, as one notorious Czech party hack put it, you buy off a third, you intimidate a third, and you jail or exile the remainder. Since the regimes have been producing an excess of university-educated personnel *that* was not even wasteful. However, it is an option clearly not available for dealing with industrial workers. A cynic could add that while the police take to cracking down on intellectuals and students with ill-repressed class resentment and therefore move joyously to the task, it is an entirely different kettle of fish to beat up miners or steel workers;

3) there is the problem that regime legitimacy, defective as it is, still does rest at least theoretically on the claim that these are some kind of workers' states.[5]

All this adds up to a formula promising continued stagnation and a continued checkmate between the class forces, and to a consolidation of class consciousness on the part of the workers, on the one hand, and self-consciousness by the ruling strata of their separateness, on the other. These are increasingly obviously class societies.

If the explosive potential of industrial unrest represents the general crisis of ruling Communist regimes in the long run, the short run is not rosy either. The gap between promise and performance in the economy, the stagnant repressive miasma affecting all spheres of intellectual and cultural activity, the lag in technological innovation and progress and the growing gaps between the top leadership, on the one hand, and the managers and the bulk of the population, on the other, make these societies unattractive and uninspiring. The effect is felt even within the party cadre itself. Decent worker Communists have long lapsed into inactivity or been pushed out by new, mostly white-collar, party membership.

The Betrayal of the Clerks: Regimes and the New Intelligentsia

One of the proudest achievements of the Eastern European Communist regimes has been the massive system of higher education which developed in the first decades of their rule. The explosive growth of the universities was meant to fill the gap between the need of the regimes for newly educated and technically competent cadres and the existing state of things where the top slots were filled with untrained party cadres and loyal time-servers. The aim was to create loyal experts who would be both expert and grateful to the regime. The massive expansion of the universities absorbed the children of the more reliable industrial and white-collar workers and all studies make clear that the universities have become the primary vehicle for social advancement.[6]

From the very beginning this was, however, a mixed blessing. The more prestigious faculties have remained those of humanities and social sciences and tended to attract, disproportionately, children of intellectuals and of the older urban middle class. Workers' children generally went into the engineering and technical faculties. Now, technically, it is true that the Eastern European Communist regimes continued singing the praises of the engineers and scientists and it is obvious that promotion into the technical and managerial strata was an enormous leap forward for the children of those who could never have aspired to such advancement before the establishment of Communist rule. However, in terms of prestige (for a series of reasons having to do both with the traditional intelligentsia and the fact that the Communist intellectuals themselves were in a way part of the humanistic intelligentsia) the prestige of intelligentsia remained higher, and remains higher, than that of technicians and engineers. This is so even though economic rewards are allocated differently. For that matter this is so even in cases where blue-collar skilled workers are paid better than university-educated personnel. As in much of the Third World, one of the legacies of the historical underdevelopment of Eastern Europe is the continued contempt towards any manual work or even administrative jobs associated with manual work.

Studies of social prestige in Poland, Hungary, Yugoslavia and Czechoslovakia are depressingly similar. At the very top of the scale are university professors, lawyers, writers and intellectuals, despite decades of party efforts to change the prestige scale.

Since the regimes have settled into a routine there are no more rapid promotions, and worker cadres cannot expect to have meteoric careers moving into the heights of the economy and society. Advancement now goes through slow bureaucratic ascent to established hierarchies where the requisite pieces of paper, diplomas and certification of political reliability (or at least harmlessness), are needed. On the other hand, there is no more need for endless additions to the white-collar officialdom. So what, then, is to happen to the masses of university-educated philosophy, economics, political science and law graduates? For years the regimes have postponed dealing with the issue by permitting the continued expansion of the universities. But that in turn creates underemployment of graduates who create a surly, unproductive and above all ungrateful stratum of lower officials and administrators, since they are obviously not going to become manual workers if they can help it.

The options of what to do about this overproduction of university-trained 'generalists' are quite limited. One can drastically cut down on admissions to the universities, at which point the critical question is just who is to be admitted. If the universities use competitive examinations, as has been suggested in several of the countries, they would clearly then discriminate in favor of the children of the middle class and intelligentsia, and the yawning gap between the new professional middle classes and the workers would increase. There is not even the heuristic side-effect of increasing the gratitude of the middle classes by this, since they tend to be quite cynical about regime politics and take it for granted that their class should continue reproducing itself. If the state uses class quotas, as has been the case in several countries, then one dooms a substantial number of the children of the new middle class to downward mobility, which increases disaffection with the regime and which tends to get the entire intelligentsia to regard itself as victimized since, of course, they have always regarded access to the university as their legitimate class perk.

Political Subjugation of Eastern European States

Beginning about a decade and a half ago, there has been a shift in the fundamental relationship between the Soviet Union and its Eastern European allies, in that Eastern Europe is no longer an economic asset to the Soviet Union. If anything, it is a drain on Soviet resources. The potential political instability of the Eastern European states is also a problem to the Soviets themselves. Today there is primarily an ideological rather than an instrumental reason for maintaining the bloc. And probably, at least in the short run, no Soviet leadership would survive its factional opponents if it 'lost' Eastern Europe.

A major part of the legitimacy of the Soviet elite, in its own eyes, is that it sees itself as being the head of a world movement toward socialism, not merely the Soviet state. It is therefore enormously important to them to maintain countries other than the Soviet Union as close allies, and to keep ties with as many Communist parties as possible. It helps maintain their legitimacy in their view of themselves and within what remains of a world movement. Military advantages may also still exist for maintaining the Warsaw Pact, although more dubious than either the US or Soviet analysts think. Given the real prospects for major cut-backs in armaments in Europe on the part of both military alliances that advantage becomes less relevant and is worth less.

There are political imperatives for maintaining the bloc and Soviet leadership within it, although the problems with obtaining effective support for Gorbachev's reforms are a warning about the difficulties with fine-tuning that support. In the longer run, increasing Eastern European autonomy may evolve into a general 'Finlandization' of the area where Soviet strategic and security interests remain protected as greater political and social differentiation of the Eastern European states takes place. An increasingly popular metaphor among Soviet bloc analysts of the process leading to the possible Finlandization of Eastern Europe is the historical comparison of the 'Ottomanization' of the empire, that is, the parallel of the century-long process of decay of the Ottoman empire where province after province on the periphery gained *de facto* independence while maintaining a purely *pro forma* acceptance of Ottoman overlordship.[7]

The Soviet model has in the past tended to emphasize heavy industry as critical for any developmental strategy. Most of the Eastern European economies, having followed the Soviet model of development, have become heavily dependent upon the Soviet Union in two respects: cheap energy and cheap raw materials. Consequently, for almost three decades the Soviets have been subsidizing their Eastern European dependencies by selling them energy – oil and natural gas, as well as some raw materials – well below the world market prices. By the 1970s, they could no longer afford to continue these subsidies, and began to renegotiate the trade agreements, moving closer to the world market prices calculated in hard currency. Since the Eastern European economies are hooked on both cheap energy and raw materials, those societies now face economic disaster.

Even more harmful is the archaic, authoritarian top-down over-centralized economic system itself. Reforms will be very difficult to achieve since of course the Soviet economy faces the same problems. That explains the urgency and seriousness with which Gorbachev is pursuing economic reforms as well as the detente with the US which is essential to provide the breathing space and economic resources for those reforms to have a chance to succeed. Due to the bottlenecks in their own economy, the drop in the world price of oil and their own need for large-scale imports of western technology (which will have to be paid for in hard currencies), the Soviets are less able to aid their allies than in the past.

The high cost of their commitments in Afghanistan and Cuba did not help. This explains their obvious and public reluctance to increase their aid to the Sandinistas in Nicaragua and their continual advice for moderation in that country. It also explains their willingness to liquidate the Afghanistan adventure on terms which are a disaster for their allies there.[8] The increasing technological and economic burden of the arms race launched in the last two years of the Carter administration and continued with such fanfare by the Reagan administration had of course exasperated the already dismal economic scene for the Soviets and consequently for their allies.

The basic stereotype about Soviet–Eastern European relations, reinforced by generations of Eastern European political exiles, is simply wrong today. The Soviet Union does not exploit the Eastern European states economically. Czechoslovakia, Hungary, Poland are all economically in miserable shape for a number of reasons which are too complicated to go into right now. However, the Soviet supply of raw materials has allowed them to maintain a relatively higher standard of living than that in the Soviet Union itself. The subsidies to Poland, for example, have created a situation where the Poles live at a standard of living higher than that of the Soviet citizens. This can be seen as adding insult to injury, since the Poles are much freer than the Soviet citizens and use that freedom in good part to complain about Soviet–Polish relations. Romania is in even worse shape than other Eastern European states, among other reasons because of their own absurd shock-treatment strategy for dealing with foreign debts which has devastated living standards.

The chains linking the Eastern European regimes to the Soviet Union today are still there, but they are above all political, ideological and military rather than economic. Eastern Europe is not exploited economically by the Soviets today, however politically it remains subjugated. Of course, *insisting* on Soviet-type centrally planned command economies did politically impose an economically inefficient system. In that sense the Soviets are clearly historically responsible for the present economic mess in Eastern Europe. Above all they are held to be responsible by the Eastern European population for the present miserable economies and unloved political leaderships. The fact that the reality is, as always, a good bit more complex does not help much in practical political terms. It remains to be seen how far the political and economic reforms in the USSR itself will loosen the political and economic dogmas and lead to an opening of those societies.

The cost of the *status quo* for the Eastern European regimes is a political, moral and social one rather than an economic one directly. The most devastating cost is the moral and spiritual one. These are above all unloved regimes, tolerated at the best. One, not-so-incidental, cost has been that the concept of 'socialism' has been devastated in Eastern Europe.

In places like Hungary and Poland, not even the party elite believes in socialism or even 'currently existing socialism' any more, if it ever did. The cost of this increasing ideological vacuum has been widespread cynicism and apathy about politics and even about oppositional politics, particularly among the young. This has also spread across the class barriers so that there is a genuine youth subculture. The problem is that this culture is mostly apolitical, hedonistic and materialist. Certain 'fashionable' topics, currently ecology, and human rights (as distinct from democracy), can serve as a focus for single-issue activities, particularly if it is an issue which is fashionable among the young in the West. On the other hand, it is not clear that the rejection of the *language* of socialism also necessarily extends to the basic values of socialism: democracy, equality, community and participation.

Resistance and Opposition in State Socialist Systems

Only a small part of the opposition in Eastern Europe still works within an explicitly socialist theoretical and political framework. Mass opposition like Solidarity does not use socialist terminology. Rather it is a mass working-class movement with an inchoate pre-socialist program mixed in with a great deal else, including nationalism and religion. In practice, much of the struggle of the opposition in Eastern Europe has, quite rightly, centered on the question of democratic rights and liberties. This is a very good thing despite the ambivalence of a generation of miseducated Marxists in both Western and Eastern Europe about so-called 'bourgeois' democracy. I do not accept the notion that there is such a thing as 'bourgeois' democracy or liberty. These are democratic rights and liberties which have been won in over a century and a half of bloody struggles from the bourgeoisie. In any case the struggle for democracy and liberty predates the struggle for socialism. These are democratic rights and liberties which today happen to exist mostly in bourgeois societies. These liberties and democratic rights are, however, safest in those bourgeois societies with the most powerful workers' political parties and movements.[9] These are not 'bourgeois liberties', and one of the not-so-minor problems with the contemporary socialist project in much of the world is that some socialists still think of those liberties as time-bound and relevant only for bourgeois societies. Even worse is the prattle about democracy and individual rights being a culturally specific 'western' preoccupation. The struggle for human rights is therefore dismissed as a form of western cultural imperialism. That is refuted by the immense size and importance of the repressive institutions in 'non-western' states and in Third World 'socialist' societies.

It seems to me not unreasonable for the working-class movements and activists or for any other popular democratic movements in Eastern Europe and the Soviet Union to say, 'We want at least *all* of the liberties which workers have in the western world, and then we want more.' What is certain is that they do not want *less* rights than the workers in Western Europe, they want more rights. That would seem a reasonable thing to demand from a government calling itself a socialist government ruling in the name of the working class.

The widespread criticism of Polish Solidarity in 1981 is that it overloaded the agenda of demands to a point where it was very difficult to win specific immediate demands which could be maintained before moving further ahead. It should be remembered, however, that the first round of regime–Solidarity confrontations occurred in 1980–81, before the advent of the reforming Gorbachev administration in the Soviet Union. It also occurred at the point of increasing US–Soviet confrontation. Clearly trade union gains, even the legalization of alternative unions, which did not include a relatively autonomous judiciary and some political freedoms, would not be worth the paper they were written on. They could have been taken away the next morning. Thus one cannot completely separate trade union demands, particularly in politocratic regimes, from certain broad democratic political demands. It is very doubtful whether the Polish regime would have actually granted even limited trade union rights if Solidarity had not also appeared as a larger social movement with very wide social and political legitimacy.

That the regime wanted to chop away at the workers' gains as soon as the situation quietened down seems to be clear.

The negotiations for the legalization of Solidarity in the spring of 1989 occur with the background of Soviet internal reforms and in the context of a successful foreign policy offensive by Gorbachev. The negotiations also occur when the economic situation is far worse than in 1981 and where the regime is desperate to get Solidarity to share in power and above all responsibility for maintaining the economy and moving on to some rationalizing reforms. That is happening in a framework where Soviet intervention, against the legalization of Solidarity as an alternative union, is very unlikely indeed.

Despite its tactical ambivalence, Solidarity has become the protest movement of a very wide sector of society – the peasantry, the intelligentsia – for example, they raised women's demands in the Gdansk agreements which were far more advanced than anything usually granted in terms of women workers. It is also the case that in regimes of a state 'socialism', the demand for democracy is the primary socialist demand. That is, everything begins with that, with freeing the society from the total domination of the party and the state. This creates the space for building autonomous social, cultural and political and popular institutions and thus a civil society.

The road to democratization and the possibility of an Eastern European socialism probably leads through a set of popular struggles which inch forward through many defeats. Reformist struggles against authoritarian state socialist regimes may well depend more on autonomous social movements, which are harder to repress, than on explicit and therefore visible and repressible socialist opposition.

But reformist struggles, as has been shown in the past, can be enormously militant, particularly as popular movements gain a sense of confidence and empowerment through limited but real victories. The problem with Western European reformist socialist and social-democratic parties is not that they *were* reformist but, on the contrary, that they were *not even* reformist. Under the authoritarian state socialist regimes of Eastern Europe, that may well be the only strategic possibility – the struggle for democratic reforms short of either a kamikaze policy of confrontation or the old forlorn hope for elemental upheavals from below appearing like *deae ex machina* as full-blown transformational movements.

A Brief Prescriptive Summary

1) The Soviet and other state socialist politocracies are today in major economic, social, and in some cases political, crises. The presence of

a large, increasingly unsatisfied, industrial working class will produce continual pressure from below in these systems, encouraging both liberalizing and technocratic reform movements from above and openings towards more democracy.

2) In part in response to this economic crisis the Soviet leadership under Gorbachev is extraordinarily open at this time to proposals for radical cut-backs in military expenditure and arsenals. Historically unprecedented opportunities are thereby opening for the socialist and peace organizations and activists. This strengthens the western advocates of disarmament and the tendency for Western Europe towards greater independence and assertiveness towards the United States. These factors lead to a possibility of an end of the Cold War as it has existed since the late 1940s and opens exciting possibilities for change in Eastern Europe.

3) The aim of radical democrats and democratic socialists should be to help both the chances of successful reforms in the Soviet bloc and the end of the present Cold War confrontation which has been the linchpin of the post-Second World War social and economic order. While supportive of the liberalization and economic reforms from above, socialists should be particularly active in contacting and encouraging the tender shoots of democracy from below and the possibility of developments towards genuine civil societies. To do this, extensive contacts, official and unofficial, with government and opposition should be encouraged and expanded between the socialist, peace and labor movements in the West in general, and Western Europe in particular, and with those in the Soviet alliance. The Soviet leaders should be told amicably but firmly that the degree of contact and friendliness is linked to the continued opening-up of these societies and expansion of democratic and individual human rights. Extensive long-range credits on very favorable terms should be offered to the Soviet leaders to help the process of modernization of their economy and society. This would of course also help the Western European economies much like the Marshall Plan in the 1940s helped the US economy.

Chapter 3

Yugoslavia: The Present Limits of Communist Reformation[1]

The longest existing experiment in the reform of ruling Communist politocracies is in Yugoslavia. The practical problems of combining market mechanisms with public ownership and planning and workers' control, or self-management, on the enterprise, local and national levels under a Communist regime have been addressed in that country for almost 40 years. Yugoslavia has also been the pioneer in the liberalization and decentralization of the state and the party as well as the development of an open and undogmatic Marxism. It is therefore an excellent place to examine just how far Communist ruling party systems, that is politocracies, can be transformed without breaking down. Lessons can be learned from the Yugoslav experience by both analysts of, and democratic reformers in, the Eastern European states and the Soviet Union.

Comparisons have to be made with caution since the Eastern European Communist regimes, with the exception of Yugoslavia and Albania, have been imposed from the outside and are more recent than the Soviet one. The order of scale itself is also important. However, there are sufficient similarities in the types of regimes involved for Yugoslavia to be at least a cracked mirror of the Soviet Union's possible futures, or at least more probable future. I do not accept the notion that the social, economic and above all political system of the Soviet Union is *sui generis*. That is why we should look at a range of these systems if we want to be able to speculate about the direction in which they may be evolving as we approach the twenty-first century. Yugoslavia represents the most radical departure, over almost 40 years, from the state 'socialist' or politocratic model. It probably marks the outer limits of Communist reformation. I think the best way to describe these systems is as *politocracies*, that is *systems in which the political elites, ruling through the single Communist party, control the state and the economy and through those, society*. This is not the place to develop an extensive rationale for my present preference for the term 'politocracy' to describe societies diversely known as state socialist or currently existing socialisms or authoritarian socialism. I borrow the term with considerable gratitude from the well-known Yugoslav political theorist Svetozar Stojanovic.[2] I think it is superior in explanatory power to the other independent Marxist (generally Troskyist influenced) attempts to describe the societies which emerged after the isolation of the Bolshevik revolution when the counter-revolution led by Stalin in 1929/30 created an unprecedented new social and political order. Politocracies can have a wide range of possible forms with more or less autonomy for independent organizations and trade unions and more or less political rights and individual liberty. Almost like bourgeois societies, in fact!

The Particularities of the Yugoslav Case

Yugoslavia is the only country in Eastern Europe (here defined geographically rather than politically) where major criticisms and discontent are still generally expressed within an explicit and conscious socialist framework. Socialism, democracy and specifically democratic socialism are very much on the intellectual and political agenda of a major section of the intellectuals, academic experts and of large sections of present membership and even in some cases the leadership of the League of Communists. Most of the Yugoslav 'public intellectuals', including most democratic and socialist critics of the regime, argue that the road to reform and democratization in their country runs through the party (the League of Communists of Yugoslavia or the LCY) rather than outside and against it. Most of what remains of the old *Praxis* circle,[3] and various democratic or humanist–Marxist groupings, still talk in terms of a democratic federal Yugoslav state based on social ownership and self-management. They are sometimes more skeptical about the place of the market under socialism than the official LCY and government spokesmen. They may object to current policies: they may call for the resignation of the Prime Minister and the entire Cabinet. But most critics in Yugoslavia accept the basic normative foundations of the system: a decentralized form of federalism, workers' self-management combined with a socially owned market economy, and non-alignment. What they reject is the LCY's continued monopoly of power.

At least eight 'factions' in the League of Communists exist at any given moment, based on the powerful autonomous league organizations of the republics and provinces. This power is all the more real since these units reflect the multi-national character of the state and are not mere administrative units.[4] In addition, there are at least three or four 'cross-cutting' political 'tendencies' or currents: liberal technocrats, hard-liner traditionalists, populist nationalists, democratic pluralists, etc., all expressing themselves through the press and media and engaged in a highly contentious debate about the future of the Yugoslav system.

The local leaderships of the various republics in Yugoslavia argue publicly for alternative policies. The Yugoslavs do not accept a monolithic party, even theoretically. They assume that there will be disagreements and contradictions in a socialist state, competing interests which reflect legitimate differences which have to be negotiated in political life. Much of the debate is still among the rival or competing local leaderships. One cannot, for example, as yet form legal and open factions within the LCY. However, the party as a monolithic ruler is hardly convincing when stormy sessions of the Central Committee are shown on television. In addition to the sharp and explicit differences which various republic parties express over policies in economy and society, there are public journals which violently polemicize with each other over economic policy, more centralization, more decentralization, more power for workers' councils, more centralized planning, more democracy, less democracy, and these issues are debated in the mass media, including television. The degree of internal democracy within the LCY varies enormously from republic to republic but it is clear that a wide diversity of views now does openly exist within the League of Communists. In short, 'glasnost' has been firmly established.

Liberalization and Democratization

In one-party politocratic systems it is important to distinguish between *liberalization* and *democratization*. The first, acceptable to new middle classes and technocratic elites as well as to the more modern sections of the party leadership, exists in Poland, Hungary and now in the Soviet Union. It most often comes from the top down, although sometimes in response to the existing or anticipated pressures from below. The second, democratization, is a far messier, more turbulent, uncontrolled and contested process. The first presupposes the maintenance of the party monopoly, a sort of Communism with a human face; the second presupposes independent unions and social movements at least as a step towards party pluralism. Some of that mess and turbulence is evident in Poland today and is characteristic of what is happening in Yugoslavia.

Both require major moves towards a state of legality, or a Rechtstaat, and development towards a civil society autonomous of the party and the state.[5]

During the struggle for democratization, more people may be jailed than under the classic one-party dictatorship, since the boundaries of what is legal and permitted dissent are continually being challenged, tested and expanded. Also the forces and groups which come to the surface during the opening up of a society are by no means only those who are for more democracy. In the Soviet Union liberalization brought a Great Russian nationalist and hard-line faction into public life as well as a rebirth of Armenian and other nationalisms. In Yugoslavia mass rallies in Serbia are heavily influenced by an intolerant nationalism and the demand for a tough line against the Albanian majority in Kosovo. Democratization is the battleground for a civil society and a legal social order, which is why Yugoslavia should be of such interest to all who speculate about the limits of the evolution of the state 'socialist' societies.

The Yugoslav Economy: Market Socialism at Bay?

The Yugoslav economy is in very deep trouble today. It is not at all clear how much of the trouble is the result of bad decisions made by the Yugoslav national and regional political leaderships against what is undoubtedly the influence of a very unfavorable international economic climate since the oil shock of 1973. Whatever the assessment of the responsibility for the economic situation, it is obviously in need of drastic rescue measures: hardly any growth of the national product since 1980, an inflation rate of over 500 per cent moving into four figures. Continued decline of living standards and growing unemployment among the young give no evidence of improving in the visible future. The drastic rescue measures now prescribed by the Federal government, with the World Bank's and other western creditors' hearty approval, are a social and political disaster for any popular government. They are the old free-marketeer nostrums of producing and exporting more while cutting down on social spending and real wages of workers. These measures would also require laying off masses of 'unproductive' workers, particularly in service industries.

In a highly politicized economy what is and what is not 'productive' or 'efficient' is very often determined by political decisions about taxes, import restrictions and pressures on enterprises to add to their workforces.

There is hardly any objective impartial allocator in a market under conditions of party monopoly. Exporting more, the other cure-all being offered, in an era of growing protectionism on the part of both the European Community and the United States, removing familiar hard-currency markets, is ever more difficult. The Third World customers of Yugoslavia are themselves over their heads in debt and are incapable of paying for the past orders.

Cutting the standards of the workers, even if that were a desirable policy, is hard to achieve given the already low living standard in most of the south and the very large and expensive administrative apparatus in both the economy and political institutions which would have to be significantly pruned for workers to be willing to accept any sacrifices. Since this is occurring in the contexts of expanding democratization, workers' protests and strikes are not only predictable but will continue to expand in scope and size.

The cumbersome federal structure makes unpleasant and difficult decisions all but impossible to make within the existing system which is based on consensus between the political elites of the republics and provinces. But this complex structure reflects the reality of the distribution of power in a multi-ethnic state with vast differences in tradition, history, economic development and consequently political culture. It also unfortunately means in practice that no one and no specific institution or elected body can be individually or collectively held responsible for the mistakes in economic decisions and allocations. That is, the diffusion of economic and political decision-making has made it impossible to fix responsibility for incompetent, politically motivated or just wrong decisions. This leads to considerable cynicism about the constant official calls for more responsibility. Those calls are less effective as grotesque waste and inefficiency come to light, given a more independent and critical press. To give just one example: major journals have publicized the fact that in the middle of this economic crisis when belts are supposed to be tightened all around, there are no less than 160,000 cars, many with chauffeurs, owned by the government and its bureaux and services! The upkeep of this monster car park and wages for the personnel involved comes to just about the $2 billion a year which it takes to service the Yugoslav international debt. In the months which followed this expose no one has denied either the facts or the figures. The rage of the workers facing wage cuts reading about this scandal is easy to imagine.

On the other hand, the socio-economic system of self-management and decentralization which is commonly, and I believe mistakenly, blamed for the present economic mess in Yugoslavia is also the identical system which works successfully in the more developed northern republic of Slovenia. This is the system which had produced spectacular growth, matching that of Japan and South Korea, during the two and a half decades before the year of the oil shock and the world recession. The question is: is self-management combined with market-socialism, that is, that which is specific and different about the Yugoslav socio-political system, more typical of the successful republics like Slovenia or of the unsuccessful ones like Macedonia? Or to put it in another way, is it because of or despite self-management and market socialism that Yugoslavia is in its present mess? My argument is that the cure for Yugoslavia's ills is more, not less, self-management and, above all, *more, not less, democratization*. That must include the removal of the constant non-legal, informal but ever-present political interference in the economy and economic decision-making of self-managed enterprises by the local, county and republic political party elites who form the informal *nomenklaturas*.[6]

Another serious problem that bedevils both the Yugoslav and other reformers in Eastern Europe is the tendency to apply abstract universal norms rigidly to proposals of how to run economies and societies. Thus the absurd counter-positions: plan or market, rigid equalitarianism or the *dolce vita* of the West, complete abolition of the federal central agencies of the state or rigid centralism, etc.[7] Alec Nove's modest and reasonable book, *The Economics of a Feasible Socialism*, represents an excellent antidote for the usual dogmas about the plan and market under socialism. Nove argues that a properly organized socialist economy would be a combination of central planning, self-management, regionally owned public enterprises, cooperatives and a small-scale private sector. The decision of which form of public or private ownership and administration one chooses should be based not on abstract general principles but on the nature of the activity.

Presumably in Yugoslavia the railroads, posts and telegraph would be run federally as public utilities, the banks and power companies as public utilities by the republics, the plants as self-managed and publicly owned enterprises, smaller plants and workshops and above all services as cooperatives or privately owned. A fair and universally applied tax structure would prevent excessive accumulations of wealth, high inheritance taxes would prevent the entrenchment of economic privilege. Independent trade unions run by workers would protect general working-class economic interests, especially above the enterprise level, and an autonomous network of enterprise committees with freely elected shop stewards would defend workers in the plants and other workplaces and run strikes when necessary.

All such basic economic reforms have as their precondition the destruction of the stubbornly entrenched pockets of privilege of the politocracy, their families and allies. The greatest of all privileges for most people is a large, modern house or apartment. Those are distributed through political channels and are not generally obtainable through mere 'income differences'. That is why so much of the talk about the dangers of economic inequalities increasing through the expansion of the private sector voiced from politicians from the less-developed parts of Yugoslavia is so demagogic. While substantial economic differences exist today, they have existed and in a far more virulent form during the harsh orthodox and centralist period immediately after the war. It is demagoguery in Yugoslavia to attack the present privileges and social differences as the product of democratization and decentralization of the society since the 1960s. Privileges *are more visible today*, because there is more property and consumer goods available and they are distributed differently. The press writes about the privileges of the elites with a freedom which could not have been imagined during Tito's lifetime. Further, it is no longer just the political elite, the *nomenklatura* and their favorites, who now have privileges.

Politics is no longer the sole or even the primary method for living better than others. There is now a growing middle and professional class which is not dependent on politics for its income and status. This group is not the creation of market socialism so much as of the greater prosperity and consequent division of labor. On the other hand, today there are no capitalists. Soccer stars and pop singers can be individually wealthy but no enterprise with more than fifteen workers can be owned privately, and any joint venture established must still have workers' councils and trade unions. This might explain why there has not been a stampede of western capital to establish joint ventures in Yugoslavia.

To improve the economy the small-scale private sector in Yugoslavia should be expanded considerably, above all in the fields of crafts and services. The problem is essentially one of power: the small private sector is not a base for the restoration of the power of the capitalist class. On the contrary, when raising the question of power, it is clear that a form of effective public, popular and legal control over the power exerted by those controlling the public sector is a desperately urgent necessity. This is particularly true since those who hold power, through the manipulation or intimidation of the elected bodies of the workers' councils, are invariably linked with the local and republic party-power structures. Control of this all too real power is a far more urgent problem than the fear of the potential power of the phantom of capitalist restoration.

The Ghost Which Keeps Reappearing: Managing Nationalism

The Communist-led partisans won the civil war and revolution during the Second World War because, unlike their civil war opponents, they accepted the fact that theirs was a multi-ethnic society and proceeded to organize federation on that basis.[8] The major Yugoslav national groups each have their national republics: Slovenia, Croatia, Macedonia, Montenegro, Serbia and Bosnia-Hercegovina. In addition to the six republics there are two autonomous provinces within the republic of Serbia: Vojvodina in the north, with a Hungarian minority of some 25 per cent, and Kosovo in the south, with an Albanian majority of close to 90 per cent of the population. The top federal positions of the state and the LCY are filled through rotation between the republics and provinces.[9] The system pays overwhelming attention to the federal units, not citizens as individuals. The real political subjects of the Yugoslav federation are the republics and their political elites as well as the official mass organizations rather than either the citizens or cross-cutting autonomous institutions of the working class.[10]

The only genuine federal institution today is the Yugoslav National Army (JNA). Centrifugal nationalism increasingly seems to try the patience of the LCY and of the armed forces. (That of course is what one means by the abstraction, 'the army'.) They have not taken sides in major political disputes except to show reservations about the rapid pace of democratization occurring in Slovenia, which seems to imply a surrender of the party monopoly in that republic.

The great ethnic complexity of Yugoslavia is today its best-known feature and its best-publicized problem. Here too, many valuable, positive *and* negative, lessons can be learned by more countries than we are accustomed to think of as being multi-ethnic polities. If the neo-corporatist model is applicable to Yugoslavia, the group identity which is 'privileged' is the nation, expressing itself through the republic in which it is dominant, supplemented by the group identity as a member of a group in associated labor in a self-managing enterprise, and in a more attenuated and indirect manner as a member of the working class. That last, which could have been a cross-cutting and unifying identity, has been submerged in the vaguer category of 'working people', which in effect includes everyone employed. That is therefore a 'soft' and general identity, whereas the national identity, particularly with the growing secularization of political faith in socialism and Marxism, comes ever more strongly to the forefront. That is a dangerous lesson for other multi-ethnic politocracies which are reforming. The long-lived party-power monopoly which eliminated other genuine political alternatives may have left traditional national and religious identification as the most salient and passionately held ones by an increasingly depoliticized people.

The current national problems are found in two unpredictable places and one, alas, all too predictable. The predictable place and the problem which makes the most stout-hearted optimist quail is Kosovo. The unpredictable places are Slovenia and Serbia. Since this is not an article on the intricacies of the national question in Yugoslavia, I will be brief and simplify.

Slovenia is the most economically and socially advanced and prosperous republic in the federation. With less than 2 per cent unemployment in contrast to the Yugoslav average of over 14 per cent, close to one tenth of its workforce are immigrant workers from the less-prosperous southern republics. The presence of these immigrant workers from the south, who are often Muslim, poorly educated and speak Serbo-Croatian, has awakened a Slovenian nationalist alarm since the Slovenes are a small and prosperous nation of less than 2 million out of 24 million in Yugoslavia. The Slovenian popular resentment has been fueled by their assumption that they pay an unfair share of the common federal budget and that those funds are systematically mismanaged by the local political leaders in the less developed regions. It does not help that the leaders from the less developed republics keep attacking Slovenia for its greater tolerance of social movements, political opposition and a somewhat counter-cultural and activist official youth organization and journal. Consequently Slovenian public opinion is at the moment defensive of its special role which includes *both* greater democracy and legality than the rest of Yugoslavia, combined with a growing local intolerance towards 'uncultured southerners'. The bias against raw material producers and high import duties on manufacturing has long subsidized their economy, but since that subsidy is invisible, while their contributions to the federal funds for the underdeveloped are politically very visible, the Slovene public opinion regards their republic as a victim of the Yugoslav economy and political system. The Slovenian youth organization's lively journal *Mladina* has been attacking the entrenched sacred cows, including the army and the revolution itself, and is at this moment the cutting edge of civil society and civil liberties in the country as a whole. As a consequence it has also been the target of an army trial of a non-commissioned officer and three journalists for supposedly handling secret army documents. With the delicacy usual to all armies, they insisted on holding the trial in Serbo-Croatian in the capital of Slovenia, offending both Slovenian linguistic sensitivities and violating the Slovenian law, and then proceeded to dish out sentences ranging from six months to three years, which outraged the entire democratic public opinion of Yugoslavia. It is important to note that democratic protests and alternative movements in Slovenia are backed by both the government and party of Slovenia.

Serbia: A Popular and Populist Nationalism

Serbia is a more complicated case. It is the one republic whose nationalism can be fatal for the federation as such. Serbs are the largest national group in the federation. Potential nationalist problems have always existed, one of which has been the fact that Serbs are divided between four republics and two provinces, which Serbian nationalists have regarded as a loss. All that had led to minor nationalist unhappiness in the past, mostly on the part of writers and academics. There were historical, if not ethnic, grounds for such division. No republic is nationally homogeneous and, for that matter, Croats are divided between three or four federal units.

The developments over the past decade in the province of Kosovo have led to a fundamental realignment of politics in Serbia and the growth of a dangerous, defensive and populist, officially sanctioned nationalism which is publicly mostly focused on the defense of their fellow nationals from demographic pressures of the local Albanian majority in that province. Increasingly Serbian nationalism is directing its attention to the real or alleged grievances of Serbs in the other republics, in Bosnia-Hercegovina and Croatia above all, placing strains on the federation itself. However, the main attention is focused on Kosovo and the pressures from the Albanian majority against the Serbian minority. That pressure, including some cases of rape, murder and vandalism, has been all too real.[11]

Increasing use of the term 'genocide' to describe the present situation of the Serbs and Montenegrins in Kosovo is an obvious hysterical and chauvinist exaggeration. The danger signal was reached when the responsible political leadership of the Serbian LCY and government and leading intellectuals and academics took that grotesquely abused term over from a hysterical yellow press and thus legitimated it. The present leader of the Serbian state and party, Slobodan Milosevic, has based his growing power on the swing towards populist nationalism. His support includes that of many well-known previous democratic and socialist critics of the LCY in Belgrade. He has also drawn the support of the neo-Stalinists with a nostalgia for the old days of firm administrative control as well as the support of nationalists who are revising the history of the revolutionary war of liberation.

The growth of this officially sanctioned national populism in Serbia has terrified the leaderships and public of the other national groups and the other republics. They fear for the future of the federation itself, if the largest national group in the federation is going to throw its weight around and insist on its right to use extra legal and extra systemic means to resolve complex national and constitutional issues. In effect the struggle for democratization of Yugoslavia is now being held hostage to a reborn Serbian nationalism which in turn is mesmerized by Kosovo which has become charged with a symbolism so powerful that it seems impermeable to any rational solutions. Politically the closest parallel is the situation of the Israelis on the West Bank. A heavy historical responsibility for this lies at the door of the Serbian League of Communists' leadership which instead of fighting the mystic and fundamentally undemocratic romanticism of Serbian national populism has chosen, to its discredit, to try to control and use it. *But one cannot have a police regime in Kosovo and democratization in Belgrade.*

These developments have nasty associations with 'Pamyat', the Great Russian hard-lining nemesis of Gorbachev's perestroika in the Soviet Union, as well as the growth of nationalist and populist sentiments in Poland and Hungary. That is why the specific Yugoslav problem of national populism in Serbia may turn out to be a part of a more general wave of a less pleasant future as the politocracies face ideological disintegration under the pressures to reform.

However, the mass demonstrations in Serbia and Montenegro also represent a distorted attempt at a popular, communitarian and grass-roots expression of the growing disenchantment of a very broad layer of the population with a sclerotized political system which seems incapable of change. It cannot manage the economy and cannot even assure the one legitimate demand around the situation in Kosovo, law and order, and personal safety and safety of property for all citizens. Demonstrations are the penalty for the blocking of the political system for far too long through ever more complex structures designed to avoid genuine political democratization and the possibility of alternation of power. In short, the mass demonstrations are a plebicidary bastard form of democracy in place of a genuine democratization of the system itself.

Kosovo: A Present and Historic Tragedy

If Serbia is complicated, Kosovo is tragic. Everything about that region, from its history to its present social and economic situation to its future prognosis, is tragic. It is the cradle of Serbian nationalism, the battleground where the medieval Serbian kingdom was conquered by the Turks, ushering in almost 500 years of Turkish, that is to say Muslim, rule over Serbia. It is the region where the most important monuments of Serbian medieval culture are located. Kosovo has become, to Serbia, an emotional equivalent of a combination of Northern Ireland and a Wailing Wall. But it is also an area in which modern Albanian nationalism was born in the nineteenth century and an area which, whatever its history, today has an absolutely clear and undisputed huge Albanian majority of over 90 per cent which must obtain the degree of self-determination which the other Yugoslav national groups have.[12]

Albanians in Kosovo have the highest birth-rate in Europe. Since they are both heavily rural and overwhelmingly Muslim, they resist birth-control and the emancipation of women. The social pressure of the traditional patriarchal society continues to be for marriage before the legal minimal age and for women to be kept out of the non-domestic workforce. Attempts to enforce Yugoslav laws and norms are regarded as an assault on Albanian culture and religion. Unless women are pulled into the workforce, the birth-rate will continue to explode and an ever-larger pool of ever-better-educated, bitter, unemployed young people will be created.

The same Yugoslav political elites, police and courts, which had been all too willing to jail demonstrators, student and intellectual dissidents, irreverent poets and writers, have tolerated child marriage, the removal of female children from the school system and other illegal patriarchal practices in areas like Kosovo and Macedonia. These legal violations have deprived and continue to deprive women in the less-developed areas of Yugoslavia, particularly in Muslim and Albanian-inhabited areas, but also in Macedonia, Bosnia-Hercegovina, southern parts of Serbia and Montenegro, of the rights guaranteed to Yugoslav citizens by the constitution. This is just one more argument why, in a state with a wide range of cultural divergences, individual rights cannot be left to *local* courts and police to protect. The enforcement of women's and civic rights and laws by local county courts and police is often a part of the problem. Then these same authorities act surprised that they face Third World birth-rates among the Albanians in Kosovo and Macedonia! Female emancipation and modernity go hand in hand.

Kosovo has been receiving the lion's share of federal and republic economic aid for decades, but it has also steadily fallen ever further behind the rest of Yugoslavia, in good times and bad.[13] Poor as it is, and its *per capita* income is *one sixth* that of Slovenia, it is still better off than Albania. Quite properly, the Kosovars do not compare their living standards with the country they do not live in but with that of the country in which they do live. Unemployment and lack of development led to nationalist demonstrations in 1981 which were repressed with massive arrests and which have left the province smoldering with the resentment of the Albanian majority and fear of the Serbian and Montenegrin minority. There is little or no popular sentiment for unity with Albania at this time. Thus Kosovo and Yugoslavia are fated to remain together and the solution of the problem of Kosovo is a burden which Yugoslavia has to carry in addition to that of a faltering economy and the problems of democratization.

They *must* solve that problem, since Kosovo is a time bomb. Consider: as a concession to their national pride and rights, Albanians in Kosovo complete their education in their own language, a language understood by no one outside of their ethnic group. Young Albanians have failed to learn even the minimum of Serbo-Croat, the language spoken by 20 million out of 24 million in that country. The result is that they are locked into a partially self-made ghetto as far as employment is concerned. All of this has to be solved while not enraging the largest ethnic group in the federation, the Serbs, who feel that Kosovo is historically theirs and, with considerable validity, that their co-nationals are being driven out of Kosovo by threats of force and pressure by the Albanian majority. This has to be done without outraging the Slovenes and Croats who have to pay a considerable part of the economic bill. And all this has be done through a consensual political system where individual republics can veto unacceptable measures!

National Confrontation Jeopardizes Democratization

The increasing nationalist confrontation has led to strikes by Albanian miners, a campaign of massive civil disobedience by the general Albanian population, and the purge or withdrawal from political life of the remaining pro-Yugoslav Albanian Communist leaders. By the spring of 1989 limited martial law had been declared in the province and the dreary familiar statistics of death and injury began to mount. As in the Palestinian *intifada* on the West Bank and Gaza, the casualties are overwhelmingly civilian.

The less visible casualty is seen in the remarkable overall coarsening of political debate and life in Serbia and increasingly shrill, intolerant and nationalist tone in the press and politics. All criticism of the present disastrous nationality policy is attacked as treason if engaged in by Serbs, and as 'Serbophobia' when it comes from other republics. The Serbian political leadership has rammed through legislation which substantially reduces the autonomy of Kosovo and subordinates the Kosovo authorities and political organizations to those of Serbia. The result is increasing alienation and hostility of the Albanian majority in Kosovo. The seeds of further national conflict have thus been sown and democratization and economic reform have been subordinated to a passionate, uncompromising romantic nationalism.

The immediate problem with that nationalism is that it cannot win without violating the right of the Albanians in Kosovo and alienating the other national groups in Yugoslavia. There is no other way for Kosovo to be 'Serbian', and that in essence *is* the central demand of the officially sanctioned mass demonstrations in Serbia. There is a choice: Kosovo (temporarily) at the price of democratization, or further democratization, which means that Kosovo cannot be Serbian. It can be an equal part of Yugoslavia but it cannot be Serbian. The Serbian political and legal authorities are a part of the conflict in Kosovo. Therefore, insisting on the present Serbian domination of Kosovo not only threatens democratization in Serbia itself but jeopardizes the continued existence of the federation. Ultimately Kosovo can be subjected to Serbia only by force and that means playing with fire, or more precisely playing with policies which may provoke the army, much against its instincts, to take a hand. After all it is the army that would have to pick up the pieces if the disastrous courting of national populism in Serbia provoked an explosion of defensive nationalism in Kosovo and elsewhere.

If some of this reminds readers of the tangled mess of Israeli-Arab relations on the West Bank, it should come as no surprise that nationalist Serbian intellectuals formed the Serbian-Jewish Friendship Association in 1988! However, that this is not a situation arising out of the peculiarities of Balkan, Serbian and Albanian history should be clear to any observer of the difficulties which the reformist Gorbachev leadership faces in Armenia, Georgia and Azerbaidzan.

In each of these Soviet republics martial law had to be declared and troops sent in after mass nationalist rallies exacerbated historic national intolerance between local national groups. Interestingly, in each of these cases, as in those of Serbia and Kosovo, national intolerance and a history of grievances are reinforced by *religious* differences, between Islam and Christianity, where 'religion' has acted as the surrogate for national identity for centuries. Again, one can argue that religious and national identity becomes central after decades of top-down modernization combined with repression.

When God is dead and the largest secular world faith, Marxist socialism, is in crisis, a moral vacuum is created. In the absence of a vibrant civil society, that vacuum can be filled by xenophobic populist nationalism, the form of populist nationalism which puts forward one's own nation as the victim of history and oppression by 'others'. That is one of the historic penalties being paid for years of Stalinism and repression and emerged during the opening up caused by limited democratization or 'glasnost'. Why should it be assumed that after years of political repression democratization will bring to the surface politically tolerant pluralistic democrats? On the contrary, prolonged rule of one-party politocratic regimes has created crude and warped political cultures within which *traditional* linkages, such as those of nationality and religion, surface with a vengeance when they get the chance.

Yugoslavia Must Get into Europe

A special current political problem is the lack of realism of the Yugoslav political leaders, who still seem to think that Western Europe is waiting for Yugoslavia to come in. On the contrary, Yugoslavia will have an uphill battle to convince the European Community that it should be taken in out of the cold. There will be two minimum requisites: that major steps be taken to improve the condition of the economy and, above all, that no gross violations of human rights take place. Both are difficult conditions today. There is little evident will to engage in major economic and political surgery. The Kosovo situation is a minefield of potential human rights violations waiting to happen.[14]

It is a grim prospect either way: staying outside of a more united European economy means facing greater tariff barriers and falling behind in both technology and the needed help for the Yugoslav infrastructure. Yugoslavia never suffered from the kind of limitations placed on Austria by the peace treaty, nor was it subject to direct Soviet influence as the Warsaw Pact allies were. There was no valid reason whatsoever, except ideological blinkers, Cominternist nostalgia and a grand illusion of a special mission in the Third World, to keep Yugoslavia from developing much closer relations with the European Community. A fundamental re-examination of the attitude towards the Socialist International and its parties is also overdue. When the Soviets seek to improve the relations with 'world social-democracy', when the Italian Communist party deputies in the European Parliament become a part of a socialist parliamentary group, it would seem that the Yugoslav LCY must go a great deal further in improving their relationship to the Western European socialist, social-democratic and labor parties. Such a move would be a signal that the LCY regards itself as closer to the mass democratic workers' parties of the advanced industrial democracies than to the Eastern European Communist parties. The problem is that the very idea is a highly contested one in Yugoslavia today, reflecting the fact that there are *two* parties inside the League of Communists. One is a slightly modified old Communist party still committed to the party monopoly in the society and 'democratic' centralism inside the party. The other is a democratic socialist party struggling to be born.

Eventually Yugoslavia will have to get into the European Community with some status or other. It can only do so with the help of the socialist and workers' parties of Western Europe. Those parties are quite properly sensitive to questions of human rights, trade union rights and democracy. Without that shift towards Europe there will be no long-range solutions for the problems of the Yugoslav economy and society. But then there is another reason for moving towards Europe, for such a realignment would greatly strengthen the development of a civil society and autonomous institutions in Yugoslavia. In other words, the political conditions which a unified Europe tends to insist on for new entrants are far from a burden, they are a positive good and will immensely help those who want to democratize Yugoslavia. These conditions are not that Yugoslavia enter a military bloc with NATO, a condition which would be quite properly rejected out of hand. For that matter, that condition would bar the EFTA countries like Sweden, Austria and Switzerland which are now collectively negotiating an entrance into the European Community.

This is not to say that integration in Europe would not have economic problems of its own. It is, after all, a Europe of multi-nationals, and the free flow of capital and goods will appear terrifying to those presently running the Yugoslav economic and fiscal system. However, the world economy itself is one dominated by those same multi-nationals and financial institutions, so there is after all only one world market today. Being a part of Europe does not isolate one from the effects of the world economy any more than being outside does. Or to put things a bit more positively, it is only by allying itself with the forces of the essentially social-democratic Euro-left within Europe that Yugoslavia has any chance at all of working out a relationship with the multi-nationals and the international banks which is not one of utter dependence.

This only brings into sharper focus just how harmful has been the official Yugoslav practice of treating concern with human rights in Yugoslavia by democratic forces elsewhere as some kind of illegitimate interference in their internal affairs. On the contrary, the presence of such pressure in international affairs is something which should be welcome, just like the presence of international peace or ecology movements.

It is a sign of genuine progress when the Soviets under Gorbachev propose to hold a human rights conference in the Soviet Union. It is also progress when the Yugoslavs set up an official body, through the Socialist Alliance of Working People, the 'broad non-party front', to deal with human rights.

Where Is the System Going: What Can One Learn from It?

Since the 1948 break with Stalin, and consequently the world of Communist international orthodoxy, Yugoslavia has evolved in increasingly interesting and heterodox directions. That development began as a search for an 'authentic' Marxist-Leninism which would free first Yugoslav and later world Communism from the distortions introduced into the world movement by Stalin. This is why the Yugoslav Communists, despite their fragile economy, pushed so hard to develop a systematic theory and practice of workers' self-management which led to the economic reforms of 1964. These were designed to weaken the centralized power of the party and state over the economy and society by introducing the idea of a *socialist* market economy. The Yugoslav Communists believed that they were not moving away from Communism but towards what they considered a more consistent and authentic Communism than the Soviet model which they characterized as either state capitalism, state socialism or quite simply statism.

The Yugoslav League of Communists today leaves large areas of civic and cultural life outside its direction and concentrates on the few narrow crucial political matters where it does try to maintain firm control. Thus, for example, a gay disco club exists in the capital of Slovenia, journals like *The Economist*, *Time*, *Newsweek* and *Playboy* are on sale in the major cities. There are translations of numerous anti- and non-Marxist social scientists, and the publication of the *collected* works of Trotsky.

Violent polemics take place among the economists about the appropriate economic programs and theory, heretical books are published on the theory of historical materialism, decadent and non-objective art and poetry. At the same time Yugoslavia has had an average of three hundred or so political prisoners at any given time.

This creates a very curious situation whereby the society which is by all evidence the freest in Eastern Europe has more political prisoners than the obviously more repressive Bulgaria or Czechoslovakia. The critical point for the other Eastern European reformers is that it shows that the party can permit a great degree of autonomy in the civil society, culture and economy and yet retain political power. With a given degree of decentralization and an explicit assertion by the party that it does not run everything, every challenge to authority is not automatically a challenge to state power.

A more pessimistic description of the way Yugoslavia is evolving is to consider it to be a new and interesting form of neo-corporatism, rather than a polity developing towards democratic pluralism.[15] The Yugoslav system has many features of neo-corporatism, with the major players being the elites of the republics and from the largest socially owned enterprises. Leo Panitch's description of corporatism in the west is a not bad approximation of how the Yugoslav system works:

> . . . corporatist programmes advocated a universal scheme of vocational, industrial or sectoral organization whereby constituent units would have the right to representation in national decision-making, and a high degree of functional autonomy, but would have the duty of maintaining the functional hierarchy and social discipline consistent with the needs of the nation-state as a whole. A limited organizational pluralism, generally operating under the aegis of the state as the supreme collective community, would guarantee the major value of corporatism – social harmony.[16]

The more general question which this raises is whether or not neo-corporatism is not the logical end result of most of the proposed reforms in Eastern Europe and the Soviet Union, and if so is it a step forward. My own, very tentative, answer is yes to both propositions with two reservations. The first is that clearly neo-corporatist arrangements will differ from society to society and over time, given the balance of class and other political forces; that is, it can be more or less advantageous to the working class and democratic forces in general. Secondly, neo-corporatism is preferable to authoritarian state 'socialist' stagnation but not to the democratization of a society achieved by massive struggles from below. Therefore, whether this is a step forward or not depends on one's estimate of the possibility for successful popular mobilization around democratic and socialist goals in a given society and time.

Most strikes in Yugoslavia today are wildcat strikes, usually against the local government, or against decisions of the central workers' council. However, beginning in 1988, there have been massive workers' demonstrations outside Parliament attacking the present policy of austerity. They represent a reaction to the pressures from Yugoslavia's creditors for economic policies which lower the living standards and attack job security. These pressures are particularly explosive in a context where the political and economic elites are making no equivalent material sacrifices. The party (LCY) and the local government authorities do not usually intervene, and the demonstrations were not forbidden. A strike is a strike, no more and no less threatening than is a strike in Western Europe. Powerful autonomous social movements exist, primarily in the north. Mass demonstrations and petitions have stopped the construction of a nuclear power center near Zadar and the Federal legislature has voted to phase out nuclear power within a decade despite sharp objections from the government. Well-known dissidents like Djilas can today travel, get published, are interviewed in at least the youth press, speak publicly and appear on TV. The government prosecutors repeatedly lose censorship cases in courts, but they also sometimes win. Such cases no longer have predictable outcomes. What are missing are two vital things: the defense of general rights of the citizen *as an individual* and the ability to posit general rather than particularist interests. The last is still reserved for the party, the League of Communists, 'the collective intellectual' of the society as a whole and of the working class. This has also diffused and almost fatally weakened all potential opposition, except localist and nationalist ones, since the opposition, as well as power, is broken up into many localized compartments. This is one of the reasons why localism and nationalism have been tacitly tolerated if not encouraged over all these years. This in turn underlines the pernicious role of the one remaining inheritance from the Soviet Communist system, the local and republic *nomenklaturas* which, while informal in Yugoslavia, still play a dominant role in determining cadre policy in political organizations, local governments and at times industry.

Whether one agrees with the in-party reformers or the critics who are outside the party, it is clear that the road to a reformed and democratic socialism lies in good part through the LCY. It is within the League that much of the battle for the establishment of a civil society and for a pluralistic democratic socialism will be fought out. Yugoslavia will, unless the party hard-liners carry out a currently unimaginable coup with the help of the military, continue evolving towards a more pluralist state and a democratic and socialist polity.

By a socialist polity I mean a society in which the working class, both traditional and new, controls the means of production and distribution through its democratic control of the state, which has a major role to play in planning, at least on a macro-economic level. I also mean a society where the demands of the various sectors of the people are democratically fought out or mediated in a political arena in which there is the posing of alternative policies. Whether Yugoslavia will evolve into a society with a plurality of parties is less certain in the relatively near future. Multi-party competition is regrettably way down the road, but there will be open tendencies and factions in the party and the broad front, the Socialist Alliance, and increasing legal and constitutional protection for free debate and organization of autonomous social movements. Questions central to a pluralist polity and democratic socialism are being posed openly and ever more urgently and acrimoniously in public debates in the Yugoslav press and society.

Chapter 4

The Third World: Socialisms, 'Currently Existing Socialisms', the United States and Democratic Socialists[1]

The three decades after the Second World War were years of stability and economic growth for Western Europe during which the prospects for radical social transformation beyond the existing welfare states became increasingly remote. At the same time, as more information came to light, it became increasingly clear that the Soviet Union and Eastern Europe were authoritarian, drab, politically and intellectually repressive and economically stagnant societies. During that same period massive and historic change was taking place in the former colonial countries and the less developed parts of the globe, that is, in what was to be known as the Third World. As the more orthodox Communist and Marxist movements began to run into ever-increasing ideological and organizational trouble in the late 1950s and early 1960s in Western Europe, many of their theorists and intellectuals and fellow travellers turned to the Third World for hope.[2] At that time the development of the Third World paralleled the growth of the influence of Maoism and the non-aligned movement. This development thus was a critique of the orthodox Communist parties and of the alliance led by Moscow: anti-imperialist but not pro-Moscow, therefore the *Third* World.

The term is a philosophers' stone: it could and does mean too many things. It was obviously a political invention meant to be used in whatever way was most convenient. Thus, for example, was Argentina in the Third World? It was a nation not only rich in natural resources but also one which had all but wiped out its native population to replace them with European settlers. How about South Africa? Or for that matter Japan or South Korea; or is North Korea in and South Korea out of the Third World, as for example, the absurd semi-official Yugoslav doctrine holds? Where does Yugoslavia itself fit in, for that matter? Is the Third World just a synonym for the non-aligned countries? Just how non-aligned does a country have to be to *be* a non-aligned country?[3] And then, what are we to make of the term 'Third World peoples' when it is thrown around in political debates by African-Americans whose ancestors have been living as a part of an English-speaking culture for some four centuries? My own somewhat shame-faced use of that term in this work is limited to the former colonial countries and to the underdeveloped – yes, that too is a tricky term – countries.

One of the many painful ironies in the Third World is that the influence of Soviet and Eastern European models of development and growth became most influential at a time when those societies and economies had become subjected to ever sharper criticism of official and unofficial domestic reformers. The effective advent of the Soviet Union as a genuine world-class military power occurred during the years after Khruschev in what will probably be remembered as the good old times in future Soviet histories. That was a period of slow and unspectacular but steady growth of the Soviet economy which was clearly ever increasingly in need of reforms which in turn were being blocked by what seemed to be an immovable gerontocracy. However, it was also a period during which the Soviet Union had poured vast resources into building itself up to match the United States as a world power militarily.[4]

The irony is that the present line of the Soviet Union is to de-emphasize the utility of force in achieving change in the Third World and to urge the Third World radical regimes to adjust to the existing, necessarily capitalist, world market. It is among regimes which have been the closest to the Soviet Union that the strongest reservations are heard both about the Soviet *glasnost* and *perestroika*, that is, liberalization and economic reforms, and to the new Soviet international line of avoiding confrontation with the United States and the capitalist world. In this respect Cuba's Castro speaks for a range of Soviet allies and friends when he criticizes the current Soviet policies.

The Lesser Evil and the Arms Supplier

Soviet influence in the Third World grew during the period when the United States became more and more enmeshed in an endless and obviously politically unwinnable war in Vietnam. That was also the time of the increasing US identification with reactionary right-wing regimes throughout the Third World. The Soviet Union did not have to be attractive: growing hatred for the US as the prop of neo-colonialism and increasing contempt for its more and more evident hypocrisy as that liberal capitalist democracy which backs most of the reactionary regimes around the world made the Soviets appear at least a lesser evil.

While that lesser-evil argument carried little or no weight in Western or even Eastern Europe, it did seem to make good sense in the Third World. The oldest of old political illusions is that the enemy of my enemy is my friend. And at least where arms were concerned the Soviets were friends of most radical and revolutionary regimes and groups in the Third World. They were also many other complicated and non-obvious things as well, but that was less relevant during the past 25 years in the poverty-stricken Third World where change was desperately needed and the US was aggressively active as the enemy of radical social and economic change.

In many of the Third World countries, however, the Soviet Union and its bloc were seen as active allies against neo-colonialism and imperialism, and less often, as possible models for the organization of the liberation movements and parties and even of the state and the economy. The widest-spread basis for supporting, critically or otherwise, the Soviet and Eastern European state socialist countries within the Third World has been two claims made on their behalf: that they are progressive and anti-capitalist, having abolished private property in the means of production and distribution, and that they are anti-imperialist, since they are the most powerful rival of the existing imperialist world system dominated by the United States.

The mere abolition of private property is, of course, not socialism. That was clear to the founders of Marxist socialism, to Marx, Engels, Kautsky, Luxemburg and even to Lenin. It only raises in the most acute form the question of who or what groups control the state, who now 'owns' or controls formerly private property. In these societies the working class, new and old, has less power than in the industrialized capitalist democracies, where, granted all limitations on effective democratic participation and power, the workers at least have their own parties, trade unions, organizations and press. What one would expect to see in any society which was moving towards socialism is the growth of many and varied and above all independent cultural, civic and social organizations and movements. What is crucial for the protection and the continued existence of individual and collective rights and freedoms is the existence of elements of a civil society such as is found in the capitalist democracies of the advanced industrial world and is under the very best conditions a new, highly problematic and contested battleground in the state socialist politocracies.

The term politocracies is perhaps the clearest way of describing the Soviet-type societies. What it emphasizes is that these societies are not any kind of worker-run states, that they are not 'dictatorships of the proletariat' but that they are societies run by the political elites which base themselves on the single ruling party. That is, the politically dominant groups, working through the *de facto* single ruling party, hold the basic political, social and economic power.

However, this description of the Soviet-type states does not unfortunately make them *less* attractive to the modernizing political elites in the Third World. On the contrary, despite all their egalitarian and populist rhetoric, these regimes are essentially ruled by small coteries of political activists or young army officers, therefore the non-democratic character of Soviet-type societies is one of their major *attractions*. This is especially so since this non-democratic character is often pointed to as evidence of serious radicalism. The masses, and it is usually the rural masses or at best the non-working-class urban masses since workers are few in those societies, are expected to participate, that is, they are going to be appropriately educated and politically developed but they are certainly not supposed to interfere with the wielding of political power and the determination of economic and social goals. Above all, they are not supposed to develop or maintain any independent institutions and organizations.

Participation in mass and popular organizations under the control of the ruling party is highly encouraged under radical Third World regimes, and is cited as evidence of regime support. It is also counterposed to the inferior 'bourgeois' democracy of competing parties, organizations and independent unions and press. That is the point of convergence between the state socialist and Third World 'socialist' realities. There are, of course, a great many differences, not least the immense poverty of the Third World 'socialist' countries and their lesser efficiency at repression.

The absence of genuine competitive democratic political traditions as well as the past caricatures of Western European parliamentarianism (which have all too often proved to be a shell game with parties representing the old elites alternating in power, thus excluding representatives of unprivileged and poor rural groups) have helped give democracy, and particularly parliamentary democracy, a bad name.[5]

Military and Economic Aid in the Cold War

Soviet military and economic aid to Third World countries has been mostly conditioned by the major axis of their foreign policy, their imperial rivalry with the US, which determines where that support is to go, how much aid and support is to be given, and which movements are to be supported. This does not make that aid, even military aid, a bad thing necessarily, but understanding the basis for that aid can spare Third World movements and governments considerable disillusionment.

Note that I write *imperial, not imperialist*, rivalry. The traditional definition of imperialism is difficult to apply to the Soviet Union or for that matter today even to the United States. Military strategic considerations, even mistaken ones, quite often explain much more. If one looks, for example, at the relationships the Soviets have with the Yemens, to the varying attitudes to the Eritrean liberation movements, Ethiopia and Somalia, it is very difficult to come out with a political rationale.

The answer there is basically strategic. This is true for both the Soviets and the United States. Creating a regime more like that of the US has also been a part of creating a safer environment for survival for the Soviet Union in this extremely dangerous world. The political and economic advice of Soviet policy-makers is meant to help socialism as a world process as they understand it. But they find nowadays that their guns are still accepted where, increasingly, their economic and political advice is not.

The Ethiopian military 'Marxist' leadership, for example, has consistently refused to set up a genuine mass Communist party on the Soviet model. They are a military modernizing regime, and have no intention of setting up a genuine party, despite the urgings of the Soviet advisers. On the other hand, they will continue to accept Soviet arms. Why shouldn't they? Those Soviet weapons, incidentally, are not gifts, they are sold – on generous long-range terms perhaps, but sold. There is no evidence that other nations' weapons would not be acceptable as well.

The immediate effect of the ongoing reforms in the Soviet Union and Eastern Europe will certainly *lower* the amount of help which the Soviets make available to national liberation and revolutionary movements in the Third World. That help was mostly military in any case, except for the subsidies of Cuban sugar. The prospect of a new detente with the United States and Western Europe implies much lower levels of military expenditures and consequently military aid.

The Soviets have demonstrated that they are ready to betray and abandon the national liberation movements, even when led by Communist parties, when reasons of state dictate. They have also historically proved themselves capable of having perfectly cordial relations with right-wing regimes, such as the military in Argentina, the Shah of Iran and various squalid and repressive anti-Communist and anti-democratic regimes in the Middle East, Africa and Latin America. While the Third World governments and movements cannot count on long-range consistent support from either of the superpowers, they would be taking leave of their senses if they did not accept aid when it is given.

The anti-imperialism of the Soviet Union, one of the two rival superpowers, should not be particularly surprising. It *is* both interesting and useful if you do need, or believe you need, weapons and the Soviets are ready to supply them. National liberation movements and movements for social change driven into illegality and armed struggle are obliged to accept arms from whosoever is willing to give them.

There is an unpleasant hypocrisy and dishonesty on the part of US and other western journalists and politicians in criticizing the African National Congress (ANC) of South Africa and movements like SWAPO, or for that matter the Sandinista government, for accepting arms from the Soviets and other Eastern bloc countries. It is not as if the capitalist democracies were lining up to offer arms and other aid to these liberation movements and they, through some inborn perversity, were showing a preference for Eastern bloc arms!

The social-democratic parties and trade unions also offer aid to national liberation movements, but they tend to be shyer about offering direct military aid than about tolerating the sale of arms to some fairly repulsive Third World governments. While still on the questions of arms, it might be as well here to remind some of the more articulate neo-conservative intellectuals in the United States that Israel's very survival had depended on arms obtained in 1947/8 from the Soviet bloc countries, primarily Czechoslovakia. That does not seem to have fatally affected the new nation or its prospects for development as a democracy, although other very different internal threats to that democracy have developed in later years from different sources.

The Soviet leaders also seem to think, like the American policy-makers do, that giving military aid and advice will produce reliable friends. Trying to achieve these aims through military and other aid has been a very expensive proposition and they will discover that it is a mistake.[6] In any case governments which receive military aid do not necessarily remain friendly, as Egypt has proved spectacularly in its time. As the level of confrontation between the superpowers is lowered, Soviet military aid as well as military aid in general will become less important. The prognosis, therefore, should be of less aid to the African countries from the Soviets in the future. On the other hand, the new Bush administration in Washington may be more willing to place pressure on the racist white South African regime, and move to a *de facto* recognition of the ANC.

Guns, or rather guns, tanks and planes, have also been an instrument of Soviet diplomacy with Jordan, India, Iraq and dozens of regimes in the Middle East, Africa and the Third World in general. In that respect they do not differ that much from the United States, France, and Israel, or even Sweden, Yugoslavia, Brazil and Holland. It should not take the present Pope to remind us that arms sales to the Third World nations are a scandal and a standing reproach to the prospects of decency and development in that impoverished part of our world.

The Devil You Know: The Role of the United States

The role of the United States in propping up reactionary regimes which often had only the tiniest figleaf of democracy has become ever more widely known. This has obviously not been helpful to the US when raising issues of democracy and human rights in the Third World. This was particularly so when conservative regimes were repeatedly 'certified' to be democratic and respectful of human rights in counter-position to more democratic and far less repressive radical regimes which the United States happened to oppose.

The US treatment of Guatemala, which has waged a murderous war against its Indian majority, in contrast with Sandinista Nicaragua, immediately comes to mind, as does military aid which went to Islamic fundamentalist 'freedom fighters' in Afghanistan, in contrast to the lack of aid to SWAPO or the ANC. The mild pressure for free elections in Paraguay and Chile contrasts markedly with the repeated, insistent and highly detailed demand for free elections in Nicaragua backed up with outrageous illegal acts of war such as the mining of harbors and arming of 'contra' insurgents against a government with which the US was legally at peace. All of these, quite typical, acts of the United States reflect current policy and are not part of a mystified colonialist past.

In the interest of fairness, one should add that the United States, as the major *status quo* power maintaining the present unequal world economic arrangement almost automatically, and often to the surprise of its own political public, supports conservative stand-pat or at best moderate reformist regimes. The USSR and its allies are more likely to support those forces challenging the *status quo*. Since that *status quo* is, as the Pope pointed out recently, fundamentally unjust, the Soviet Union often ends up supporting the forces which at least promise progress. The problem is that all too often that ends up being a false promise, even if sometimes for reasons completely beyond control of the local actors.

There are many distinctions between the roles of the United States and the Soviet Union. For one thing the US is still by far the most important world power and the world capitalist world market is basically sustained by it. As the weaker power, the Soviets are more likely to back groups which oppose the *status quo* and therefore the US and its allies. On the other hand, there is a near-symbiotic relationship of the two superpowers in much of the world which has repeatedly bent and twisted various Third World situations and struggles to fit within their Cold War competitive relationship, greatly exasperating already bloody and complicated realities.

It is hatred for the US and its local allies which builds support for local revolutionary movements and parties, and it is a justified hatred. On the other hand, it is fear of local or Soviet-supported proto-Stalinist repression and revolution which creates allies for the 'West' and the United States in the Third World. Most of the allies of the United States in the Third World, however, are not motivated by their fear of authoritarianism, but by the more naked fear that, whatever else a radical change of their societies would achieve, the property and privileges of the small pro-western elites would be destroyed. This is why the repeated proposals for US-sponsored democratic, social or economic transformation of Third World economies, which re-emerge under liberal democratic administrations, are so illusory even when well meant. US allies in the Third World may be – very rarely – for more democratic and law-abiding governments but they are hardly ever for fundamental economic redistribution and social equality.

Under President Carter the US was helpful in the settlement in Zimbabwe and in fighting human rights abuses in many countries which were friendly to the US. To be sure, most of the regimes engaging in those human rights abuses, like the military dictatorships in Chile and Uruguay, had been set up with active subversion by US agencies like the CIA. The police forces of some of these less lovely regimes had been trained and financed by the US as well, which surely should go some way in explaining why the US is not taken all that seriously when it raises issues of human rights, not even on those occasions when it is quite accurate and telling the truth, which became increasingly rare during the long dusk of the Reagan administration. Central America is a particularly ugly example where death squads and massacres by the military and landowner cliques in Guatemala and El Salvador hardly rate as news and certainly do not seem to rate the ire of the Department of State, while the Sandinistas, who, warts and all, are immeasurably less repressive than any of their neighbors except Costa Rica, have been repeatedly denounced as major human rights violators not just by the Reagan administration but also by the Democratic party. All this may help to explain why Third World revolutionaries and reformers are sometimes insufficiently sensitive to issues of democracy and individual freedom, particularly when raised by westerners, and find the devil they do not know at least potentially attractive.

The United States has done as much damage to the word democracy in the Third World as the Soviet-type regimes have to the word socialism in Eastern Europe and the Soviet Union. But it is the *overall* role of both superpowers as such that is reactionary. Both superpowers share the responsibility for the grotesque over-armament of the fragile and economically weak states in the Third World. They both, therefore, share a responsibility for the ever-growing power of the military elites – whether 'right-wing' or 'left-wing' – in those countries.

Drugs and Destabilization of Popular Regimes

A particularly glaring example of the devastating role which the United States has played within Third World economies and societies is its absolutely central role in the international drug trade. While administration after administration declares verbal war against the drug traffic, it is clear that the United States plays a major role in the development of this twentieth-century plague. This is most clearly so through the uncontrolled demand of the American domestic market for drugs which financially fuels the entire industry in its present malignant form. Even more irresponsible has been the role of the US agencies like the CIA in cultivating the drug producers in the Asian 'golden triangle' of Afghanistan, Pakistan and Turkey, so that in case after case it turns out that it is the clients of the US who are involved in the production and refining of narcotics.

In addition to the US clients in the Latin American military and the Afghan 'freedom fighters',[7] most of the trade originates from governments and groups friendly to the US. The vast sums involved in international drug traffic are now creating a new problem of immense-scale corruption in Third World countries, which acts as yet another barrier to social change and democratization.

All the sins and errors of commission and omission of the various US administrations are less important, as far as the Third World is concerned, than the central and indispensable role of the United States in maintaining the *status quo* of the present world economic system. It is that system, the world capitalist system, as such, which remains the major problem of the would-be reformers and democratizers in those countries and not the particular policies of given administrations in Washington. In that role the United States remains bi-partisan, as it remains bi-partisan in its self-selected role as the policeman and law enforcer in the Panamas and Persian Gulfs of this world.

So long as that remains the case, the greatest single source of instability in the Third World is not caused by Communist subversion but by the pressure of the world banking system on those fragile economies. In country after country it becomes clear that the US policy towards the debts to the US and international banks has imposed a moratorium on any policies which would deal with poverty, inequality and injustice. It does so by insisting on austerity in already miserably poor countries. It does so also by a dogmatic and rigid insistence on introducing fiscal austerity and market-type economies with the same rigidity that the primitive Marxists had insisted on collectivization of land and central planning.

The Historical Communist Road to the Third World

From the October 1917 revolution up to the mid-1920s, the Soviet Union and the Communist International, more often than not, backed revolutionary movements throughout Europe and in those underdeveloped countries which were in revolt against imperialism.[8] This became a life-and-death question for the Soviet Union when it became clear by the early 1920s that the anticipated revolutionary wave in Central and Western Europe had been defeated in country after country, through varying combinations of repression, cowardice and timidity of the traditional social-democratic parties, and adventurist mistakes of the newly formed Communist parties.[9]

Survival of the Soviet Union in a hostile world was necessarily the first priority during the first decade after the Bolshevik revolution. This necessity was imposed by a relentlessly hostile capitalist world which, in Churchill's own words, tried to strangle the newborn regime at birth having failed to abort it. Ironically enough, and significantly for the future, such allies as the Soviets found in the 1920s, outside of the Communist parties, were the anti-colonial nationalist movements which opposed the existing imperialist world order but were at the same time ferociously and murderously anti-Communist at home.

In practice, alliances in what is now called the Third World were quite problematic for the Soviet Union before the Second World War. The fledgling Communist parties were very weak and the nationalist and anti-imperialist movements were often inconsistent and dangerously opportunistic. The result was that these parties were often abandoned for reasons of state. The Communist International had great difficulties developing an effective policy to deal with Chiang Kai-shek's Kuomintang in China which, despite generous supplies of Soviet arms and advisers, turned on the Chinese Communists in one of the more spectacular massacres in 1929. The Communist International's support for the armed Muslim resistance in Morocco and Algiers produced no immediate visible results or useful friends in the Muslim world. Nor did the attempt to work out a limited alliance with Kemal Ataturk's nationalist regime in Turkey produce increased security for the Soviet Union.

However, something must be added when assessing the role of the Communist International in the Third World before the Second World War. With all their weaknesses, adventurousness and mistakes, the Communists had developed far more substantial work and even cadres outside of Europe in 20 short years than the much larger parties of the Socialist International had in their entire existence. The Communists were the first to break with the historic burden of Euro-centrism in the international workers' movement. While the alliances with Third World nationalists and anti-imperialists proved to be illusory in the intra-war years, *pursuing these illusory alliances* produced long-range effects. For one thing it made international Communism an attractive potential ally or even mentor for a generation of Third World revolutionaries.

Such an alliance became much more common after the Second World War when the language and symbols of Third World nationalism became pseudo-Marxist, just as it had been pseudo-liberal democratic in the nineteenth century and sometimes fascist or at least corporate-statist between the two world wars, without much changing its essential character. That character remains at best essentially radical-populist where the nation, the oppressed nation to be sure, sometimes defined in religio-cultural terms, becomes the substitute for the role of class in the socialist and Marxist movements. Islamic populism or Arab socialism or, for that matter, most branches of left Zionism are all good examples. But then both Mussolini and Peron stressed the concept of the have-not exploited nation, whose interests were more urgent than those of the selfish contending classes, in ways very reminiscent of the more contemporary Arab 'socialism' or African 'socialism'.

In the post-world war period the Soviets have aided anti-colonial and anti-capitalist revolutions like the Cuban one. They have also helped a number of the African nations and independence movements, essentially after the death of Stalin, who had combined ferocious tyranny at home and in the bloc with conservative caution in international affairs. In recent years they have also helped the Angolans, Ethiopians and Nicaraguans as well as somewhat more modestly some of the other radical Third World regimes and movements. Many of these movements and regimes are also aided by the social-democratic parties and trade unions of Western Europe, particularly by the Swedish, West German, Dutch and Norwegian parties and trade unions.

For Soviets, helping the spread of national revolutionary regimes and, where possible, pro-Soviet-type regimes, has been a way of moving towards a progressive and eventually socialist world. It was not just a question of the rivalry with the United States. It was a desire to help regimes which are on the road to 'socialism'. Failing that, 'progressive' or at least friendly regimes will do. There have been grotesque examples in recent history of which regimes were considered 'progressive' by the Soviet policy-makers; to give just two examples: Uganda under Amin, and former Spanish Equatorial Africa which was ruled by a mad despot who managed to kill or drive out more than a quarter of the population. One of the more cheering results of Gorbachev's *glasnost* is that this past set of misjudgements about African despotic regimes which use radical oratory about international affairs, particularly in attacking the United States and/or the World Zionist 'conspiracy', is being gingerly acknowledged by Soviet African experts today.

The Urgent Need for a Sane Socialist Agricultural Policy

Despite the present economic and political reforms in the USSR itself, many African and other Third World left-wing states still stress bureaucratic centralized planning, collectivized agriculture and the rule of a single party, which have together and separately proved to be a disaster. While Soviet advice on economic and political development has been generally bad, if sincerely given, the other sources of advice or experience have not been all that helpful either. The current fetishization of the market by most western economists with repeated references to the Pacific Rim countries is not particularly helpful for societies which are far poorer and less centralized. Though correct, socialist strategies stressing the need for flexibility and a variety of economic approaches through a mix of ownership and management forms appear to be slow to the more desperate of the Third World political leaderships facing immediate economic and social catastrophes.

Beginning with Marx and Engels themselves, orthodox Marxists have historically harbored a deep and abiding prejudice against peasants. Most

Marxists have shared a general feeling that collective agriculture was both necessary and a good in itself. In reality collective farming has proved to be generally disastrous, although there are some exceptions.[10] China's most radical and effective agrarian reforms consist essentially of blending collective farming on the communes with individual initiative. This is far more radical than anything even proposed in the Soviet Union at this time. A central problem remains that, because of the artificially low prices maintained for grains in China, there is always the fear that peasants will turn to growing vegetables and other products which are economically more inviting, thus creating shortages of basic foodstuffs. This is an almost universal policy error throughout the South and is a reflection of the widespread desire to favor the urban populations with cheap grains at the expense of the peasants. Many Marxists and socialist policy-makers now agree that the earlier fear of a prosperous peasantry, as well as the overwhelming urban and industrial bias, were exaggerated, wrong-headed and harmful and that the point was to achieve higher food production. The problem was to decide that you wanted higher food production *more* than you feared the peasants on collective farms or individual farmers getting more prosperous. But greater individual prosperity for farmers can, and in practice does, also create more corruption. That was as close as one gets to fear of original sin in Communist regimes: the fear that someone (else) may be getting more.

In most countries productivity on collective farms has been low because of an understandable lack of peasant enthusiasm and because of low prices for agricultural products delivered to the state. This is in contrast to the situation when the peasants are permitted to sell their produce at the market. The positive experience of China and the aborted experiment with more farmer initiative in Cuba both prove that peasants will produce when economically motivated. Cuba, typically the government or rather Castro, seemed more worried that a few peasants might get to be slightly richer than they were about low productivity and the chronic shortages of vegetables and meat in the cities. Supporters of centralized planned economies and collectivized agriculture in the Third World also base their position on the problem of corruption and class inequality. But the *central argument* was that such systems are more effective in producing rapid growth. That is a problem because the countries which have developed most rapidly in the Third World are not planned centralized economies. South Korea and Taiwan have had more rapid developments than most Soviet-model economies.

These are economies with a major state interventionist role in the economy, but *without* the Soviet-type centralized plan and above all *with* the market. So if support for economic and political models was based purely on efficiency, there is not much of an argument for the Soviet-sponsored Third World industrialization. On the other hand, the argument in the case of Taiwan and Korea is that they have received a great deal of aid and investment loans. That is not a particularly convincing point since many countries have received a great deal of aid but have not been able to develop stable and growing industrial economies.

Creating a climate for investments and loans, after all, is also a conscious political decision. And many of the Soviet and Eastern European sponsored regimes have tried to encourage such investment with, in general, very unpromising results. It is China which has done rather well in this respect, but, for a number of reasons, the Chinese influence in the Third World among the modernizing elites is at a low point these days. This is rather a pity since, despite their sometimes impossible politics as far as revolutionary movements are concerned, the Chinese have done well in at least two major fields of interest for the Third World economies: they have made breakthroughs in agricultural production and above all distribution and they have attracted investment capital for labor-intensive industries which permit China ever-greater participation in the world economy. The results from China are not all positive, even in agriculture. There has been a growing problem with rice and grains which are less lucrative than other crops. But that simply underlines the fallacy of assuming that moving away from a rigid centralized plan requires a total marketization of agriculture. There is an obvious need and a role for the state with subsidies and encouragement for the introduction of appropriate new technologies.

Soviet allies in the Third World often argue that while the Soviet Union is past that stage, for the underdeveloped countries it is still a short cut. Centralized economies run by single parties in power will create sufficient economic and political power to make great breakthroughs in development. This is a form of political and cultural time lag, since those beliefs or rather their consequences are being sharply questioned by Gorbachev's economic and sociological advisers like Tatyana Zaslavskaya. Since the early 1970s that perspective has become far more ambiguous as a number of Eastern European states have entered, and were forced to deal with the harsh realities of, the world market. That reality has not yet caught up with the official ideology everywhere. The USSR and most Eastern European countries will soon be knocking at the doors of the International Monetary Fund and the World Bank for membership.[11]

There is Always a Role for Socialists in the Third World but Not Necessarily to Build Socialism

It does not do much good to keep saying that authoritarian and autarchic short-cuts will do more damage than good nor that there well may be countries which are of an order of size which cannot have a developmental strategy. It is grotesque that the left in general and in the Third World countries in particular has accepted the boundaries inherited from the old colonial empires, frontiers which were obviously quite ahistorical and ethnically unfair and unrealistic as the framework within which to attempt to carry out policies of modern nation-building and economic development.

We are thus offered the roads to socialism of a Grenada, a Sao Tome and Benin or, for that matter, a Nicaragua. Poor old Leon Trotsky had dared raise the question: could socialism be built in one country as large and resource-rich as the Soviet Union? Today's leftist and socialist intellectuals are petrified even to whisper a hint that the 'socialism' which is being built in one of these micro-states might not be an appropriate model for leftists in advanced industrialized countries to follow, lest they be attacked for arrogant Euro-centrism and lack of respect and sympathy for the victims of colonialism and the present unjust world economy. They would be accused in the academic leftist press of all the above sins and also probably be denounced as racists.

That is tragi-comic since there is a great deal which can be learned from the Third World and of course a great deal which Third World activists and socialists can learn from the socialist movements and intellectuals in the advanced industrial countries. Honest and open discussion is required to do either, and self-righteous demagoguery has made that almost impossible. Devastating damage to the concept of socialism is done when it is being handled like a medal which should be issued for good intentions. On the 'left' it is considered impolite and condescending to write or say that one thinks that socialism is not achievable through the subjective will of socialist or Marxist activists alone – not in the Third World, nor anywhere else for that matter.

There is most certainly a role for Third World socialists in these non-industrial countries, a difficult and often a heroic role. It is the worst form of patronizing, pandering and illusion-mongering to talk or write about the roads to socialism in some of these countries. Third World socialists have a right to expect from their allies and sympathizers in the advanced industrial world the truth as they see it, not endless manipulation of that truth in the interest of Cold War maneuvering or from a useless and debilitating burden of guilt which permeates all left discussion of the Third World in Western Europe and the United States. If socialism is in crisis in Western Europe and the Soviet-type societies, surely we must say the same thing for the various socialisms of the Third World?

A Lost Tradition: Rural Anarchism and Grass-Roots Self-Help

One of the obvious roles for socialists in the Third World is to lead relentless struggles for the expansion of democracy and empowerment and the mobilization of the broadest layers of the population to decide their own destiny and political development. That means the fight to build democratic and participatory unions and popular organizations of peasants, women, minorities and youth, run by their own members. Typically they engage in mass efforts to spread literacy and establish popular education and cultural institutions independent of the state. That is after all what much of the work by radical or revolutionary Catholicism has emphasized in building the bases for communities and the self-help networks among the poor in the countryside and the slums of Latin America.

Much can be learned from the theology of liberation movements in Latin America, and for that matter the women's and other community organizations of the African liberation movements before they took power. It was the vitality of organizations developed during the struggle for national liberation against colonialism which made me so optimistic about the prospects of the post-revolutionary regimes in countries like Guinea-Bissau, Angola, Mozambique and Algeria.[12] This is in contrast with the countries which gained their independence without a prolonged struggle requiring mass mobilization. That optimism turned out to have been premature. But it *is* a fact that the potential of mass organization from below has been repeatedly illustrated in the Third World. So, unfortunately, has been the capacity for revolutionary elites to take over these societies.

That is one of the forgotten lessons which the Spanish anarchists tried to teach the revolutionary movements of the poor and rural masses in authoritarian societies: the need to be suspicious of the bureaucrats, officials and the state. In some ways a useful model could be the heroic activity of the anarchists and rural socialists in the poorest regions of Spain before the 1934 civil war, when Spain resembled a Third World country. These iconoclastic activists spread a genuine sense of empowerment and self-confidence and pushed previously silent Spaniards into the front lines of political and social activism, including the women who are all too often ignored by the Third World liberation movements and represent a major resource for democratic change from below.[13] The historical rural anarchist tradition, in Spain and Italy and in Mexico and other Latin American countries, is a part of a precious lost dimension of grass-roots popular radicalism which seems far more in tune with the realities of oppressed underdeveloped societies than the centralized models imported from Fabians or Soviets.

Above all, what Third World socialists should do is to reject the implicitly racist and neo-Darwinian notion that democracy is something for the developed industrial societies, that the rights of peasants and workers should be sacrificed to some abstract notion of progress as defined by self-selected vanguards or that the emancipation and empowering of women should be postponed into the vague future. I have always found it strange that radicals in the Third World, who have been willing to outrage peasants and workers asserting their rights, are often so reticent and diplomatic when dealing with issues of gender oppression. Even more astonishing is that Third World political activists, especially women who are educated in the industrialized west and who enjoy all the individual liberties of western democratic societies, including sexual emancipation, often argue that equality for women is a 'culture-specific' form of western cultural imperialism, as is the defense of the most elementary democratic rights. Clearly it does not help for the democrats and socialists in those countries to agree with that rubbish in the name of solidarity with the Third World.

Academic Third Worldism

The entire debate on the prospects of democratic social change and socialism in the Third World has been confused by competing schools of academic Marxism or radicalism which have specialized in issues of development and the Third World since the 1960s. Third Worldist doctrines were almost all developed by radical or Marxist academics who had no further, if they had ever had, connection with any socialist, Communist or labor movements or organizations in their own countries and who had developed a completely pessimistic view about the prospects for socialism in their own or any other advanced industrial country. That pessimism about the advanced industrial societies was more than compensated for by great expectations from the Third World countries. The workers of the advanced capitalist countries, whether organized or not, were considered to be totally co-opted by their economic and social systems, and the living proof was that they were not as radical as these armchair revolutionaries, but were interested in mere material gains.[14] Struggles by socialist or labor movements in advanced industrial societies were therefore either useless, or harmful, since the working class of the advanced capitalist countries participated in the exploitation of the Third World. Therefore any struggles which would increase their political, social and economic power were in fact reactionary.

On the other hand, the workers and peasants in the Third World do not have a rosy outlook either since their countries are doomed to underdevelopment by the immutable fact that the world market would always impose terms of trade on them which are unequal and therefore exploitative. What they must therefore do is break from the capitalist world market (never mind that the Soviet Union and many of its allies are just now knocking at the doors of that market to get in) and try a path of development which can at its most charitable be described as autarchic. That is, they would have to go it alone. Since going it alone would impose great privations on most of these economies and societies, it is unlikely that that path would be followed if there were any vestiges of democracy – bourgeois, proletarian or whatever – left in these societies and if the people (that is, peasants and workers) had any say or independent institutions of their own. Therefore what is presumably needed in those countries is the stern tutorship of an enlightened elite, somewhat like the Third World graduate students of these professors, who would not flinch at the task in hand. Since these students, however, are unlikely to be capable of carrying out the tasks under most circumstances, their real-life role is to be the ideologues of the various existing repressive Third World mobilizing elites. There is to be sure another possible, although very theoretical, option, which is to hold out for a world proletarian revolution and denounce everything short of it as a hopeless utopia or worse – a sell-out.

The views in question have been somewhat caricatured, but good caricatures should have a resemblance which accents the essence of the object or person. I believe that this caricature is useful, since it should show that there is more than a family resemblance between these 'Third Worldist' academic views and the views respectively of Mao and Trotsky. The only problem is that the originals were both more stylistically powerful and clearer.

This is very harmful stuff indeed, particularly since it appeals to Third World radicals frustrated by the real-life situations of their societies. One reason why these theories are so appealing is that they address the not-too-deeply-buried elitism of the western-educated intellectuals from the Third World. The world market, or the world system whichever you choose to stress, happily relieves the participants in these societies of any responsibilities for their economic and political choices and actions. If decent civil societies and democratic paths to development were never possible in the first place, how can one be blamed for not taking them? It is gratifying to be able to argue on the basis of academically certified theories that it is the western world since the industrial revolution in general, and the United States since the Second World War in particular, which are alone responsible for the disastrous situation of socialist experiments and movements in the underdeveloped world.

There is a further heuristic bonus for holding such views: since the western working classes are so hopelessly enmeshed in the system of unequal exchange between the developed and underdeveloped, from which they consciously benefit, one is relieved of any responsibility for political engagement and activism in the advanced industrial countries. The amazing thing is that professors propagating these views are rewarded with distinguished chairs in elite bourgeois universities. That, of course, is no bad thing since they at least challenge the prevalent conformist theories of modernization and development.

Third World Countries Need Genuine and Massive Solidarity

The issue of aid to the underdeveloped countries is complex, since many of the forms which that aid took historically have done more harm than good to the recipients. Some of the aid has been so crudely and directly linked to the interests of the major Cold War protagonists that the political price has been to drag the recipient countries into the superpower confrontation. A part of the price of that confrontation has been to speed the already existing built-in tendency for the newly independent countries to spend increasing shares of their grossly inadequate resources on arms. This has not only diverted precious resources, human as well as financial, but has also strengthened the military in these fragile societies with only rudimentary civic institutions.

The prospect of a major detente between the superpowers may also end up, in the short run, being dangerous for the South since the cuts in arms expenditure for the superpowers may increase the pressures to sell arms to the Third World. It is a multi-billion-dollar industry in the West and a major Soviet hard-currency-earning export which is at stake. A number of countries, east and west, including quite a few NICs, are heavily committed to arms production.

Since the 1970s the Socialist International and its affiliated labor, socialist and social-democratic parties have paid increasing attention to the problem of providing both short-term and long-term aid to the countries and movements in the Third World. Since the 1950s, there have been a number of bilateral arrangements to send aid and advisers and to provide training for individual movements, parties and trade unions in the Third World which had historical ties with the Western European socialist parties and trade unions. The Fabian Society and British Labour party experts have been involved in a number of African, Asian and Caribbean Commonwealth countries, while the Scandinavian unions and parties, most particularly the Swedes, have been very active in aiding unions and independence movements in Africa, Asia and Latin America. The West German trade unions and social-democratic foundations have deployed their massive resources on behalf of socialist and trade union groups in the less developed parts of southern Europe and in the Third World. All this is desperately needed solidarity, and is just a drop in the ocean, given the overwhelming and urgent needs of the South.

Willy Brandt's *Independent Commission on International Development Issues*, the two-volume report *North–South* (1980) and *Common Crisis* (1983), followed by the Michael Manley report, *The Global Challenge*, published by the Socialist International in 1985, break new ground because they posit the issues of aid and North–South relations on wider and more solid grounds than those of inter-movement solidarity or international charity. This is not at all to denigrate solidarity and charity, both of which are basic decent values which need to be strengthened, but to assume that genuine alliances based on mutual self-interest are a sounder basis for long-range policy in North–South matters. Brandt and Manley, as well as the Socialist International, argue that it is in the immediate as well as long-range self-interest of the workers' movements and indeed the economies of the North systematically to take on the vast task of helping to build up the economies and societies of the South. The obvious reason is clear even to many enlightened non-socialists, that an impoverished South cannot participate in world trade by purchasing the manufactured goods and services of the North. What little hard currency is earned by the South goes to service the huge debts which have been swollen by high interest rates. Attempts to meet these payments de-stabilize any moderately decent regimes in the South since that involves cut-backs in already poor societies with inadequate social services. They also require drastic cut-backs in imports from the North and thus help prolong the present recession in the North. Obviously, the first step would be wiping out these debts which were often thrust on the societies of the South by banks anxious to invest the huge surplus resulting from the oil shock of the 1970s. Socialists and progressives should support a flat moratorium on the debts. Failing that, a cap should be imposed on the percentage of its foreign trade de earnings which any country should be expected to pay to the international (read, often US) banking community.

The present arms reduction negotiations between the superpowers provide a historic chance to propose that all or most of the savings achieved through the cut-back of arms budgets be funnelled as aid to the South. That aid, in turn supplemented by increased contributions from the industrialized countries, could create an equivalent of the Marshall Plan which so successfully helped rebuild the economies of Western Europe and Japan. The analogy with the Marshall Plan cannot be pushed too far, since the measures would be in substance different and should be funnelled through international agencies, which include the Soviet Union. What is essential is a massive systematic effort over time, as distinct from *ad hoc* aid.

To be effective that aid must produce egalitarian growth leading to self-sustained balanced and *ecologically sound* development. That in turn would be a major shot in the arm of the stagnant industries of the North, and that is also the first reason why such aid is in the self-interest of the Northern workers' movements. The second reason is that it is illusory to think of peace being possible for any prolonged period of time if the vast majority of humanity is doomed to hunger and need. Military technology can make desperate poor countries dangerous, so if for no other reason than self-preservation the more prosperous societies of the North must help the South. The third is the most complex reason and yet I believe it to be of utmost importance. The workers' movements and parties of the North desperately need a moral equivalent of mobilization for war. I can imagine no task more appropriate, more likely to fire the idealism and imagination of the younger and better-educated public which the labor and socialist parties must now address than a war on hunger, exploitation and need in order to create the first genuine human world community.

In this project the socialist movements of the North join with the most massive international movement of them all, the Catholic Church. If such a task is undertaken by the socialists of the North they will soon find opposite numbers in the countries of the South to join with in this genuine massive international effort to create a democratic and non-exploitative world order which will make increasingly irrelevant the petty dictators and tyrannical elites, whether using the language of Marxism or religious fundamentalism.

A Brief Prescriptive Summary

1) The North–South divide has been increasing the differences between the industrialized North and the underdeveloped South. The most important single reason for this is the maintenance of a world system of exchange which has historically discriminated against the less-industrialized countries. The United States is the main military, political and economic prop of that system. It is that, rather than various policies followed by individual administrations in Washington, which pits the US against the forces of social change in the Third World. These policies have essentially been bi-partisan and are even more harmful than occasional interventionist adventures.

2) The Soviet Union as the competing superpower has backed movement for social change and national independence in the Third World essentially for its military and political interests. This has, however, also been a part of a historic drive to aid national independence and radical movements which could help the Soviet Union end its isolation and emerge as a supreme power. Soviet military aid has often been useful; its economic and political advice has been a disaster.

3) In many of the Third World countries local elites emerging from the process of de-colonization, wars of national liberation, or radical social and political revolutions, have established left-wing populist regimes which are quite often based on military cliques and use a Marxist or Marxist-Leninist vocabulary. A few have made major advances in modernization and abolition of the worst kind of poverty which is seen in the unegalitarian parts of the Third World of the same level of development. They have stressed participation and mobilization, but have been at best ambivalent about democracy.

4) The ever grimmer economic realities of the world economy and problems of development have led an increasing number of radical Third World governments and parties to re-examine their previous urban and industrial bias and to move towards a more rounded and flexible strategy of development. Massive aid along the lines proposed by the Brandt and Manley reports is needed to begin to deal with the North–South gap. That alone will make possible the development of democratic egalitarian societies in the South with prospects of stability and growth. In turn

such aid will help to create a new universalist political project capable of mobilizing support for a revitalized and non-parochial democratic left.

Solidarity with the democrats and socialists in the Third World must also be informed by the understanding that certain concepts like democracy, the right of organization, individual rights and liberties and equality for women are not culture-specific 'western' ideas that can be doled out to the South in small doses when their elites decide that it is appropriate. These are gains in the universal struggle for democracy and socialism which are desirable in themselves and worth fighting for and are invaluable tools in developing decent stable societies capable of growth. National independence and anti-imperialism are only worthwhile when their goal is to create societies in which the democratic rights and liberties of women and men are maximized.

Chapter 5

The End of the Affair: Europe Without the United States[1]

The prospects for a revival of socialist movements in the twenty-first century depend primarily on a model of socialist strategy being developed which is relevant for advanced industrial societies. One must therefore begin by examining the possibility for European autonomy from the two superpowers. That also automatically poses the problems of European security.[2] Both, taken together and separately, are critical when considering the prospects for a revival of socialism. Note, that I write 'European', rather than Western European, where autonomy and security are involved, whereas I will mainly write about *Western Europe* when I begin to deal with the problems of contemporary socialist strategy and possible renewal. This is because, as I will argue, if socialism is to have a credible prospect it will have to prove able to have one in highly industrialized countries with developed civil societies and strong trade unions and workers' parties. That is, it must develop where it is supported by a majority of the citizens, self-organized in their own voluntary political and social institutions, with both the capacity and tradition of actively participating in control of their own organizations, parties and local governments.

That means that Western Europe is crucial for the fate and future of democratic socialism. But for Western Europe to be able to assume such a role it must first free itself from the tutelage and domination of the United States. For that process to continue, and it has already begun, it is essential that Western Europeans feel sufficiently secure from military threat and potential political bullying from the Soviet Union for the US military protection to be no longer perceived to be necessary.

It helps, of course, for the price of that protection to be questioned, for it to be linked to a United States which is both excessively confrontational, and thus potentially dangerously adventurous, and at the same time weak in the ability to project its power and authority effectively. This is, of course, an almost perfect description of the Reagan administration's military, security and foreign policy. This image and reality may be somewhat modified by the Bush administration, particularly in the era of lessening superpower tensions and reductions in armaments. However, the foreign policy and security goals of the US and its Western European allies will continue to diverge. This is true of the allies as a whole, left and right, but it is above all true of the labor, socialist-democratic and socialist parties which are increasingly antagonistic to a United States with a right-wing executive controlling its foreign and military policy.

One need only dwell briefly on the US 'security' policies in Grenada, Nicaragua, El Salvador, Panama, the Persian Gulf, Lebanon and Libya to see the twin effects of excessive bluster combined with little effective usable power.

When US self-isolation is linked to an unprecedented skilled and effective foreign policy offensive by the Soviet leadership under Gorbachev, during both the Reagan and Bush administrations, the prospects for an increasingly assertive Western Europe begin to look positively promising. The Soviet peace offensive is managing to convince the Western Europeans that massive disarmament, and indeed an end to the military confrontational stage of the Cold War, are now possible. But in that case, what is the value and the price for the continued US military presence in Europe? That is a question which is increasingly being asked on *both sides* of the Atlantic. It is broadly posed in West Germany, the backbone of the NATO alliance.

East–West 'Security' Issues[3]

It is logical first to consider the present military or security relationship between East and West. The set of questions which the implantation of American missiles in Western Europe in the early 1980s opened up permit the posing of politically relevant questions even today. Were these rockets an instrument of US political hegemony, or were there genuine security issues as far as European allies of the US, or even the Soviet Union, were concerned? For that matter were the American missiles placed in Western Europe at such great political cost in the early 1980s of any genuine security interests even for the US at that time?

Posing the questions in that way opens at least one Pandora's box: what is a genuine and legitimate security interest, as distinct from an attempt to project military power? Does that distinction exist at all except in arid abstract discussions? Secondly, to what extent are the security interests of the United States and its allies, however defined, congruent? Thirdly, to what extent are the security of either or both the US and its allies also the security interests of the democratic and popular forces essential for the maintenance of Western European political democracy and for the advancement towards a democratic socialism? Defense and security policy cannot be usefully discussed unless they are located within an examination of foreign policy in all its ramifications. A security policy which wastes resources and is not in the overall interests of the country is too expensive no matter what the actual cost, while in a genuine emergency no one would cavil at the cost of legitimate defense. No security or defense policy can be legitimate from the point of view of consistent democrats or socialists if its essential purpose is to maintain by latent or actual force the present unjust and unequal relationship between the Third World and the industrialized world.

To put it simply, there is no legitimate 'defense' interest which requires interventions in the smaller ex-colonial countries of the Third World or the Middle East. There may be all kinds of reasonable political, economic or even strategic interests, so long as we live in a world of armed superpowers, in all those areas. However, armed force has proved a singularly blunt instrument for any decent policy in defending any such interests. Therefore at this time the defense interests of the US as expressed by both Democratic and Republican administrations and the Western European socialist and labor movements do not mesh. They *could* mesh were there any substantial argument that Western Europe itself was in danger of a military invasion. No such argument has been made for decades. NATO and the Warsaw Pact are both reasonably well balanced in actual strength and therefore admirably situated for mutually beneficial cut-backs in conventional as well as nuclear forces. The most recent round of deep unilateral conventional arms cuts promised by Gorbachev underlines that proposition.

It is difficult to imagine any legitimate civilizational goals, let alone democratic or socialist goals, which could be advanced by mass nuclear destruction of civilian population. In that I share the present view of the Catholic Church, which is also increasingly the view of the mass labor and socialist parties. Therefore nuclear weapons can only be justified to the extent that they lead to their own demise, that is, nuclear weapons should serve as a leverage for negotiations combined with unilateral initiatives which would lead to the abolition of all nuclear weapons. That represents the most immediate genuine security interest of both the United States and Western Europe. This has been and is jeopardized by the shredding of the doctrine of mutual deterrence and its replacement by two dangerous illusions: the possibility of fighting a 'limited' nuclear war, and 'star wars' or the possibility of developing a defense against nuclear weapons. Happily the 'star wars' boondoggle seems headed for the scrap heap.[4]

Both fatally endanger the concept of mutual deterrence which has provided a prolonged period of peace through mutual blackmail. More to the point, both endanger Western Europe more immediately and directly than the United States, since it was in Western Europe and not in the US or USSR that the scenarios of limited nuclear warfare were played out and it was the US and more particularly its command and control centers (Washington presumably) which could be protected by the 'star wars' gadgetry. The stationing of the US missiles in Western Europe in the early 1980s, in response to the stupid and provocative Soviet modernization of intermediate missiles, brought all these fears to the surface. The US was turning up the heat in the one theater of superpower confrontation where limited war was least possible since both powers had too much at stake. Either the stationing of US intermediary missiles was unnecessarily politically expensive and provocative or, even worse, Western Europe was to be targeted in the case of any conflict for stationing of weapons over which it would have no control.

The readiness with which they were negotiated away hardly argues that the missiles were regarded as essential weapons by either superpower which to date have eliminated no major strategic weapon systems. At the time of the dispute about stationing US missiles in Western Europe it did not seem to me that the issue affected the security of either the western or eastern blocs. Which is of course why Reagan and Gorbachev have been able to reach an agreement on those intermediary missiles with relative ease. There were quite different questions involved. The opposition to the stationing of missiles in Western Europe was an opposition to involving Western Europe more directly in the new arms race, begun in the last years of the Carter administration and expanded with such enthusiasm by the Reagan administration, and to the breakdown of detente. It represented the quite justified fear by the Western Europeans that it would make them the target in the case of any conflict between the two superpowers.

On the other hand, given that there are more than some 4,000 nuclear warheads already around, stationed in Western Europe, the issue was mainly symbolic in terms of actual security. The symbols were important both to the US government, which bullied its allies to go along with the stationing of the missiles despite their obvious reluctance,[5] and to the peace movement which found in these missiles a convenient symbol to link the danger of war with increasing resentment of the role of the United States as a world power. The passionate massive objections to these missiles must therefore be primarily understood more as a revolt against American hegemony and the Cold War than anything else. The peace demonstrators called for the removal of missiles east and west with none of the illusions about the Soviet Union which had characterized the peace movements of the 1950s and early 1960s. That had been taken care of by Prague in 1968 and the repression of Solidarity in 1981.

These protests represented the beginning of a more general revolt against the domination of Europe by the superpowers. In practice the mood in Western Europe is moving steadily towards a form of neo-Gaullism on a Western-European scale: this is by no means localized in France or even specific to either the left or the right. This 'Western-European scale' will by 1992 create a Western Europe which transcends the Europe of Nations which the good General envisaged, but it will therefore be even more a Europe which can be assertive towards the United States and unafraid of the Soviet Union. A sea change in the mood of Western Europe in general is taking place.

The issue of the missiles arose in part as a response to Kissinger's well-known statement that Europe should not necessarily count on the US nuclear umbrella in the case of a 'local' war in Europe. That is, the US would not necessarily risk New York to defend, say, Hamburg. In response to that 'problem' the missiles were proposed as a way of linking Western Europe's defense more directly to the US. The argument now has gone way beyond that issue and E.P.Thompson of European Nuclear Disarmament (END) has quite rightly posited the issue of the missiles as an issue of European independence from superpower rivalry. This is why such groups had opposed the placing of US missiles *and* had called at the same time for the removal of the Soviet SS-20 and SS-22 missiles. The momentum gained during that mobilization remains in the form of a network of groups and activists throughout Western Europe, with even some Eastern European contacts, thus creating a non-parochial, supra-national movement for peace and individual rights.

From the point of view of the Eastern European regimes and populations the missiles had never made much of a difference. For the Soviets themselves it is clear that they were at best mildly politically useful although militarily non-essential. That is incidentally why there had not been much mobilization on the part of the Eastern European regimes or for that matter by the anti-regime opposition around the missile question. The Eastern Europeans were more concerned about the break-up of detente since it is during the detente, during the period of better relations between the Soviet Union and the US that liberalization and reforms in Eastern Europe are maximized. That is also the time during which loosening the ties to the Soviet Union and improving economic, cultural and political relations and trade with Western Europe is possible. The last is primarily why, whatever they may or may not like about Gorbachev's 'glasnost' or economic reforms, the Eastern European regimes are delighted with the success of the present Soviet diplomatic peace offensive.

This is why Gorbachev's diplomatic breakthrough and the real possibility of further US–USSR disarmament agreements to be followed by deep cuts in conventional forces in Europe is so exciting and cheering. The cheering has been modified by a degree of wariness since the major actors remain the superpowers. When it comes to detente the Europeans, East and West, quote the old African saying 'pygmies get hurt when elephants fight'. To which the appropriately cynical Yugoslavs add, 'but they also get hurt when elephants make love'. It is important to realize that important though the INF (Intermediate Nuclear Forces) Treaty might be, the superpowers remain superpowers and remain nuclear giants with the capacity for overkill and world destruction many times over. What it does represent is the end of the acute stage of the new Cold War which Brezhnev and Reagan launched in the early 1980s. Bush has now inherited a momentum of negotiations over arms cuts which will be difficult to resist. But that also means that it will be impossible effectively to demand more arms expenditures from the Western European allies.

The Increased Obsolescence of the Cold War[6]

The less noticed but potentially more important development for European security, and for that matter security in general, has been the growing acceptance by the Soviet military experts of the doctrines of *sufficiency and deterrence.* With a more reasonable US administration this may lead to major cut-backs in military spending being grudgingly acceptable to both military establishments as at least not endangering the national defense. But then there is always a danger when discussing security issues of getting sucked into a peculiar mind set which clashes with common sense and even common decency. For example, were any of the intermediate missiles ever conceivably needed? Since the days of the Berlin blockade, if even then, was there ever even a remote possibility of a Soviet attempt at a limited war in Europe? Or for that matter a NATO attempt to alter the post-Yalta and Teheran treaties by military force? Why, then, did an entire generation of otherwise reasonable people in Europe, the US and USSR end up playing this idiotic tit-for-tat minuet with the cyclical arms race in Europe which had made no one more secure?

It is when questions like that begin to be asked that a beginning of the end of the Cold War as we have known it becomes possible. Lions will not lie with lambs, even if it were all that clear who is whom. Dirty little repressive colonial and semi-colonial conflicts on the peripheries of the interest spheres of the superpowers will take place. Third World countries will continue waging murderous civil and international wars. But a limited war in Europe with conventional and/or 'tactical' nuclear weapons will not take place. And even if it did, by some malign miracle, it is not at all clear that NATO as it now stands would not win a smashing victory with the support of the Eastern European population which certainly would not fight on behalf of the systems it hates.[7] It probably makes more sense to pay attention to massive civil defense strategies of the sort the Dutch peace movement has developed, and the all-people's defense of the type the Yugoslavs propose if there is to be anything left worth defending at all.

The current lowering of tensions between the superpowers is of course most welcome but one must speculate on the consequences of a rapprochement between the US and the Soviet Union on a whole variety of economic and political issues, for example, on opposition movements in Eastern Europe and in any part of the Communist world. Another example is resistance and revolt against US-supported right-wing regimes. Would the detente mean that there would be mutual suppression of criticism of the other bloc?

The Soviet officials have tended to link progress in disarmament with the easing of public pressure on questions of human rights and democratization.[8] The US policy makers have also repeatedly raised the issue of 'linkage' of disarmament agreement to Soviet 'restraint' in the Third World. That is, would mutual arms cuts be dependent on the Soviets cutting off military aid to radical Third World governments and revolutionary movements? That would be both absurd and dangerous.[9] *Arms agreement should be justified because they are defensible in themselves and not as a reward for supposed good behavior of the competing superpower.* Otherwise the implication would be, as the hawks argue in both the US and the USSR, that one is doing the other side an almost unpatriotic favor rather than agreeing on mutually acceptable and beneficial cut-backs in military hardware and spending.

Those would be fragile agreements indeed, subject to every whim of domestic political opinion. There is a further and crucially important factor which makes the present arms negotiations between the superpowers, welcome as they are, a symbol of the obsolescence of the world dominated by the superpowers. There are only two real actors in the present military conversations, since the Warsaw Pact countries outside of the USSR do not count in policy matters, and it is a standing grievance of the Western European allies of the US that they are informed, often *post factum*, of the US negotiating posture.

That is both ironic and obsolescent. It is a reflection of a world power relationship, bi-polarity, which is in the process of disintegrating. The world has moved well into the new, more complex, and perhaps dangerous, relations of multi-polarity, of a number of power centers, as far as the economy and technology are concerned. It is only in the field of military power that the world has remained essentially bi-polar and it is only a question of time before the realities of the new power relationships, above all the new economic power relationships, begin to impinge on the consciousness of the political elites and political publics of the two superpowers. In a way both superpowers have lost, or rather failed to win, the Cold War.

A New Detente and Support for Democratic and Human Rights

Quite clearly there are several models of rapprochement. One would be a second Yalta, a second Teheran. That is, the two superpowers agreeing that each be left alone to manage their own spheres of influence. All one would haggle about here would be what those spheres are. That is, that the Soviets would not help with opposition movements in the sphere which is defined as Western, and that the West not give support to oppositional movements in Eastern Europe. That would be an imperialist agreement at the expense of various national liberation movements and of all smaller states. It should not be acceptable to socialists or consistent democrats, or the peace activists for that matter. But one of the curses of the Cold War is that is has also calloused the consciences and sensitivities of many peace and socialist activists when national independence and democratic rights seem to interfere with the possibility of peace.

Decent men and women of the peace-oriented left, who understand perfectly well why they must support the rights of the Nicaraguans, Grenadians and Palestinians to struggle for their rights and independence, suddenly become extraordinarily 'responsible' when it comes to the rights of the Eastern Europeans, or for that matter the Baltic nations, the other Soviet and Eastern European minorities or the Soviets themselves. They have been hesitant about supporting the rights of repressed minorities in Third World and former colonial countries as well, as can be seen from the scandalous neglect of the plight of the Kurds, the various minorities in Ethiopia, the non-Muslim Blacks in Sudan, the oppression of the peoples of East Timor, the Indonesian-occupied New Guinea, to mention only a few of the more obvious cases.

This double standard has been very harmful to the left in the West, and has contributed mightily to the suspicions held over the years by the human rights and democratic activists in the East. Whatever the other reservations I have about French foreign policy under Mitterand's first and second presidency, he did a superbly decent thing when, on a state visit to Prague in December of 1988, he insisted on seeing the Czech embattled human rights activist from Charter 77, Vaclav Havel. That is exactly the kind of signal which the socialist and democratic Western public figures should be giving to the Eastern Europeans and Soviets. That signal should be combined with genuine offers of armament cuts and economic aid.

Even if it were not harmful in instrumental ways, this double standard is certainly immoral. One should always make the distinction between the 'west' and the West: the 'west' of the governments, trade and immigration barriers and capitalism, and the West of the trade unions, party pluralism and social movements. An argument could be made about long-range futility of the first 'west' interfering in Eastern Europe and the USSR, although there is nothing at all wrong with protesting at outrages against human and democratic rights. After all, the same persons who object to such 'interference' with internal affairs in the Soviet Union and Eastern European countries find nothing at all objectionable in pressures and protests directed against the South African government. On the other hand, much more active and consistent involvement by unions and socialist parties and social movements with both official and unofficial organizations in Eastern Europe and the USSR and their continued support of democratic struggles, human rights and dissidents' rights is urgently needed. It would contribute to creating European movements for democracy, peace and social justice.

In the United States years of right-wing Republican control over the White House make it possible to forget that the Democrats at the present time are not that much out of the old Cold War consensus. In opposition they sound much better than when they are in government. However, if there had been a Democratic victory in the 1988 presidential race, one should not underestimate the changes which even a modest pro-human rights policy such as the one which existed during the Carter administration could have made in the lives of thousands of victims of right-wing oppressive regimes.

An easing up of the arms build-up, or, even better, cut-backs in the military budget, would ease that military and economic pressure on their own population and on that of Western Europe as well as on the Soviets. That is a good thing. On the other hand, one should be skeptical of superpower agreements which simply abandon Nicaragua to the mercies of the Americans, and the Afghans to the mercies of the fundamentalist Muslim 'freedom fighters'.

When it comes to the fate of the Eastern European dissidents in the case of a major detente, it is hard to speculate but the past is not an optimistic one. The Solidarity movement is doomed to be sold out by the present-day official 'West' anyhow. From the point of view of the Western banks, the Solidarity movement, and other popular working-class resistance and movements in Eastern Europe, Yugoslavia and the Soviet Union are a disaster. Despite all the verbal outrage at the repression of Solidarity and imposition of martial law in 1981, the Western banks did not hasten to bail Poland out.

During the strike wave of May 1988 in Poland, official Western political opinion was moderate to an extreme. Western European governments and financial communities and those of the US are not interested in supporting a *working-class* opposition in Eastern Europe. All the more reason for the parties of the Socialist International to develop firm and solid links there. The Greens in West Germany have tended to be considerably better on those sorts of questions than even the social-democrats and their unions, who tend to suffer from an excess of 'responsibility' when dealing with Eastern Europe and the Soviet Union. But then that is the problem of a party which takes itself seriously as an alternative government of a major European power and as the major architect of a unified socialist strategy in Western Europe.

Western European Independence from the Cold War Alliance is Essential for a Genuine Detente

Western Europe is far less prone to military saber rattling wherever it seem convenient for domestic purposes then the US and is the most likely place for a political breakthrough by the socialist and social-democratic parties. These are increasingly less Atlanticist having learned their lessons from repeated US administrations that Washington is basically hostile to Western European socialist and social-democratic parties. Right-wing American administrations have made that point clear far more effectively to the leaderships of the labor and socialist parties than the left-wings in those parties ever could, despite their very best efforts. Reagan's Washington did produce some interesting and potentially very good side-effects in the political education of a whole generation of Western Europeans. While Bush will be a milder and less ideological version of Reagan, stereotypes and images take a long time to set and an even longer time to change.

That is an additional reason why it makes sense for socialists and progressives to support the growing independence of Europe from the United States. It is in Western Europe that powerful socialist and labor movements as well as vital alternative social movements exist. It is also there that the advanced welfare states, the indispensable terrain for an advance towards socialism, also exist. The two are of course intimately linked.

Let me put it in another way: were the Soviet Union by a fantastic turn in historical events to become more democratic, more decent and egalitarian, in short closer to being a socialist society, the rivalry between the USSR and the US would not become politically any *less* potentially confrontational. Unless the Western countries also moved towards a democratic, egalitarian and more socially responsible society, to leave out the wildly optimistic notion of a democratic *socialist* society (and the prospects for that in the case of the dominant power, the United States, are dismal), the two types of societies would remain inherently antagonistic. This antagonism will not be necessarily lessened if the more technocratic and market-oriented economic reforms are adopted in the Soviet Union and its alliance. On the contrary, antagonisms based on economic dependency and the burden of loans will exist, and have historically proved to be very sharp indeed. It is also probable that western financial and banking circles will take a far more benevolent attitude towards such a Soviet Union, that is a more market-oriented Soviet Union, than will the Western European trade unions, left and human rights activists.

By the same token, were the west to become democratic-socialist, the rivalry between the west and the Soviet Union might take different and less dangerous forms, but it would be necessarily less intense. Not unless more far-reaching changes occurred in the Soviet Union in the direction of a democratic and socialist society than even the most optimistic realists can hope for today would this be possible. It is one thing to hope that Gorbachev's reforms succeed, but quite another to base political prognoses and strategies on the assumption of that success. Unfortunately the odds are rather long for that to happen.

While everything consistent with long-range strategic goals of democratic socialism should be done to aid the Soviet political and economic reforms, the hope that these reforms will succeed should not lead socialists in Western Europe to act as if the reforms have already succeeded. They clearly have not. Nor is their victory inevitable, which is regrettable. Excessive optimism can be as treacherous a guide to political action as pessimism. But, after years of Cold War and domestic class stalemate in Western Europe, decent socialists and democrats are desperate for hope and good news from the Soviet Union. A disappointment of those hopes would have a debilitating effect on Western European politics in general and leftist politics in particular.

That is one of the reasons, and only one of the reasons, why in dealing with the prospects of reforms from above in the Soviet society one should maintain links with the opposition as well as developing sympathetic dialogue with the in-system reformers. However, the prospects of a major advance towards democracy and socialism in the Soviet Union, or towards democratic socialism in the major military power of the west, are too distant to be worth much time for speculation. The more immediate prospects are more interesting, if less dramatically inspiring.

The American ruling elite is today still divided into two basic groups. One thinks that it has to fight against any spread of Soviet-type regimes, or regimes which they define as Soviet-type regimes, everywhere. This has essentially been the Reagan administration's point of view. In a more sophisticated form that is also the view of the major players in the Bush administration, that is, they regard all anti-capitalist regimes as perpetually potentially dangerous. If they are not dangerous, these regimes are doomed to failure. The US, in the view of this section of the American foreign policy elite, may be temporarily willing to deal amicably with regimes like China or Yugoslavia, but in the long run they are deeply convinced that they are involved in a world struggle to maintain the hegemony over 'free' institutions which are identified with the capitalist market economy. The Soviets, not unreasonably, are unwilling to accept a situation in which the domination of the world remains with the capitalist market dominated by the United States. The combination of the two above views leads to the possibility of at best short-range truces between the superpowers.

The other part of the US establishment wants a genuine deal, the kind of thing which was in the air as one possibility in the immediate years following the Second World War in 1945 and 1946, a deal where the two sides really decide that they can coexist for an indefinite period, that is, a deal which accepts the Soviets as a partner in 'managing' the world. That deal was a fantasy from the beginning when initially proposed in the 1940s, since the Soviets were too eager to consolidate their gains in Eastern Europe and the US too quick to read this as the beginning of a period of Soviet expansionism and adventurism.

That in retrospect turned out to be a much exaggerated and inaccurate perception made possible by the increasing evidence of monstrous massive repression in the Soviet Union of which the concentration camp universe of the Gulag archipelago was only one facet. On the other hand, the post-Second World War decade did look like the outset of the American century as the

US replaced the French and British Empires as the guardian of the capitalist world market and developed a series of world-encompassing but illusory alliances which were to contain the Soviet Union.

Today both the US and the Soviets represent alternative and rival, but essentially secure world systems. More to the point, both know a great deal more about each other and there are few traumatic revelations left in store. Thus a deal which was impossible in the late 1940s may be possible in the 1990s. One argument against such an arrangement is that Japan and Western Europe can provide access to economic credits and technologies at a lesser political cost to the Soviet Union today, which was clearly not an option in the 1940s.

The present US–USSR rivalry, however, could take another form, short of an overall 'deal'. This would be a non-military form, and, clearly, it would be better if they competed politically. This would lower the threshold of the arms race, it would move towards the lowering of the number of nuclear missiles and the eventual abolition of nuclear weapons and there would be a fairly strong international institution which could mediate between the two. However, that is a separate issue from the fact that a struggle for socialism and democracy would still have to deal with the existence of the two superpowers as such. In other words, if Russia and America had no nuclear weapons, if they agreed to mediate all military differences, the internal movements for freedom, widening democracy and socialism in Eastern Europe and the Western hemisphere would still be directed respectively against their own superpowers.

That is what one means by saying that socialism represents a third alternative. That alternative is not neutralism, it is not the non-aligned movement: it represents the struggle against both superpowers for the right of people to fight for democratic and egalitarian societies which are not dominated from outside. The left wings of the mass working-class parties, national liberation movements and democratic social movements can have a future only insofar as they view themselves, at least strategically, as being counterposed to the superpowers and their supporters.

France: The Problem and the Asset for European Independence

The inchoate moves towards an independent Europe – independent of the two superpowers – represents a major step forward towards a world less dominated by the two blocs. Thus, although the French socialist party participates in the consensus on a policy of depending on nuclear weapons under its national control, it argues for that in terms of a potential independent Europe.[10] First Western Europe but then Europe – independent of both of the superpowers. Without agreeing with their nuclear policy either in the case of arms or energy, one can appreciate some of their arguments.

What they argue is this: the French nuclear deterrent is far too small to threaten the Soviet Union or the United States. What it does is buy France a place at any table negotiating nuclear disarmament. It precludes another Yalta without Europe participating, it precludes a deal being made at the expense of Europe, which is entirely possible given the nature of the two superpowers. However, the problem with nuclear weapons is that they can never be used. That is an additional reason for moving as quickly as possible towards nuclear disarmament.

One can concede this much to the French: they say, whenever demands are made that they cut down on their nuclear capacity, which is after all in comparison to the two superpowers laughably small, that surely it should begin with the two giant arsenals of the superpowers. Surely neither the US nor the Soviet Union are in a position to point their finger at the French nuclear weapons because, at the present time, the French and possibly the Chinese arms are only a deterrent. They are nothing else. They certainly do not have any first strike capacity, they cannot knock out another power's silos. What the French are saying is, if you Russians and you Americans make a deal that Europe will be the arena in which intermediate or local nuclear weapons alone will be used, we are not a part of that deal. We will not allow Paris to be blown up to spare Washington or Moscow. That is what deterrent means – it is supposed to deter.

Let me be clear about my own views on this issue. I think that the proper policy for the French socialists is to propose to devolve nuclearly; that is, to move towards a policy of no nuclear weapons. For that matter, they should join the Swedes in proposing to move away from the use of nuclear energy itself by a realistic but firmly set date. However, it is at least important to understand what the French political actors are saying at this point in time. They are saying, 'If you take out Paris and say that it is only a local tactical or intermediate missile that is involved, we will not accept that. We will take out Leningrad or whatever we can, therefore please do not take out Paris.' Thus the existence of the independent French force of 'dissuasion', a modest version of deterrence, makes the superpowers' grotesque arsenals' balance in Europe absurd. The French independent nuclear capacity guarantees that there cannot be a local nuclear conflict limited to Europe since once the French responded the fat would be in the fire. In practice they have answered the question posed by Kissinger by linking the US to Western Europe under circumstances where it is not the US unilaterally which determines when the conflict goes nuclear. I think that the socialist policy in Europe should demand the removal of all superpower troops and weapons, conventional and nuclear, from Europe – East and West.

Let me put it somewhat schematically, to illustrate why it is such a radical demand. If the troops of the US and the Soviet Union were removed from Europe within a moderate span of time, not a single Eastern European regime would survive and not a single Western European regime would collapse. That tells us a great deal about the claims of those regimes to be socialist, popular or even legitimate. How long would the present Polish regime survive if there were no ultimate Soviet sanction in the form of troops? What are the bets on the lifespan of an independent East German regime or any other Eastern European regime without even the present, at least potential, ultimate sanction of Soviet force. The Western European regimes clearly do not today depend on the power of the United States as a sanction against any internal political challenges real or potential.

So to repeat: if the demand, the old left-Gaullist demand, were ever fulfilled, the withdrawal of all troops from Europe, all American troops and all Russian troops,[11] not a single Eastern European regime would survive and not a single Western European regime would collapse. One must add, however, that the collapse of Soviet hegemony in Eastern Europe and the regimes which it maintains would be the death knell of the Cold War in Europe and the end of the asymmetrical alliance between the United States and Western Europe.

Nuclear energy and nuclear defense have provided the French political elites with a substitute for the post-Second World War welfare-state consensus. France is an excellent illustration of the growing trend to neo-corporatism in Western Europe. This trend has both a radical and a conservative facet and can be counterposed to the archaic free-marketist ideology of the Reagan and Thatcher administrations on the one hand, and the equally archaic traditional trade unionism of the British Trades Union Congress.

In contrast with the class-stalemated and confrontational politics of Great Britain, the continental social-democratic and trade union leaderships have had to deal with a far less confrontational business community and with a social Catholicism which has been as ambivalent about capitalism as it is about socialism. This has created room for a very wide consensus around an extended welfare state, an interventionist state as far as the economy was concerned and a general commitment towards a welfare state economy which has attenuated class conflict.

The French nuclear consensus acts to form a terrain where future-oriented French technocratic elites can posit a program which simultaneously offers the option of greater French and therefore European independence from the US as well as the alternate option of a France which is a more equal and solid ally of the United States. Which option one picks depends on one's political predilections. Clearly whether one chooses the left-Gaullist approach of stressing the need for an independent Europe capable of defending itself without depending on the American nuclear umbrella, or the more egalitarian alliance which in the era of nuclear power is taken to mean that you will not be taken seriously unless you do have nuclear weapons, the French nuclear policy provides an answer.

It also provides France with a short-sighted but momentarily effective answer to the scarcity of energy resources. What interests me at this point is not why the French are wrong, and they are wrong for a great number of reasons – not the least of which is the fit between nuclear energy and high centralization – but rather the evident disintegration of the old consensus around an American alliance which, beginning with France, is spreading throughout Europe and affects the social-democratic parties, the left, the social Catholics, and the traditional European nationalists.

In examining this process more closely, it may well be that the sea-change in Catholicism in the last few decades will turn out to have been of enormous significance in providing broader and increasingly trans-class opposition to the continued role of the superpowers in maintaining an unjust and exploitative world order. This growing hostility to the superpowers as such presents a fertile terrain for ideas about a Europe outside of the alliance and more assertive on the world scene. Therefore I view a renewed Euro-centrism on the part of the European political publics as an essential step towards breaking up the frozen alliances created by the Cold War and therefore the creation of space for new political and social alternatives. The crisis of the Atlantic Alliance noted, if not hailed, by observers from both sides of the Atlantic is a part of a re-examination not only of the role of Europe in the present world order but of a serious discussion of the appropriate future roles for the United States and the Soviet Union.

Even such conservative and hawkish institutions as the Pentagon think-tanks are positing defense needs today and for the next decades in terms of marginal conflicts in the Third World, that is, on the periphery of the two rival alliances, rather than in Europe. But if Europe becomes increasingly unlikely as the scene of military confrontation between the two alliances, and I have argued that the least likely place for a limited military conflict is Europe, then one can begin seriously to talk about truly massive cut-backs in military expenditure on the part of both alliances. Massive cut-backs are possible which would fundamentally alter assumptions about the nature of the competitive relationship between the Soviet Union and the western alliance. In such a world, one less dependent on the military strengths of the leaders of the two blocs, the differences of interests within the alliances are more likely to become salient.

The time for major cut-backs of military expenditures and commitments of both NATO and Warsaw Pact seems almost ideal: no imminent threat of military conflict, Europe is the area in which the bulk of the heavy armaments of both blocs are concentrated, the Soviet elites are currently preoccupied with the problems of modernizing and radically reforming an inefficient economic system, while a growing part of the American political establishment is questioning the continued viability, purpose and above all costs of NATO as well as the rationale for keeping large US forces in Europe. In the meantime Spain asks the US to withdraw its F-16 planes, while the Western European social-democratic and labor parties (always with the exception of the French) move towards near-neutralism and a posture which emphasizes openings towards the possibility of a post-Cold-War Europe and world. The old concern with what the US political public opinion would tolerate no longer acts as the limit of what European socialists can do politically.

The Germanies and European Autonomy

The new prospect of a general detente in Europe always revives the question of the Germanies. It is, after all, the United States and its allies which are primarily responsible for the existence of a divided Germany. The Soviets under Stalin had shown an almost indecent willingness to sacrifice their East German party loyalists in their haste to achieve an Austrian-type settlement in Germany.

This deal for a unified and de-militarized and neutral Germany, exactly like today's Austria, has been offered again and again and is of course the nightmare of the supporters of NATO and the notion that the Cold War must last for ever. How could one even imagine a NATO without West Germany, which provides half the ground forces and the physical ground on which the conflict would be fought? What was a possible objection, and probably the only possible objection from a German point of view, was the potential danger of a militarily aggressive Soviet Union dominant on the European continent.

But what happens in the case of a very major set of military cut-backs? What if the danger of military conflict in Europe is reduced to a vanishing point? Why would the West and East Germans agree to a continued and artificial separation in the name of non-existent security considerations? The old seductive Austrianization deal, the Rapacki Plan, versions of the Palme proposals, all essentially propose the same thing: to improve conditions for peace and European unity by creating a huge neutral zone in Europe separating the two military alliances. This would be a block of neutral states starting with Sweden in the north and moving through the Germanies to Austria, then on to Yugoslavia and Albania.

There would be all kinds of heuristic side-effects of such a step. To mention only a few: it would deal near-fatal blows to both NATO and Warsaw Pacts, it would be likely to spread the zone both eastward and westward; Czechoslovakia, Hungary and Poland on the one hand being obvious candidates and Denmark, Norway, and the Benelux countries on the other. Free elections would be possible, for the Federal Parliament in a unified Germany would almost certainly produce a near-permanent social-democratic majority. Of course this would make the probability of trade between the Soviet Union and a unified Germany even more likely, since the chances of political strings being attached to such trade would be minimized. This all makes one wonder just how long it will take for the social-democrats to link the campaign for German re-unification on a democratic and peace-strengthening basis with the old Austrian model and to call for a Finlandization of Eastern Europe. This would be not a bad trade: military security of the Soviets in Europe, in exchange for internal political freedom for the Eastern Europeans and a unified neutral Germany. What is the argument against this: loyalty to the United States, the same United States which in effect guaranteed the permanent division of Germany, and which was willing to strip NATO of troops when engaged in its own little adventures in Vietnam and which gives lessons in respect for little countries' sovereignty throughout Latin America? I believe those days of loyalty are fast going.

West Germany could probably have its unification and be able to stay in a European Community since the Soviets have raised no objections towards Austria's moves in that direction. Times are changing and the old cosy arrangements in West Germany may not last. I can imagine few more powerful electoral platforms for the social-democrats in West Germany than to call for a unified democratic Germany in an independent and peaceful Europe. The right would have to counterpose to that the good old alliance with the United States. West Germany, which has been the sturdiest pillar of the western military and political alliance, does not look so sturdy today.

The social-democrats have been pushed steadily to the left by the relentless hostility of Washington under Reagan, on one side, and the pressure from the Greens and the new social movements, on the other. In the meantime both the Christian Democrats and Strauss's Social Christians emphasize the special relationship between the two Germanies. Neither bodes well for any increased West German military and financial effort to bolster the alliance. These trends have been encouraged by the development of a Soviet diplomatic offensive which is increasingly successful in projecting the image of a Soviet Union which is genuinely interested, for its own economic technological reasons, in massive cutbacks in military expenditures and a prolonged detente. Given the natural trade focus of the German trade towards the east, that is welcome news indeed.

By the same token those who would interfere with the three desiderata of West German policy will not be bearers of welcome tidings. The three propositions are: no increase in military spending or military manpower; an expansion and deepening of the special relationship between the Germanies; and an expansion of long-range trade and access to raw materials and markets in the east. The key to all three rests in improved relations with the Soviets and a development of a real detente. The current (1988 Fall) standing in West German opinion polls respectively of Reagan and Gorbachev is evidence of a sea-change in attitudes towards the US and USSR in relation to the questions of peace and stability. This change is not accompanied with any particular admiration for Soviet and Eastern European state socialism.

There is an intrinsic truth in the stereotypical images of the US and USSR as the Athens and Sparta of our age, but one should remember that it was Athens that started the immensely destructive Peloponnesian war. There are, after all, many historic precedents to show that jingoist democracies have often been more dangerous for peace than repressive authoritarian regimes. The histories of Great Britain, France and of course the United States abound in examples. History, that is to say the story of human-made societies and activities, has ways of moving in complicated patterns which defy the simplicities beloved by today's politicians and political publics, increasingly shaped by an age of televised political campaigning and the systematic depoliticization of public life and debate by the mass media.

A Brief Prescriptive Summary

1) The most probable place for the revival of socialist energies, projects and politics is today in Western Europe. This is for a number of reasons but the essential ones are the presence of mass democratic socialist parties,

unions and organizations in societies which have a high level of civic culture and advanced welfare states.

2) For Western Europe to be able to play this role it must become independent of the political, economic and above all military domination of the United States and the real or potential military and political threat from the Soviet Union. The ideal time for this is a period of major military cut-backs and disarmament of the superpowers in Europe. For this to be convincing, evidence of the Soviet Union's needs for the resources tied up in the military sector to help an ailing economy is essential. Thus nothing depends on goodwill and sincerity.

3) The growing autonomy of Western Europe has been accelerated by the military and economic recklessness and dogmatism of the Reagan administration and the successful diplomatic peace offensive by the reformist Gorbachev administration in the Soviet Union. The Soviet acceptance of a zero option in intermediate nuclear weapons for Europe and an independent French nuclear capacity further reduces the dependence of Western Europe on the nuclear umbrella of the United States.

4) An essentially conciliatory posture by the Soviet Union increases the internal strains on the reactions between the US and Western Europe. This in turn raises several specific issues: the possibility of a neutral zone separating Europe from north to south along the lines of the Palme proposal for a nuclear-free zone, or more radically a unified neutral and de-militarized Germany much like contemporary Austria, and a Findlandized Eastern Europe in the context of the complete withdrawal of all conventional and nuclear military forces from Europe by both superpowers.

5) A unified de-militarized and neutral Germany is likely to be a social-democratic Germany: this is only one reason why the left in Europe should begin to push for it. The other is that it is both unreasonable and undemocratic that the German people should, 40 years after the Second World War, have separation imposed on them by treaty. A unified neutral and de-militarized Germany could begin the necessary process of massive reflation of the entire Western European economy through a huge long-range program of exports of goods and technology to the Soviet Union and Eastern Europe. These exports in turn can buy the time necessary for the successful reforms and liberalization of those economies and societies. These are essential in turn for any hope for the eventual democratization of these societies and re-creation of a Europe no longer divided between the east and west. That is a possible future and one well worth working for.

Chapter 6

The Eternal Bridegroom: Western European Labor and Socialist Movements

A Brief Historical Sketch:[1]

The Second World War represents a major historical break within the mass social-democratic[2] and labor movement of Europe. After the war, it lost its near-monopoly on mass workers' organizations, parties and unions and was forced to face the prospect of wielding state power under the two very restricting conditions imposed by the power realities of post-war reconstruction of Europe and what appeared to be the inevitable and irresistible onset of the American century.

The vast majority of the organized workers during the inter-war years had remained within the socialist parties and their unions despite the historical Communist-socialist split. The only mass Communist party in Europe which did develop during that period was the Communist party of Germany which was driven into exile and underground by the Nazi victory in 1933. It had been by far the largest and most significant Communist party outside of the Soviet Union, with the possible exception of China, which was in any case on the periphery of the consciousness and attention of the international workers' movement in the years before the Second World War.

Another smaller, but militant and romantically attractive part of the radical workers' movement was the anarchist and anarcho-syndicalist organizations and trade unions which, after the defeat of the Republic in Spain, where they had a mass base in the intra-war years, faded into political and organizational insignificance.[3] The remnants of the remnants were the far Marxist left, which until the 1960s meant, for practical purposes, the various fragmented and fragmenting Trotskyist, or Trotskyisant, groups and parties which were always small but sometimes played an ideological role on the fringes of the socialist parties and unions.[4]

The defeat of the Popular Front government in Spain by Franco's right-wing military and clerical forces, with the help of international fascism, represented one more defeat for the anti-fascist forces of the left and demonstrated the unwillingness of the western parliamentary democracies to defend democracy against fascism. It was thus doubly demoralizing, particularly since it was followed by the craven betrayals of Czechoslovakia to Hitler by the western democracies at Munich and the grotesque alliance of convenience to partition Poland and Eastern Europe between the Soviet Union and Nazi Germany.

The victories of fascism over the left and labor movements in Italy, Germany, Austria and Spain, followed by the Nazi and Italian occupation of most of Europe during the war and the resultant brutal repression, had a devastating impact on the socialist labor movement. Socialists and Communists had filled the concentration camps and the lists from which the hostages to be executed were drawn. Perhaps even more debilitating was the political problem posed by the victories of fascism *precisely in the countries where the labor movement has been the strongest,* namely Italy, Austria and Germany. The connection was not lost on the socialist and Marxist theorists. While it was clear that the divisions within the working class between the Communists and socialists had played a major role in the victories of fascism, two other things were also of considerable significance – the absence of an immediate and usable program on the left for dealing with the economic crisis and an insufficient willingness to defend ('bourgeois') parliamentary democracy.[5] Now, to be clear in the latter case, no one on the visible political horizon of inter-war Europe seemed to be that passionately attached to parliamentary democracy. The First World War, the repression of the radical upsurge which followed, and above all the demoralizing and prolonged depression since the late 1920s had left a heritage of deep cynicism about a democracy which was both limited and very class-specific. The general strikers in Britain in the 1920s and workers throughout Europe discovered those limitations quickly enough. That far worse horrors were not only possible, but were lurking in the near future, was not yet clear – these were, after all, the years before the unimaginable, the Nazi Holocaust and the murderous operations of Stalin in the Soviet Union.

Nevertheless, no one had been more attached to parliamentary democracy than the socialists in practice.[6] One very good reason for this was that the very right of suffrage, for the workers and the property-less, and later for women where it existed, had been the result of prolonged militant struggles of the socialist and labor movement. The middle class, centrist, Catholic and conservative parties proved all too ready to jettison the burden of bourgeois parliamentary democracy when capitalism itself was threatened.

The socialists defended this limited democracy with arms in hand in Austria and in Spain, and politically in France and less competently in Germany. By the time of the Spanish Civil War the international Communist line had changed and the Communists from a number of countries, as well as other leftists, rushed to defend the democratic republic there. This was in sharp contrast to their previous unwillingness to do so, in either Austria or Germany, where settling accounts with their socialist rivals appeared more urgent than any united actions against fascism.[7] That was the time (1929–34) when the socialists and social-democrats were denounced as 'social fascists'. That was also the period on the eve of the Nazi take-over, when the Communists joined with the Nazis in the general strike toppling the social-democratic government in Prussia in 1931.

The whole left, as well as the world, learned a bloody lesson for the grotesque underestimation of the danger of fascism in Germany by Stalin and his supporters. It took a great deal of blood, much of it shed by the peoples of the Soviet Union, finally to destroy Nazism. It is also true that the rise of fascism was also due to the cowardly and treacherous role of the bourgeois governments, notably those of Great Britain and France, who regarded Hitler and Mussolini as lesser evils than Communism or the threat of workers' political and class assertiveness. The bourgeois democracies proved to be poor defenders of democracy when they conciliated fascists and Nazis in the name of social order. They also proved poor strategists as they kept trying to get Hitler to turn his appetites eastward towards the Soviet Union. The results were the débâcles of the Munich agreement in 1938, a synonym for ineffective appeasement, and the Hitler–Stalin pact of 1939–41 which guaranteed the start of the Second World War. The pact also provided for a partition of Eastern Europe between Nazi Germany and the Soviet Union and vital supplies of wheat, oil and other raw materials to the Nazi war machine for the first two years of the war.

Despite the disgraceful machiavellian episode of the Hitler–Stalin pact, during which the Communists avoided resisting the Nazi occupation and soft-pedaled arms production in Britain and the US, the Second World War proved an immense asset to the Communist parties throughout the world and in Europe in particular.[8] The Communists played a major and heroic role in the Resistance against the Nazis throughout Europe, east and west. They also benefited immensely through their association with the growing prestige of the Red Army and the Soviet Union which had taken on and destroyed the bulk of the Nazi armies.[9] Resistance, and even more so, the mythology of the Resistance, had helped the Communists become mass parties in Italy, France and Greece and for a while serious parties in Belgium, Holland and Britain. The Communist parties used this new good fortune with varying degrees of skill in the years which followed and of course met with varying degrees of repression and opposition. In Eastern Europe, with the exception of Yugoslavia where the Communist-led partisans took power on their own, the Communist parties had power handed to them by the occupying Soviet armies carrying out what they claimed, and very likely were, the agreements of Yalta and Teheran. In Western Europe the Communists with their tighter organizations, far more adaptable to clandestine and underground existence, proved more capable of functioning and surviving in the Resistance. This helped them emerge as mass parties after the victory over the Nazis, replacing the socialists as the largest parties of the left and in the unions in Italy and France, and as serious factors in labor in Belgium and Holland.

Only in what later became West Germany, where they were outlawed by 1956, and in Austria, where they associated with the unpopular temporary Soviet occupation, were the Communists a negligible force on the left. They also remained organizationally and politically weak in the Scandinavian countries, where the social-democratic parties and unions maintained their huge majorities within the working class. The exception was Finland, which had been forced into a special relationship to the USSR as a consequence of having been allied with the Axis during the war.

Thus when the post-war dust settled, there were no social-democratic parties or unions left in Eastern Europe at all: they had been forcibly merged with the Communists into the new Communist-dominated parties and unitary government-controlled unions.

In Western Europe the socialists had been replaced by the Communists as the largest and most important parties of the working-class only in France and Italy, although the Communists were also present in a number of other countries as significant elements in the trade unions. This increasingly bitter division of the working-class parties, unions, organizations and political publics in the post-war years hardened during the first Cold War, from roughly 1948 to roughly 1968, immensely weakened the left, and made left-majority governments impossible in some, and more difficult in other, countries.

Post-War Reconstitution of the Socialist International

The post-war reconstitution of the Socialist International took place slowly, since the dominant socialist parties in Western Europe remained quite disparate, with rather limited and formal links. The dominant socialist party in the first years was the British Labour party which was both arrogantly insular and committed to an imaginary special partnership with the United States in the post-war world. Nevertheless the post-war period was also the beginning of a golden era for the socialist parties.[10] The classical parties of the right had been by and large discredited during the war, and the Communists were soon isolated as a result of the beginning of the Cold War and the Marshall Plan in 1948. The centrist parties could not form majorities by themselves in most Western European countries.

There were limitations, very great limitations, for what the social-democrats could achieve, but these were not evident at the time. In addition to the dominant role which the United States had in post-war Europe and the leverage which Marshall Plan aid gave the US over economic and social policies of Western Europe in the first years after the war, there were other serious limitations that the socialists had in developing successful reformist socialist programs. Two should be mentioned: the socialist parties had considerable experience as parties and movements of opposition but little practical experience as government parties. More seriously they had no transitional program of any sort, not even a reformist socialist one, and only a very vague program of immediate demands beyond the broad outlines of a welfare state. The latter had been sketched out in the Beveridge Plan in wartime Britain, which provided the blueprint for the social welfare program of the first British Labour government.

In dealing with the economy, the British socialists made the first of the almost classical mistakes of post-war social-democracy. In the name of consensus, *they nationalized industries which were losing money and which were terribly undercapitalized over the years* – railways, coal-mines, shipyards. The result was that these industries, essential for the general infra-structure of the British economy, had to be run at a loss, subsidized by tax-revenues, thus 'proving' the economic inefficiency of both nationalization and socialists in government. To make things worse, the British public enterprise provided a structure of authority in the nationalized industries which was almost as authoritarian as the one in the private industry.

For workers in those industries the advantage of nationalization was abstract, and the Labour party's emphasis on bureaucratic nationalization rather than macro-control of the economy, combined with workers' control in industry, helped erode its initial massive support. By the early 1960s British socialism began to enter its long-drawn-out programmatic crisis. This crisis was exacerbated by a foreign policy influenced by the two special relationships, that to the United States and to the Commonwealth.

While the British Labour party was in government, its internationalism tended to be directed primarily towards the Commonwealth. It was also restrained by the special relationship assumed to exist between Britain and the US, a relationship made all the more significant by the devastation of the wartime British economy and vast economic and military power of the true victor of the Second World War, the United States.

The French socialist party was factionally divided as usual but participated in the cabinets of post-war France, gradually becoming ever more complicit in the doomed attempts to retain the French colonies. The West German social-democratic party was trying to rebuild with cadres returning from concentration camps and long exile and lived politically within the parameters of what the occupation authorities would accept, and that was not a great deal of militancy. Thus, while the US and other western occupation authorities were willing to accept trade unions and even the co-determination legislation with workers and union representatives on the corporate board, the US pro-consul Lucius Clay declared nationalization of the industries owned by war criminals and Nazis to be 'premature'. The process of taming the post-war German social-democracy had begun and it led to the Convention at Bad-Godesburg in 1959, where it voted against the last symbolic vestiges of being a party based on class-struggle and designed itself as a 'people's' party working for an advanced and egalitarian welfare state in a mixed, essentially capitalist economy.[11]

It was not until the 1960s that the German SPD began to become more self-assertive and convincingly to put itself forward as the alternative governing party of West Germany. It achieved this status first by painfully reconstructing the most successful and massive labor movement of Europe.[12] But to achieve the status of the alternative legitimate governing party, the German social-democrats had to go through a long process of adaptation. This included years in coalition with the Christian Democrats in the 'Grand Coalition' in the 1960s and then government under both Willy Brandt and Helmuth Schmidt in the 1970s, during which the SPD proved that it could govern competently and do so in the interests of a far wider political public than industrial workers. The social-democrats proved capable of taking widely supported foreign policy initiatives in Eastern Europe and the Third World which set West Germany and the social-democrats on a long-range collision course with US foreign policy and with the dominant American role in the Western European alliance.[13] This makes the SPD a very major player in the future of a unified European Economic Community after 1992.

Last, but far from the least, of the major parties, the Swedish socialist party had been the government through all these long years. Alone of the socialist parties, it had headed a neutral government and had not participated in the anti-Nazi war, which left it somewhat guilt-ridden and defensive in the immediate post-war years. While developing the most advanced welfare state in the world, and the closest approximation of the political and organizational hegemony of the working class in a capitalist society, the Swedish socialist party was initially isolated. This was because of its neutrality in the new division of Europe. Sweden is, and was, no part of the supra-national West European alliances, economic, political or military, which pushed the other West European socialist parties into cooperation.[14]

The socialist parties of Denmark, Norway and Belgium were also significant and were busily engaged in reconstructing their countries and helping with the French and Germans to lay the foundations for a European Community. One should note that the Community was not at all accepted as benevolent by the British Labour party, the Norwegian social-democrats or the Swedes. In any case the first post-war decade took place in the shadow of the dominant role that the United States had assumed in the world economy and the enormous successes of the Marshall Plan in getting the European economic 'miracle' started. This was accented by the increasingly visible harsh repression in the Eastern European countries in those years of high Stalinism. In terms of economic and social policies, the link with the United States obviously did place restraints on what could effectively be done. Nevertheless, fairly generous social welfare state measures began to be the Western European norm.

This was for several reasons: the junior partner of the US was Great Britain, whose Labour government was itself engaged in development of a welfare state, much admired and less copied. Secondly, there had already been a heritage of fairly generous and extensive corporatist welfare state legislation under Mussolini and Hitler, plus the laws passed under the Popular Front government of Blum in France and never repealed. Further there were social-democratic governments in power in Norway and Denmark and a powerful socialist influence on post-war legislation in Holland and Belgium. Mass Communist and socialist parties in Italy and the presence of social Catholicism and Catholic unions underpinned the welfare-state measures in Italy, while in Austria these issues had not even been politically contested.

During the first post-war decades extensive social welfare states had become the norm throughout western and northern Europe and the tasks of reconstruction and the take-off provided by the Marshall Plan provided both unprecedented full employment and steady and high growth. Even through a mere trickle-down system of distribution, this would mean steadily rising living standards for the working class without excessive efforts on the part of their parties and unions. But there was more than a mere trickle-down working, and this for two important reasons. To begin with, the traditional parties of the right which could have been normally counted on to object to progressive social legislation and to the growing influence of the unions had been in good part discredited through their collaboration with the Nazi occupation during the war or their lack of enthusiasm for the Resistance. This weakened them for at least the first post-war decade during which the Western European welfare policies began to take form.

The whole mythology of a war against Fascism, and the Resistance had helped create a general left-wing 'progressive' political culture and atmosphere in the years immediately after the war. To be sure, this process had been slowed down somewhat and restrained by the onset of the Cold War in 1948/9 but a momentum for progressive social legislation had already been obtained. In any case the US was considered to be a liberal hegemonic power, hostile to nationalization of industry, but not necessarily to (non-Communist) trade unions and welfare state measures. This turned out to be a dangerous half-truth.

US hegemony, it is sometimes conveniently forgotten, could be complex and ambivalent, in the immediate post-war period. In Japan, for example, the US imposed a very liberal Constitution, with free trade unions, freedom of the press and a destruction of the old landlord class in the countryside. Perhaps more to the point, those were the years of Keynesian orthodoxy and self-confidence, when it was generally believed that the capitalist cycles and depressions were now a thing of the past. It was broadly assumed that a social compact between the major class contenders could now be reached based on creating huge internal 'Fordist' markets throughout Western Europe, through increasing the incomes and thus the purchasing power of the working classes. Finally, there was pressure, precisely because of the Cold War, to make substantial concessions to the socialist and Catholic trade unions so that they could effectively replace the Communist ones. In any case the economies were no longer perceived as zero-sum games, where the gain of one group could only be at the expense of another. On the contrary the economy and society were a growing pie with plenty for all.

Thus the foundations of the Western European welfare state were laid in the optimistic productivistic post-war years and since then have become gains to be defended by their beneficiaries. That automatically vastly expanded the clientele of the socialist and labor parties throughout Europe and therefore the era of the 'end of ideology' never resulted in the lowering of the left vote – quite the contrary. What was less clear than the stability and growth of the left vote was what that vote meant. However, if nationalization of industry became a dubious trumpet for the British Labour party and the socialists on the continent, the welfare state was, and remains, immensely popular. The programs of social entitlement and the steadily increasing living standards revolutionized the conditions of the working class throughout Western Europe. This was almost 20 years of prosperity and growth, unprecedented in the history of modern capitalism.

Euro-Communists: Breaking out of the Ghetto[15]

The increased bitterness and rivalry of the parties of the left made it mathematically impossible to obtain left majorities in at least two countries, France and Italy. No majority was possible without the Communists, and no coalition was electorally possible with the Communists after the bitter disputes over the Marshall Plan in 1948. This was all the more so under conditions where the Communists were so much the larger party that a coalition government would have to be dominated by them. This remained the situation until the French socialists under Mitterand's tactically brilliant leadership, beginning in the late 1960s decided to gamble that it was possible to form a left majority which would not be dominated by the Communists. When the gamble began the odds looked very long indeed against it. Another of history's surprises!

The division of the left also produced the pernicious dual effects of hastening the political evolution of the socialists towards the center, while locking the Communists into what was for practical purposes a self-contained and sterile political ghetto. Both processes contributed mightily to the inability of the Western labor movement to develop an effective strategy in the years of the European economic miracle. The break-out of the ghetto in France took place very late, and the French Communists proved unable to use it to salvage their rapidly collapsing political organization and fortunes.

The vast resources of the Italian Communists remain on the margins of national political life, although they have played a major role in city and regional governments. No government of the left is possible without them in Italy. The irony is that the evolution of Euro-Communism,[16] that is a Communism which would not be politically and ideologically bound by the dictates of the Moscow 'center' of the world movement, occurred at a time when a far grimmer and more difficult terrain for class politics of the left emerged, after the oil shock of 1973. *That was not a period for daring experiments with structural reforms leading beyond the limits of capitalism, at least not in single, middle-size countries with relatively fragile economies.* The greatest historical significance of Euro-Communism will probably have turned out to have been the removal of the obstacle which orthodox Communist parties and unions had represented to the very possibility of any unified action by the left which could have obtained majority support in France or Italy. A possibility is not always also a reality. But the present Italian Communist party is, for example, a possible partner both for a joint socialist-Communist government in Italy and for a European left majority within the European Community, which would include the socialists, Greens, and Euro-Communists (meaning today the Italian Communist party for practical purposes).

The orthodox Communist parties were not possible partners for such an alliance for a host of historical and organizational reasons. Of these their relationship with Moscow represented only one. Breaking that dependence and subordination was essential if the masses of voters and activists within the western Communist parties were to emerge from their political ghetto and into mass democratic politics.

Revival of a Reinvigorated Socialist International

The Socialist International's revival immediately after the war was of no immediate great significance since the dominant party, the British Labour party, was insular and the other parties were busy with the tasks of governing or participating in governing the Western European capitalist welfare state democracies. The real revival of the International had to wait for Willy Brandt to stop being the Chancellor of West Germany and to become President of the German social-democratic party in 1973 to breathe real life into the previously moribund body. Brandt managed to pull together two socialist heads of state, Kreisky of Austria and Palme of Sweden, into the International. Ever since then it has been the clearing house for the heads of states ruled by socialist parties or heads of the parties themselves. The effect was to increase the visibility and prestige of the Socialist International enormously and to make it possible for it to move out of its central and north European stamping grounds.

By the 1970s the International was well represented in the Mediterranean, where the German and Swedish parties especially played significant roles in helping the socialist parties which developed after the collapse of the military dictatorships in Portugal, Spain and Greece. Led by Brandt and a Swedish General Secretary, Bernt Carlsson, the International developed close ties with movements in Africa and Latin America and witnessed by the 1980s the growth of parties affiliated or friendly to the Socialist International in non-European countries. This was partly because the long sterile romance with guerilla movements seemed to be coming to an end and more importantly because the process begun in Spain and Portugal seemed to be spreading to Latin America.

Democratic regimes began to replace military dictatorships by the middle 1980s, including the two most important NICs, which seem destined to develop mass worker-based parties and socialist-led unions. The Latin American and Mediterranean experiences highlight one very significant role of the democratic socialist movement, or the democratic left more generally. Whatever the fate of the socialist project itself in those countries, or in general, the special vocation of the socialist parties in these countries seems to be to help carry out their long overdue process of political modernization and democratization. Their role is to push the armies firmly back into the barracks and keep them there, and to permit democratic institutions of a civil society to grow and mature. This may well fail in a number of cases but is certainly a worthwhile and noble vocation or project for Latin American and Mediterranean socialists at the close of this century.

This will require all possible aid from the parties of the Socialist International in the advanced industrial societies, but that help cannot be sufficiently massive unless backed by social democratic governments and a socialist-dominated European Community. In this vocation the Catholic Church will probably be a major ally, but parties of middle-class and moderate capitalism are weak reeds when it comes to defending democracy and social justice in the south. They have too many interests at stake and they are too indebted to a United States which is increasingly ambiguous about democracy in the Third World when it is not directly complicit with the forces of right-wing repression.

What is clear is that, despite all their radical oratory, these Latin and Mediterranean parties are not more radical than the central European and Scandinavian social-democratic parties. They cannot have been expected to be that, given the much weaker organizations and trade unions in their societies. All talk of a radical anti-capitalist French socialist program was less relevant than the small percentage of unionized workers and the weak party organization. The same is even more the case in Greece, Portugal, Italy (where the *real* social-democratic party is the Italian Communist party) and somewhat less clearly Spain. Greece is a clear example of a pseudo-radical socialist party. The Greek party PASOK and its leader Papandreou, have been the darlings of Western European and American–European leftists, not to speak of the Greek electorate, because of their nationalist, populist, anti-American and Third Worldist demagoguery which was a substitute for an effective and egalitarian domestic program.

The socialist parties of Western Europe appear to be recovering from the doldrums of the early 1980s. Their steady organizational revival, backed up by the electoral trends and trade union strength throughout Western Europe, with the exception of Great Britain, is paralleled by greater confidence in a Europe independent of the superpowers. Mitterand's electoral victory in France, the increase in socialist strength in Belgium and Norway, should give pause to those who hastened to see the present crisis of socialism as a final one. A crisis is both a challenge and an opportunity.[17]

Beyond the Welfare State: The Potential Case of Sweden [18]

If one had to guess today which European country is most likely to have to deal with the real-life problems of building a socialist society in an imaginable future, the most reasonable answer would be Sweden. It has a highly developed and widely popular welfare state and a mass party and movement at least formally committed to moving beyond the welfare state.[19] In Sweden the enormous majority, over 85 per cent, of the working population – blue-collar, white-collar, and pink-collar, old working-class and new working-class – are organized in trade unions. Sweden is therefore a society in which the organized workers' movement has organizational and moral hegemony, although it does not, alas, as yet have a clear program of how to push beyond the welfare state.

If one contrasts the Swedish movement with that of Great Britain, certain quite mundane but striking differences emerge. The most obvious and measurable one is the simple difference in size, and therefore of density, of the two socialist movements. The SAP (Swedish social-democratic party) had a membership of 1,229,703 members, of which some 300,000 were individual memberships and 900,000 were affiliated through the unions. The Labour party in Britain had about 295,000 members in 1983 and about 6,100,000 trade union members. The individual membership of the two parties was almost identical but, given the huge population disparity between the two countries, this means that the individual membership is *seven times greater* in Sweden.

The membership–population ratio is even more unfavorable in the Mediterranean countries, which may explain the equally large ratio between the maximalist oratory and performance of those parties. Social-democratic parties with a high membership density produce a thick network of allied organizations, women's, youth, and cultural. Trade unions are also far more massive than in Britain or the European south, which helps create a sub-culture, not unlike that of Italian Communism and the classic social-democracy preceding the First World War. This essentially egalitarian political culture makes them more resistant to the influence of the mass consumerist culture or the so-called Americanization of the Western European political scene. But there is a second, less obvious, difference. A labor movement as massive as the Swedish one is markedly less narrow and trade unionist in its demands precisely because it has a far larger percentage of workers organized. It speaks to a large section of the population and uses the language of universal entitlement and the trade union strategy of pattern bargaining which does not favor the strategically better-placed skilled workers at the expense of the ones who are in a weaker position. The unions raise general societal demands and are therefore not perceived as narrowly selfish defenders of specific small sub-groups of workers. This creates other problems, including the discontent of the more skilled and strategically better-placed workers, who often bridle against the egalitarianism of the Swedish union strategy, and pattern bargaining, which does have a secular tendency to reduce income differences both between skill levels and sexes. However, those problems are obviously far preferable to the problems which, let us say, the British Trades Union Congress has with its image, unjust as it sometimes is, of short-sighted, narrowly economistic and individual, union-based particularistic selfishness. To state this more positively, the Swedish labor union federation (the LO) is the defender of the *general interests of those who work in Swedish society.*

The Swedish unions have defended full, well-paid and secure employment for all, not particular, specific jobs. The result over the decades has been that the Swedish unions have not been an obstacle to the modernization of their economy and the massive shift from traditional smoke-stack industries to the more modern mix of high-technology and services. Whatever else the Swedish unions can be accused of, being a brake on technological development is not one of the charges. This has given the labor movement a greater legitimacy and political leverage than exists in any other advanced industrial country and has produced neither high unemployment nor high inflation, nor for that matter, technological backwardness. It has also produced a trend of a steadier lowering of the hours worked per week and during a life-time. This increase in leisure has also led to the continual emphasis on discussion circles and adult engagement in education. In turn this continually expands the number of persons involved in the vast network of organizations, study-circles, people's parks and all of the rest of the popular institutions which help make the Swedish social-democratic movement politically and morally hegemonic in their society. In sharp contrast to the British Labour party's situation where a fundamentally undemocratic electoral system permits a party with 40 per cent of the votes to have a large parliamentary majority, the Swedish socialists come by their majorities honestly in a democratic system practising proportional representation. The effect is that it has far greater political legitimacy as the natural party of government.

The Swedish labor movement has had the ability to veto hostile legislation through extra-parliamentary pressure, which is normally wielded by capital, both national and international, in most of the rest of the world. This was demonstrated rather clearly during the brief period in the 1970s when for the first time in 40 years the social-democrats lost their parliamentary majority. The coalition of bourgeois parties in parliamentary power was not capable of carrying out any of their social or economic program since the trade unions had effective veto power and blocked any cut-backs in the welfare state and social spending measures. What the Swedish labor movement argued, in a way which might profoundly shock proceduralist liberals, was that the welfare state is just as much, and as unnegotiable, a part of the social compact as parliamentary rules of the game themselves. That is, like parliamentary democracy itself, it is not reversible without struggles which would not be limited to the electoral field.

At this time, unlike most other socialist parties, the Swedish social-democratic movement has a very specific socialist project, although it is also a very modest, moderate and clearly reformist project. The labor movement was forced to retreat from its imaginative proposal to take over the bulk of the Swedish economy through the 'wage earner funds' an ingenious device to turn over the voting majority in the Swedish corporation gradually to elected committees of employees, unions and local governments.[20] The vicious frightened campaign of the 'bourgeois' parties in Sweden and the chambers of commerce against this proposal, known as the Meidner Plan, showed that a most sensitive, even vital, nerve had been touched. The Meidner wage earner funds proposal is currently on the political and legislative back-burner in Sweden. But a precedent had been created: a ruling social-democratic party actually proposed to move irretrievably beyond the boundaries of capitalism and a welfare state to the unknown territory of social ownership. The plan is postponed for now, though its revival is a certainty; the only real question is when. In the meantime the Swedish socialists are firm in defending the welfare state with its concomitant full employment and social and economic egalitarianism at a time when those modest victories of the workers' movements are under general attack in so many of the advanced industrial societies of the west. This is in a period when many of the other labor and socialist parties have accepted, no matter how reluctantly, the necessity of at least some cut-backs in social spending.

Even more depressingly, this is also a time when many self-defined far-left academic Marxists write lengthy treatises *proving*, no less, that under the present conditions of the world economy, an advanced welfare state, particularly in a small country, is impossible. That work should be put on the shelf, next to the equally learned and Marxist works *proving that full employment is (a) impossible under capitalism or (b) impossible under capitalism at this time. Those are among the reasons why it is so useful to have a Sweden around – it helps maintain not only morale but some sanity on the democratic left.* Almost alone in Sweden today one hears elected non-fringe politicians explain that unemployment is not inevitable, or god-given, but the product of human-made policies. Therefore full employment, or the closest equivalent which can approximate it under even a welfare capitalism, is also the product of human agency.

Of course the program of the Swedish social-democrats is 'merely' reformist. But then most European social-democratic parties have not even been reformist in the past 30 or 40 years. The classic debate about reformism in the historic social-democratic movement was not about whether it was the aim of the movement to move ahead to a dismantling of capitalist economic, social and political relations, that is towards socialism. Rather, the debate was whether it was *possible* to make that transformation gradually, through basic reforms of the existing capitalist system and through the peaceful parliamentary road. There was no question at all about the desirability of moving on beyond capitalism, even a highly reformed welfare-state capitalism.

Post-Second World War reformist parties were really in a different, although in itself quite worthwhile, business. They were parties which primarily sought to develop socially advanced welfare states, and major wings of the German social-democratic and the British and Belgian labor parties have even quite explicitly argued that in reality there was no specific goal or goals beyond a welfare state. *That is the meaning of the thesis that socialism is primarily, if not only, about equality. That is, the welfare state itself has become the goal and not a strategy.*[21]

The Swedish social-democrats do not accept that. That is, they *do* think you need to move and can move beyond a welfare state towards a socialist society, and have a project to take over the basic needs of production and distribution in Sweden, and give it into the hands of elected bodies representing workers and the local communities. Therefore they are today more politically and programmatically advanced than any other Western European workers' party. They are more advanced than most of the Greens, for that matter.

The distinction between a socialist project and a Green project is important, since it divides much of the left public in the advanced industrial societies today. It is the difference between the transformational and universalist orientation of a socialist movement and a movement which sees the new social movements of ecologists, feminists, gay liberationists, and in the United States, Black and minority activists, as a far horizon of political oppositions. That is, as defenders of *particularistic and specific group interests and demands* rather than as those who pose an alternative vision of what is the general good and interest of the society as a whole. The distinction is in part artificial since, for example, the Swedish social-democrats have probably won more equality for women in the economic and social sphere than any other movement in the world at the present time. There are fewer differences in the economy and society. But more to the point, in addition to a generally egalitarian wage structure, an extensive set of social measures exist, which directly affect women, although they are intended for the whole population. *That is, the measures tend to be universalistic rather than gender-specific.* They are presented as universal rights rather than measures aimed at specific oppressed groups.

The Swedish socialist and feminist activists complain that women earn only 87 per cent of what the men do. That figure is even more impressive when one remembers that in Sweden, and most of Europe, East and West for that matter, one is dealing with a welfare state and a system of supports for women and children which simply do not exist and are not even proposed for the political agenda in the United States. Thus the gap in material conditions between the women living in the European welfare states like that of Sweden and those in the United States is even greater than mere income figures indicate. This was achieved by movements which did not define themselves as feminist, but which pushed for whole series of universalistic, social and economic demands which properly belong in any feminist movement. For example, in housing, unmarried mothers get a priority because single parents get a preference in housing whatever their gender. The fact that most are women is an artifact of cultural attitudes which change more slowly. The social-democratic welfare states have developed free and accessible child-care centers. They have developed a whole range of social legislation and educational policies to try to wipe out sexual inequalities in society. Little boys learn how to cook and little girls learn how to be carpenters and machinists. It is simply not true that 'economistic' socialists in the Scandinavian countries ignore other vital questions such as gender discrimination and racial inequality.

Swedish social-democrats have done more to clean up the countryside than any government has in Western Europe. This was done without much bombastic talk about ecology and has therefore all but passed unnoticed by the ecological groups in Western Europe and the US. In so far as it has been noticed by social-movement-oriented intellectuals, it was only to express the worry that the social-democrats would co-opt the Greens' program. Why this would not be a very good thing to happen for politics of the left in general is not at all clear. Of course such co-option of the more relevant parts of the Greens' program and subculture by the social-democrats could weaken the Green organizational challenge to the organized workers' movement. It could, but did not, since the Greens did surprisingly well in the 1988 election which returned the social-democrats to power in Sweden. But while it is a good thing for the left to develop a more politically pluralist structure in the capitalist industrial democracies, *excessive* organizational fragmentation makes it difficult to move on more than individual issues of reform. To move further towards the social transformation of the society as a whole, the strategic core of the left needs to be massively organized and to be able to draw in large-scale active participation of the type we find in the 'thick' social-democratic political cultures like those of Sweden, Norway, Austria and around the Italian Communist party. That *includes, but is not limited to, a mass electoral party.*

Both the programmatic innovation and the increasing awareness of the sensibility of the younger and better-educated can therefore only be helpful to the classic workers' parties. The Norwegian socialists have moved to make the majority of the cabinet women, with a woman Prime Minister, and will reserve 40 per cent of the leadership positions in the party for women. The most important social-democratic party, the German SPD, has passed rules which will make 40 per cent of the leadership female in two years. It is fairly clear that within less than a decade this will be the norm in all democratic socialist parties.[22] It is true that social-democrats also talk, as Greens should talk more, about ecology in the workplace as something affecting the lives of millions, although perhaps in less visible ways than the defense of dramatically beautiful countryside.

Classical reformism, as I stated earlier, did not give up the struggle for socialism but merely argued that socialism could be achieved by peaceful or parliamentary means. That did mean, unfortunately, also that the question of the nature of socialism itself and the struggle for socialism could be conveniently postponed, although never formally given up.

Post-Second World War reformist parties gave up reformism, that is the struggle for socialism through structural reforms of the bourgeois societies, for neo-corporatist Keynesian welfare-statist compromise. It is useful to remember what that compromise appeared to be and seemed to offer in its heyday. It was generally agreed, left, right and center, that the compromise had succeeded in solving the problems of the capitalist crisis, that unemployment was a thing of the past for advanced industrial societies and that the formula for stable and permanent growth had been discovered.

Today it might be ironically appropriate to raise the slogan, throughout Europe and the parties of the Socialist International, as well as in the democratic movements in Eastern Europe and the Soviet Union: *forward to classical reformism*. That may well be the terrain of the future socialist strategy, and we will need a theory for that strategy if the traditional socialist vision of the struggle for socialism as the great, unprecedented conscious social transformation is to be possible.

But that transformation is towards a new human civilization and must therefore be informed, and permeated, by modern feminism and socially responsible, non-cultist ecology. A movement to win the devotion of millions of adherents and the commitment of new generations of activists has to deal with both the mundane reality about how effectively to organize a society and economy on a day-to-day basis, but also, and perhaps more urgently, it has to answer the question of how we are to be able to live as decent and full human beings. That is why socialism cannot be national or limited to the prosperous north.

A Brief Prescriptive Summary

1) The post-world war neo-corporatist welfare state settlement in Western Europe has not yet been exhausted, despite the neo-conservative assaults inspired by Thatcher's Conservatives in Britain and the most ideological conservative administration in Washington since the war. The effect of the attacks on the welfare state and post-war class settlements has been on the whole to push the socialist and labor parties to the left. This takes primarily two forms: greater hostility to superpower domination over Europe and a concern for a Euro-centric North–South strategy on the lines proposed by the Manley and Brandt reports.

2) The coming of European Community economic integration by 1992 and the ever-greater interpenetration of national economies by the world

market dictate less narrowly national and parochial strategies to the Western European labor movement. This is essential to deal with multinationals, the mobility of labor and the constant danger of the flight of capital. The end of the virulent phase of the Cold War, as well as the desperate needs of the south, suggest pan-national reflationary strategies involving massive credits and aid to both Eastern Europe and the Soviet Union and the South.

3) The socialist parties (including the Italian Communists) are already the largest force within the European Parliament. Internationalism is more congenial to the left, broadly speaking, than to the parties of the right, whose internationalism is more often expressed as Atlanticism. But Atlanticism is now being questioned on both sides of the ocean.

4) The massive changes in world Catholicism raise the possibilities of an alliance between the socialists and Catholicism in three major areas: a joint concern with North–South issues in the context of accepting that the North has a major responsibility to help the South; a joint agreement on a defense of the right of workers to form and control their own unions and movements; and, thirdly, a joint concern with joining social-justice and democracy. The two great historic movements also agree in defending both an advanced welfare state and the right of people to have decent jobs. Add to these broad bases of agreement a common hostility to the nuclear arms race and a world dominated by superpowers and one may well have what amounts to a historic shift in political alliances in the making. The Church no more shares the cult of market than do the socialists, despite the past alliance between Washington and the Vatican.

5) The advanced welfare state is a relatively secure terrain for further advances towards socialism. However, it is also clear that there is no broad consensus in the socialist parties of what those advances should be or what socialism itself should look like even in broad outline. Despite the ability of the socialist parties to maintain their organizational and electoral strength, that merely means that they have bought time which must be used to flesh out new programmatic proposals and alliances. Clearly one central set of new alliances must be with the modern women's and ecological movements. This must be achieved without giving up the massive base of the labor movement, consisting as it does of three elements: the classic industrial working class; the new working class produced by mass higher education; and the post-industrial and service sectors of the economies and the clientele of the advanced welfare state. What this means is the greening of the classical socialist and labor movements without accepting the elitist and anti-productivistic attributes of the Greens. The socialists must also be

ready to accept coalitions with Green parties whenever necessary and possible.

6) A major part of the socialist project is to attempt to create a modern participatory political community which has as a major aim the broadening of democratic rights and social and economic entitlement. Therefore the characteristic of successful socialist parties will be to develop a thick network of popular participatory and educational organizations giving them the nature of a movement as well as that of a mass democratic party. In that sense the Swedish socialists represent both politically and, above all, organizationally a desirable possible future for the West European democratic socialist movement.

Chapter 7

The Proud Tower or the Last of the Mohicans: The United States at the End of the American Century

A Changing International Environment[1]

The major obstacle to popular economic and political change in the Third World since the massive de-colonization following the Second World War has been the US in its role as the world policeman, apparently doomed to maintain right-wing, but presumably solidly anti-Communist, regimes in the face of ever-more-desperate opposition and revolt. That is its visible, and increasingly unpopular, role. The less obvious role, which has been the foundation of the post-war bi-partisan foreign policy, without the primitivism of a Reagan administration in Washington, has been the maintenance of the present capitalist world economic system as such. It is, as has already been pointed out, that system which exploits the Third World, not conscious policies pursued by this or that administration.

It is also that same world economic system which has done untold damage to the more unionized sectors of the American manufacturing economy and helped degrade the living standards of unionized blue-collar workers, among others. This is important, since a part of an academic Marxist critique of the official US labor movements' complicity and collaboration with American foreign policy in the Third World was to argue that American workers benefit from the unequal exchange which the world market imposes on goods from the South in trading with the North. From that, not completely inaccurate, insight, one can go one or two steps further: first, to argue that American workers 'exploit' the South by simply participating in the US economy and, through that, in the world market.[2] The second step, very popular among 'Third Worldist' theorists and activists, is that American workers consciously help exploit the Third World. So, therefore, it is reactionary to fight for higher wages and living standards for unionized workers in the US, unless they happen to be living in absolute economic misery. In effect, this would mean only farm-workers or workers in the miserable textile sweatshops in the South or Appalachia or the new sweatshops in the cities with their own Third World workers.

Since that still does represents the minority of the workers in the US, it means that one is not only happily exempt from having to support the economic struggles of most workers in the United States, but that not doing so is an act of solidarity with the Third World. The increasing internationalization of capital has encouraged the export of well-paid unionized jobs from the smoke-stack industries of the US and their replacement by mostly 'hollow' service jobs most of which are both un-unionized and low paying. In turn, this export of well-paid manufacturing jobs has helped to lock many new, young, mostly Black and Hispanic, unskilled workers in the major cities into a vicious cycle of unemployment and marginal insecure jobs. Thus a part of the price for the US world role has been an erosion of living standards of the blue-collar workers, and the creation of massive Black and Hispanic youth unemployment, with all the resultant social pathologies, in the cities. It has been used as an argument to assault the already mean and marginal welfare state in the name of increasing the competitiveness of US industries and society and it is in no small part responsible for the present flood of drugs and crimes devastating the major cities.

The imperial role of the US is increasingly now in question at home and abroad. It is in question for many reasons, but the most obvious is the changing consensus of the estimate of both Soviet power and intentions. If the Soviet Union is, as most analysts East and West, now seem to agree, facing grim internal stresses and difficulties in moving towards essential economic and political reforms, then it is hardly in a position to play much of an adventurous and expansive role in the world. Therefore the specter of an inevitably expanding Soviet empire, always dubious, given the essentially cautious and conservative nature of the ruling Soviet bureaucracies, is now increasingly difficult to maintain. One need not have any illusions about Soviet society being democratic or particularly attractive to be able to separate one's estimate of that country's domestic regime from its foreign policy.

A country can be both authoritarian and essentially militarily unaggressive, just as political democracies can be and have often been adventurous and imperialist in foreign policies. It was, after all, the Democrats, not conservatives, who have tended historically to get the US into its military adventures. This shift in elite consensus about the international role of the US can also be seen in the changing attitude of what has been the most confrontational and adventurist US administration since the Second World War towards both the possibility of major rounds of disarmament treaties and towards more civil relations between the two superpowers. After all, if you believe that the Soviet Union is on the verge of aggressive expansion you do not invest major political capital in negotiating disarmament treaties, as the Reagan administration did in its last year of power. This point has been perfectly well understood by the more hawkish right in the US, which explains their even more frantic and paranoid style than usual in political debate about disarmament treaties with the Soviets.

The US political and economic elites have only slowly absorbed the lessons of the costs of imperial over-expansion and over-commitment in terms of security responsibilities. A whole wave of new books have carried the issue of US over-extension out of the left, and the margins of academia, into public debate. None questions that the United States will remain the major world power among the advanced capitalist democracies; it is the cost and hubris of empire which are in question. The recent books by Calleo, MacNamara and Kennedy all raise the need to reassess what is possible and desirable for a major democratic power to attempt by way of defending and defining its world-wide interests.

It is a terrible pity that the lesson has been so expensive and had to be paid by not only hundreds of thousands of American draftee soldiers but also by the millions of Vietnamese and other victims of the brief and bloody attempt to make this effectively an American century. A not-so-minor casualty of that lesson has been the abortion of the brief flirtation in the US with an advance towards the welfare state standards of the Western European countries in the Great Society programs. Surely, this was one of the shortest centuries recorded of a great power's hegemony.

We are now moving towards the reality of a multipolar world where the centers of economic and technological action may well move to Europe and the Pacific Rim. The US does remain a superpower, but, alas, this is mostly in the same way that the Soviet Union also remains a superpower, militarily. It is of course also a major, but note *a* major, economic power and will remain that for the practical foreseeable future. The trouble is that public opinion and the electorate seem to be carefully guarded from this new reality by both major parties.

The closest that public debate has come towards facing the new economic power relations has been in the protectionist themes raised by Gebhardt during the 1988 primary campaign. It is also present in the understandable but dangerously simple-minded and nativistic protectionist sentiment increasingly urgently voiced by an AFL–CIO leadership, some of whose unions have been badly battered by imports. It is not the cheap consumer goods imports which should be the focus of worry for labor and progressives so much as the exports of capital and jobs.

Some of the capital exports are directed to 'reservations' where underpaid and politically repressed labor is worked at sub-subsistence wages, but that is a moral and political rather than an economic problem. It is not export of capital to the Third World and the NICs that is the problem, but rather the internationalization of capital and technology, placing both out of reach of any kind of social and political control. That, and the vast amounts of purely speculative capital floating around, argue that the primitive currently popular notion of simply letting the rich keep more money is not only a utopian program for obtaining socially necessary investments for the United States but also produces an irresponsible and immoral economy. But then in this respect, as in so much else, a socialist finds himself repeating much of what has been said by the Catholic bishops in that excellent social-democratic statement, 'Pastoral Letter on Catholic Social Teaching and the US Economy'.

A scaling down of the US economic and military role throughout the world opens up the possibility of a major political and educational campaign to redefine that role in a way more appropriate to a political democracy than that of a world policeman or an empire. This permits the opening of a debate around the proposals for a genuinely non-interventionist and democratic foreign policy which works to strengthen international agencies as a way of creating a more secure world environment. That in turn should further lower the temperature of confrontation between the superpowers.

The Jackson Campaign: Filling the Hole in the US Electorate[3]

The Jackson 1988 presidential primary campaign confirmed, in good part, the proposition that the 'hole in the electorate' of the United States, that is the massive abstention from voting, represents mostly that which would be filled if there existed a political party of the broad left, representing the interests of the working people, the minorities and therefore automatically most women. To redefine that: if a US version of a mass social-democratic party existed, such a party could either emerge from the debris of the present two-party system or, which is more likely, through those forces taking over the present Democratic party.

To be sure, that proposition has been bitterly challenged from two diametrically opposing viewpoints: one argues that the Democrats must move more towards the center to regain the possibility of ever winning the White House, while the other, more often found among left activists and intellectuals, argues that social-democracy has in any case proven inadequate in Western Europe so why bother even trying to build it in the United States. The second argument comes in two versions, simplistic and reasonably sophisticated. The simplistic argument emphasizes the undoubted truth that social-democracy has nowhere achieved or even tried to achieve socialism, and that many social and economic problems remain unsolved in countries with social-democratic governments.

The assumption, of course, is that the options in the US are between pale economistic social-democratic reformism and a red-blooded genuine radical transformation. This transformation would be more economically radical than any reformist program in Western Europe, but also more anti-racist, more feminist and more ecological. One can only ask why these radical options keep so stubbornly evading realization, and unfortunately, on the left one of the more common explanations is betrayal of the genuine radical program by the leaders of the larger social movements, the progressive unions and the socialist organizations. But then since betrayal is also invoked, all too often, in debates about European social-democracy as well as with the state socialist systems in the Soviet bloc and the socialisms in the Third World, one sometimes wonders what to make of a world movement so universally prone to betrayal.

Why this argument of betrayal by a compromising leadership selling out should be relevant in the United States is unclear, unless the assumption is that it is more possible in the US *today* to fight for a more advanced social and economic program than it is in Western Europe. That is, that the absence of a powerful trade union movement, a mass social-democratic party and a whole network of social movements in the United States make no practical political difference, and thus represent no special *disadvantage* for a broad left in that country.

The more sophisticated argument tends to emphasize that social-democracy was successful in periods of economic growth when the expanding world economy and national economies could accept major welfare-state expenditures because of the existence of near-full employment, which made generous welfare state measures relatively cheap. So, if only a small percentage of people are unemployed or on welfare, it does not matter *economically* how generous benefits are, though it may, and in the case of ideological conservatives does, matter morally and politically. They seem to think that decent social welfare standards corrupt the morals and fiber of the lower orders. That argument tends to suffer from an excessive Americo-centrism. The attacks on the welfare state outside of the Anglo-Saxon powers, the US and Britain, have done quite poorly politically and have been generally beaten off.

In any case there is a great deal of mystification about the costs of the welfare state measures as a factor in economic performance, and no substantial argument has been made that it is their cost that is the problem for the economies involved. After all, the US economy under Reagan most certainly did throw money at the problems it was interested in, like the huge military build-up much of which is now destined for the junkyards at best, or resale to Third World governments at worst. No, it was not the costs of full employment and a welfare state which were a problem for the Reagan administration in its eight years, for they showed every readiness to build up deficits with a greater recklessness than any Keynesian would have dared to suggest for their economic and, above all, political aims. Those were a huge military build-up, a domestic assault on unions and the welfare state, and the reverse of a Robin Hood policy to one of robbing the poor to give the rich the biggest tax-cut in two generations. The interest payments alone of around *$200 billion* a year on the US national debts are a massive income transfer from the taxpayers to the bond holders, that is, from the general public to the rich. Surely those were not the measures of an administration concerned with economic costs of social policy! The trouble is not that the conservatives in US politics have seized their unusual opportunity under Reagan to attempt to carry out a moral, social and economic quasi-counter-revolution in successfully assaulting the post-world-war Keynesian consensus. The real problem is that the conservatives have for most of the decade defined the very terms of the debate and have thus helped push the Democratic party, never a tower of progressive strength, far to the right on economic issues.

The Democrats are better than the Republicans from the point of view of progressives and the democratic left on almost all social, gender, racial and cultural issues. They are better in terms of defense and foreign policy or at least they are much more open on those issues. It is on economic issues that the eight years of Reaganism managed to push them so far to the right that mild technocratic liberalism is the best that their mainstream can come up with. Then they wonder why they cannot excite their traditional plebian voting base of Blacks, workers, the unemployed, in addition to those hosts of nice college educated lawyers who seem increasingly to dominate the party. There are more PhDs as delegates at the Democratic party convention than union leaders or activists. And that is considered normal!

Let us imagine what would happen if the US today, all other things being equal, had a labor movement of the relative size of the movement in – not Sweden, that is day-dreaming – but, say, Canada. Would all other parts of the political equation remain the same? What would happen if the present AFL–CIO, with its not-too-inspiring leadership, were twice as large? Would the business community be as confrontational, would there be as anti-labor an administration in Washington? Would corporations be as ready to demand 'give-backs' from the workers and the unions as to grant them? Clearly, that order of change is within the realm of possibilities of even this capitalist system.

Further, why are unemployment and the poverty of the social sector treated as a natural law? Goran Therborn, a Swedish sociologist, argued quite convincingly that both are sensitive to governmental intervention even on the relatively modest scale which the contemporary social-democracies are capable of. The Swedish and Austrian unemployment statistics are an interesting argument for that case. But, apart from arguing that social-democratic politics would be both possible and effective in the US, the more interesting question, and that is what the Jackson campaign has posed, is would it be good, effective politics? Could a candidate with such politics possibly be elected?

It would seem to me that the first part of an answer is that the US does not need two centerist parties. While centerist Democrats may well be preferable to centerist and particularly right-wing Republicans, it is clear that such a party cannot get its working-class base mobilized behind centerist candidates waging media-oriented campaigns. Jackson hit a chord which has to be hit if a party with a mass working-class base is to win in this age of media and pre-packaged candidacies. The chord was not merely a charismatic campaigner who seemed more interesting and more, yes plebeian, than the others. *The chord was economic populism or in other words, the made-in-America version of social-democracy.*

But the Jackson campaign was only a very partial test of possibilities of a mass, social-democratic type of a campaign using a native idiom, and sensitive to the themes raised by social movements, and to the central role of racism in America. It was partial because of all the very obvious flaws and weaknesses of the campaign. It was a supremely individualistic campaign attempting to raise the issues specific to movements which stress collective empowerment, organization, responsibility and democratic organization.

The campaign's weakness was its excessive, one could almost say total, identification with the charismatic personality of Jackson. Its strengths and weaknesses were both based on the fact that, while Jackson is a very real factor in the politics of the Democratic party and has become the focus of the more progressive forces in the party, there is not a Rainbow Coalition in any but the most rudimentary organized form.

Everything about Jesse Jackson's past record as an organizer, as well as his political style, argues that the Rainbow Coalition will remain in the realm of symbols rather than developing into a democratically controlled mass political organization of the broad left in the United States. It will probably not even become a genuine coalition of organizations, since charismatic authority cannot stand to be routinized and to be subjected to the process of negotiation and bargaining which is of course what democratic coalitional politics are all about.

Tactical and Strategic Debates among American Socialists[4]

The major strategic debate of all serious American socialists, organized or not, has focused on the issue of American exceptionalism. American exceptionalism refers to a problem which has bedeviled the American socialist and Marxist left from its very inception: why, in a country which had so many of the obvious heuristic conditions for the formation of a mass working-class party, was it so difficult to form one? Or, why is the United States alone among advanced industrial capitalist democracies the exception to the rule that such states have a mass labor or socialist party as a part of the political system?[5]

There are many arguments advanced, with varying degrees of subtlety and vulgarity, but the basic ones seem to center on three notions. First, the working-class in the United States did not have to battle for a democratic franchise in counterposition to other class forces, and, as a consequence, unlike Germany and the continental European countries, no mass workers' movement developed over the issue of franchise and the right to participate in the polity. This argument has been put forward both by serious non-Marxist observers such as Daniel Bell and Seymour Martin Lipset, as well as by a number of Marxists.

Secondly, the development of America as the country in which the most successful and complete bourgeois democratic revolution has been carried out was also the country of considerable economic opportunity. Thus, in the words of Sombart, a social-democratic observer from Germany writing at the beginning of this century, American socialism was wrecked on the reefs of roast beef and apple pie. A more subtle version of this would focus on the fragmentation of the American working-class along ethnic dimensions as successive waves of immigrant workers entered the American economy, usually taking the ecological niche vacated by the previous wave, that is, at the bottom of the socio-economic ladder. Thus, the US has developed an ethnically charged stratification system within the working-class, making class solidarity far more difficult to mobilize than in Europe. The third reason sometimes cited focuses on the peculiarities of the American electoral system which make it exceedingly difficult, if not impossible, for minor parties to enter into the political process. The tendency in America has rather been either for the displacement of an existing party, or for struggles within an existing party, as the arena through which new claimants entered into the politics.

Whichever version of American exceptionalism one chooses to accept, serious problems were posed for socialists in attempting to deal with the consequences of this exceptionalism. Again, the responses were predictably vague and not convincing. The early Marxists and socialists, the Communist party – at least until the 1930s – and the Trotskyists tended to work with an implicit assumption of America's backwardness. That is, *they treated the absence of a mass class-based socialist movement in America as a question of a cultural lag which would be solved in time. America then would catch up with the European experience.* They therefore basically, more or less mechanically, adapted the tried and true policies from Europe to the inhospitable terrain of the US.[6]

Thus, the early socialists placed an enormous emphasis on independent electoral political activity and a principled socialist program more or less copying the orthodox currents in German social democracy. The early Communist party in the US rushed to 'Bolshevize' itself and sought to find its salvation in a rigid adherence to the 21 points or conditions (which were required for any party to accept to affiliate to the Communist International), and to the directives of the International (Comintern). One might add that was not always a bad thing; in practice, in the early 1920s, native American Communists tended to be, if anything, more sectarian and out of touch with American reality than the Comintern directives, and it was not a matter of the Comintern imposing its will so much as the American Communists insisting that it arbitrate in their internal disputes. The Trotskyists, at least during Trotsky's lifetime, fairly vigorously followed the general world strategy of the Fourth International, with roughly the same hopeless results as all other Trotskyist parties.

The practical issues, when one cuts through the verbiage, seem to have been relatively well defined and surprisingly few. The first major issue, placed on the table even before the First World War, was whether one worked in the official trade union movement (then the AFL) or set up revolutionary industrial trade unions. The second issue was whether one stuck rigorously to running independent candidates on one's party's full program or whether it was appropriate to attempt to form some kind of a broader formation, usually defined as a labor party, as the electoral vehicle for socialist and working-class polities.

To this dichotomy, with which all three major currents of American Marxism and socialism have played at different times, Earl Browder, the national leader of the American Communists from 1930 to 1946, and the old guard social-democrats of the 1930s added a new strategic proposition: that is, that it was possible to work in the electoral field with a set of working-class and other alliances within the two-party system, while maintaining an independent organized center outside of it. Again, schematically, the range of options was independent socialist candidates, an independent working-class labor party, or any combination of the first two with an attempt to intervene in the electoral politics of the two major parties.[7]

Today, in practice, all organized socialist groups agree that under some circumstances they might run independent candidates. The real dispute is whether for one substantive main thrust one raises the slogan of a labor party or works within the coalition of social forces found around the Democratic party.

Practically speaking, the Trotskyists, Maoists and some of the smaller independent Marxist groups still hold a 'labor party' point of view, while the democratic socialists and Communists, again with all kinds of ambivalence, hold the view that it is desirable to work within the two-party system while maintaining one's independent political organization ('party' is in reality a misnomer here). To put it differently, *the political and class cleavage which is most relevant in American politics runs through the Democratic party electorate and supporters rather than outside it.*

This is not the place to argue out these propositions in detail, but it is important for the non-US reader to understand that the American party system has no analogue in Europe. Since the ever-widening, near-universal introduction of *primaries which determine the choice of candidates*, the two American major parties have increasingly little control over the candidates which run under their labels. A Democrat can be a Ku Klux Klan member, an adamant hawk and right-winger, a laborite not too different from moderate European social-democrats, a left-wing socialist,[8] or a close supporter of the Communist party, depending on which set of forces plays the most important role in the given electoral situation.

The crucial point, however, is that class-conscious and trade-union-oriented voters, Blacks, peace activists, and popular social movements, *insofar as they vote at all, vote for the Democrats*. The effect has been that the most serious attempt to bring forward a radical reformist program within US politics in decades, one which challenged the major suppositions of US foreign policy and called for the introduction of a generous welfare state, that is the 1988 massive presidential primary campaign of Reverend

Jesse Jackson did take place inside the Democratic party. *It had to take place inside the Democratic party.*

The consequence was that almost the entire left Marxist and non-Marxist as well as the major part of the progressive social movements in the United States, in some cases shamefacedly, did in practice back the Democratic party in 1988, by campaigning and working for Jesse Jackson in the Democratic party primaries throughout the country. There is no other meaning to the term 'working inside a party' in the United States, since, with very few exceptions, the two major parties have no real membership, clubs or organizations. But backing campaigns inside major ('bourgeois and capitalist') parties may end up being like losing political virginity for parts of the left which had stayed out in the past. It is impossible to go back to the original virginal state, or lose it partially.

American Socialists and Organized Labor

The trade union strategic questions for the socialist left have presented a complex set of issues, which have included the whole problem of the relationship between organization and consciousness. The most banal aspect of it was, of course, the degree of direct organizational influence which the socialist organization ought to attempt to assert over the trade unions. Or more accurately, over its members and sympathizers in the unions.

This issue had a peculiar history in the US, as it did in Britain and Canada and Australia, since, unlike on the Continent, their trade unions developed independently of the Marxists and socialist parties. It is important, however, to note that throughout American labor history, significant groups of Marxists and organized socialists were found both in the base and in the leadership of the official organized labor movement. A more salient question that arose, and keeps arising, is the relationship of the labor movement to those who are unorganized. In the period before the First World War, Marxist and socialist labor policy was to insist on industrial unions which would include the unskilled, as against the traditional craft unionism of the AFL. One side of this policy could be seen by American socialist party left-wingers' participation in the formation of independent revolutionary syndicalist unions (the IWW) before the First World War. The majority of socialists remained inside the AFL unions and opposed in principle the setting up of 'dual unions', that is to say revolutionary trade unions. That issue was an almost permanent dispute among leftists in the US. The issue re-emerged in the mid 1930s, in a more relevant form, when the industrial unions were organized in the bulk of American heavy industry. American socialists and Communists participated in quite disproportionately large numbers as organizers and leaders of the organization of the Congress of Industrial Organizations (CIO). The new federation of industrial unions emerged out of the more radical AFL unions and the mass of new, mostly mass-production workers, who were swept in by a huge wave of working-class militancy, including massive sit-down strikes, which organized the auto, rubber and steel industries. Large numbers of Blacks and women were thereby first included in the unions. They have stayed and increased in numbers, although only recently also in influence.

Many American socialists and progressive trade unionists argue that today in the US an analogous situation exists to that of the 1930s, where the official labor movement proves incapable or unwilling to reach out and organize the *new layers of workers outside of the traditional industries*. They also argue that it is the task of American socialists, not only theoretically to understand and describe the recomposition of the American working class which is currently taking place, but also to propose the strategies and tactics appropriate for organizing the vast new strata of women, white-collar workers, technicians, and hi-tech experts in the present workforce.[9] The preoccupation with the problems of class and political consciousness of the American working class by American Marxists and socialists of most perspectives attracts them to rank-and-file struggles and revolts within the official labor organizations. After all, working-class consciousness presumably develops, not from the preaching by outside agitators, but real-life experiences in specific struggles mostly in the workplace. Therefore the tumult caused by rank-and-file revolts inside bureaucratized unions is the supreme educator of workers about democracy and the need to control their own organizations, and therefore deserves support.[10]

Unfortunately, some American socialists believe that the bureaucratization of American unions has gone so far that they regard *all* rank-and-file revolts as inherently progressive and *all* labor leadership as inherently hostile to the development of working-class militancy. Just as in the case of social movements and community organizations, there are progressive and reactionary rank-and-file struggles inside the unions. There are union revolts motivated by nativism and racism, by the selfish particularistic desires of strategically better-placed workers to improve their contracts at the expense of other workers, or even to demand the nepotistic privilege that their children be able to inherit their jobs.

In a capitalist society, such as that of the United States, where individualist egoism and individual economic progress are fetishized by all the media and the entire system of political socialization from childhood on, it is unreasonable to expect class solidarity and the values of democratic collective effort to dominate. The miracle is that they emerge so often out of union and social struggles, not that there are exceptions. In theory at least, the overwhelming majority of organized American socialists have regarded working with and inside the trade unions as their major task. The assumption shared by most socialists in the US is that, without the bulk of the American trade union movement, or at the very least significant sections, agreeing to do so, no American mass labor or working-class party can ever be formed. Therefore, the fact that the American labor movement has for decades chosen the Democratic party as the arena throught which it expresses itself politically has posed the issue of working within the Democratic party willy-nilly for all American Marxist and socialist organizations which pretend or desire to have any substantial influence within sectors of the labor movement.

If a given party or group of socialists has major influence within a union such as the Machinists or the Automobile Workers union, and has, as a consequence, a number of elected officials and activists within that union, what is it to do when the political action arms of those unions enter into the electoral process, and enter almost invariably within the framework of the Democratic party? Practically speaking, the two organizations which have historically had the widest influence inside labor – the Communists and the democratic socialists – have over the years mostly either tacitly or explicitly accepted the strategy of working as a socialist wing of the labor/progressive coalition.

Other serious problems are posed theoretically and practically by the grim contemporary realities of labor and industrial relations in the United States. One is the problem posed by the prolonged economic downturn of the American and world economies. This downturn has been accompanied by a wholesale assault on the organized labor movement and on the gains made by social and political movements over the past decades. The assault on the unions has been many-pronged, not only in the expansion of well-financed anti-union think-thanks and publications and programs of the right and business community, but above all through the most anti-labor administration which the United States has had since the Great American Depression of the 1930s. The hostility of the administration has been reflected in the systematic use of the National Labor Relations Act (NLRA) and the Department of Labor to obtain anti-union administrative rulings. The resulting atmosphere has resulted in repeated losses of votes by unions in their organizing drives, and a campaign for open shops and a 'union-free environment'. The unions have had an almost universally bad press and one result is that even the public opinion of liberal Democrats has turned increasingly cold towards the unions, despite the obvious reality that their party cannot win national elections without union support.

The narrow short-sighted selfishness of many contemporary organized labor leaders has created a situation where unions can be treated as a special, by definition narrow and parochial, interest. One consequence of this is that unions have maintained and increased their strength primarily in the public sector, and there, unfortunately, their demands are often seen as counterposed to the other budgetary needs of fiscally strapped cities and state governments. That too has been a consequence of systematic cut-backs in social spending by the Reaganites in Washington for eight long years. Social meanness and zero-sum game politics are maximized, as scarce resources have to be divided among many particularistic publics uninformed by any generous program of social justice and coalition.

Inside the trade unions one particularly painful tactical issue is how to handle defensive struggles and the demands by employers for 'give-backs'; or retreats of the unions from previous gains in either wages or fringe benefits. 'Give-backs' have provoked major clashes inside organized labor, and most American socialists have taken the position that, while not necessarily excluded as a way of preserving employment in given industries, under extreme conditions, most such give-backs in practice are unjustified. This issue has generated rank-and-file revolts within some of the more progressive unions within the US and jeopardizes a whole set of relationships painfully developed over the years between American socialists and the more progressive sectors of labor leadership. Whatever the strategy towards give-backs, however, the more serious issue of how labor is to handle a prolonged period of economic decline has been posed.

Among the reformist proposals most often heard are proposals for a new social-contract approach which would in effect freeze real wages and prices and force some kind of a willy-nilly partnership between trade unions and the American industries. These proposals, current as they are in *both* major parties, may in fact create a far sharper set of antagonisms between American socialists and their past liberal allies than has been the case in the past.

The second general issue is that of the recomposition of the workforce or the rise of a new working class. While this is a matter of great theoretical interest in attempting to understand late capitalist economies, it also creates a major crisis within the present labor movement of the US. The new jobs occupied by the service sector employees tend to be non-union, and the shift from production to services also represents a shift from relatively highly paid industrial jobs to routinized white-collar and service jobs which are, if anything, even more vulnerable to automation than the blue-collar jobs were. It is sufficient to think of the impact on the American economy of the fact that the MacDonald's hamburger chain now employs more persons than does US Steel to realize what impact this has on the living standards of American workers and on the viability of the traditional trade unions.

Not only is a vast new field for union organizing opening up, requiring specific new approaches to a heavily female and Black as well as younger workforce, but the harsh consequences of these shifts has given rise to increasingly urgent calls for more planning under capitalism. As has been pointed out by a number of observers, left, right and center, the unplanned, solely market-regulated nature of American capitalism has been one of its more whimsical myths. The question, as has been repeatedly pointed out by Michael Harrington among others, has not been: planning or not planning, but rather planning by whom, for whom and under what kind of democratic popular control, for which social and economic and moral goals.

An even more pernicious recent consequence of the defensive into which organized labor has been forced over the past decade has been the popularization of the call for workers' ownership of dying industries. The attractive slogan of workers' control thus becomes a caricature of itself given the absence of political power and organization by the working class. An example may suffice: a major ball-bearing plant organized for decades by the UAW in Newark, New Jersey, was threatened with relocation and the consequent unemployment of its workforce. The corporation (General Motors, in this case) 'agreed' to sell the plant to the workers and to continue buying ball-bearings from that plant. A year later the results were as follows: the corporation had received a substantial price for a plant that had been losing money; the workers, now saddled with a huge mortgage, in order to remain competitive have been forced to cut their wages by a third and dismiss almost half of the workforce. The consequent popularity of the concept of workers' ownership and workers' control among the workers in the area can be easily imagined.

The whole issue of workers' control in the workplace or industry suggests interesting theoretical and strategic problems about the very possibility of such demands being raised in the absence of a workers' party in power. One problem for American socialists has always been the enormous gap between their subjective desires and the objective circumstances. This makes most American socialists excessively impatient with the politics of the possible while unable to engage in the politics of transformation. The effect has been an unusually intense fascination by American Marxists with what they saw as socialist experiments and experiences elsewhere. The absence of an imminent utopia in the US has led to a search for that utopia in a wide range of other countries. Depending on the individual or the group, this search ranged at different times from the USSR to Cuba, China, Yugoslavia, Sweden, Albania, and even Canada. While there is something pathetic about this search for a successful 'model', it has made the American Marxists unusually sensitive to a range of theoretical debates about the Third World non-capitalist paths to development and, of course, the famous Russian question. American socialists have also been forced to confront the reality of racism in their own society in a much more dramatic and intense form than their European counterparts. That racism is also related to the role of the United States as a superpower, which maintains an unjust social order essentially at the expense of the vast non-white majority of the world's population.

The American Left and the Struggle against Racism

A major issue within the American left which arose in the early 1960s has been the problem of Black nationalism and the general strategic relation between struggles of Blacks, and Black workers in particular, with the broad class alliances the Marxists had traditionally called for. The socialist and Communist movements in the United States have always supported integration rather than Black separatism. To be sure, the Communist party played with and even courted Black nationalism during the 'left' zigs of its line, to the point of supporting the establishment of a separate Black nation, a state with the right to secede in the south. However the major thrust of its work throughout the Popular Front period in the 1930s, when its influence was at a peak, was to work for integration and to oppose racism. As Ralph Ellison and Richard Wright's novels so clearly and powerfully show, the Communists were a major influence within the radical and more political part of the Black community throughout the 1930s and 1940s. They helped politically to form and educate, directly and sometimes indirectly, a large part of the Black trade union political cadre in the United States.

The socialists have been quite consistent in fighting for integration, from the founding of the Niagara movement, at the beginning of this century, which later evolved into the NAACP (National Association for the Advancement of Colored People). They also played an active role in the integrationist Negro organizations. Their major Black trade union figure, A. Philip Randolph, played a pioneering role in establishing the first Black union in the AFL, the Sleeping Car Porters Union which, through its journal *The Black Worker*, played a major role in developing Black trade unionist activists and cadres. That union had a crucial and unsung role in acting as a network during the spread of the civil rights movement and sit-ins during the late 1950s and early 1960s throughout the south. Bayard Rustin, a life-long socialist, who unfortunately ended his life as a very right-wing social-democrat, and other Black and white socialist intellectuals and activists, played a major role as strategists and links with the northern labor movement for the civil rights movement in the south up to the point when sections of it began to develop Black separatist politics after the assassination of Martin Luther King. King's tragic and premature death represented the major break within the civil rights movement. King clearly stood *both* for Black empowerment and for integration, and in his last years increasingly linked the struggle for civil rights, as it obviously had to be, with opposition to the war in Vietnam and the campaign to organize poor people. Poor people so very often meant poor Black people but King's campaign was always stated in terms of all poor people and the unionization of the poorly paid municipal workers. His death left a vacuum which has not since been filled. The movement was in good part fragmented and lost its universalist moral thrust; the clarity and directness of the early civil rights movement was never duplicated. His subsequent canonization should not let it be forgotten that this saintly figure was even more explictly a socialist in his last years. The practical demise of the activist and integrated civil rights movement of the mid-1960s left the political scene for radical Blacks: to nationalist, Muslim and Black Marxist–Leninist groups. Some of the fringes of the fringes turned to 'revolutionary suicide', that is armed violence against odds which were crushing and under conditions of isolation in their own community which made this a hopeless romantic gesture that managed to get some fine young Black militants killed or imprisoned. They forgot the advice of Machiavelli, 'If you would strike at a Prince, make sure that you can kill him.'

That was a tragedy which led to an increasing separation of Black and white socialists, Marxists and social movement activists. This separation is to a limited extent bridged today in what remain the major left organizations, the Communists and democratic socialists, both of which have a number of important Black activists and leaders prominent in their ranks. Most of the socialist and leftist groups in recent years have accepted a language and a view of Black political struggle which is more in tune with what the nationalist Blacks had been proposing than the traditionally integrationist view which dominated on the left until the mid-1960s. But, by the same token, Black Marxists and radicals have moved towards a politics which seeks an alliance between autonomous Black organizations and white radicals in American domestic struggles. Socialists in the US have been and are more sensitized to issues of cultural and ethnic autonomy and politics than their European comrades.

An additional new issue, or rather a reborn issue, arose in part out of the collapse of the student New Left and the integrationist civil rights movement of the 1960s. That has been, of course, the birth of an assertive new feminism, a substantial wing of which expressed itself in Marxist and quasi-Marxist terminology. It is fair to say that the debate has influenced both the practice and theory of all socialist organizations since the 1970s. Today it is inconceivable for any socialist or Marxist organization not to pay major attention to cultural, social and economic issues associated with gender-based oppression. A whole new Marxist anthropology of the family has become a part of the vocabulary and praxis of American socialists. This is even reflected in trade union work and in such larger women's organizations as the Committee of Labor Union Women (CLUW) and the repeated drives to organize white collar workers undertaken by Local 925 of the SEIU and the District 65 of the Automobile Workers of America (UAW), for example.

American Socialists: Relatively Advanced or Backward?

In recent decades new themes have entered into the discussions of American socialists. These were responses to new or renewed major social movements and forces which raised new issues. The first post-war set of issues centered on the experiences of the Cuban and other Third World revolutions and their transferability to other, and even domestic, situations in the US. The major impact of this debate had been that throughout much of the 1960s, on the left fringes of the Marxist student, Maoisant and Black milieux, an intense debate over the possibilities of armed struggle and urban guerilla activity took place. While all traditional Marxist and socialist organizations rejected this approach, some of the Maoist and post-Leninist, Guevarist or *sui generis* sects adopted them. The urban guerilla fantasies and experiences have all been invariably catastrophic for the groups involved – such as the Black Panthers, the Puerto Rican Nationalists, the Weather Underground, and the Black Liberation Army – and today these groups and their views have been completely marginalized.

The second set of new issues was posed by the rise of the student movement of the 1960s and the familiar Marcusian themes (or more fairly stated, bowdlerized and vulgarized versions of Marcuse) had currency through the early 1970s. Herbert Marcuse and Frantz Fanon helped to introduce the notion of the alienated, marginalized outsider as the principal carrier of the possibility of radical transformation in a bourgeois society brainwashed into conformity. This conformity was enforced by a repressive tolerance which marginalized and trivialized all serious opposition to the capitalist system.

By the end of the decade considerable debate about the underclass and other marginalized elements and their relationship to social change were discussed jointly with attempts to revise the traditional dependence on the industrial working class and on organized disciplined political parties of the left as the subject of the social transformation by neo-Marxists and the new left. Here one only need refer to the later writings of C. Wright Mills, Marcuse, Fanon as well as a host of already forgotten academic revolutionaries who had their day. No serious Marxist journal or socialist organization holds these views any longer, although there is at least a nostalgic remnant of them in Z and *Radical America*.

A digression might be useful here to point out that in dealing intellectually with these newer issues – Third World, racism, student rebellion, and militant feminism – the American Marxists have been, if anything, more advanced than their counterparts in the rest of the world. This, in turn, poses a more general question about the nature of Marxist and socialist analysis and debate in advanced industrial societies and whether the old paradigm about American 'backwardness' really applies. A possible, although distant, analogy suggests itself in the relationship between the Russian Marxists before October 1917, and the world socialist movement, and today's situation of American Marxism. It is useful to remember that Russian Marxism, in all of its varieties, was seen before the Russian revolution as exotic, strange, and not particularly relevant to the rest of the movement internationally. If anything, it was considered to be theoretically and conceptually backward. Yet an entire epoch of world revolutions followed during which the experiences of the Russian Marxists have been mechanically adapted by movements throughout the world.

Given the general crisis of socialism and Marxism in advanced industrial societies and the absence of commonly accepted strategies and paradigms, it is not at all impossible that, for a number of major theoretical and practical issues common to advanced industrial societies, the American Marxists may find themselves playing a significant role out of all proportion to their numbers and influence. This is so for several reasons:

one is that there is more of a richness and variety within American Marxism than almost anywhere in the world today. It is, in some questions of theory, on the cutting edge of serious Marxist and socialist debate. It certainly has had more of an experience with dealing with new social, generational, gender-specific, and ethnic movements than its counterparts in other advanced industrial societies.

Further, a number of industrial and social processes of late capitalism occur earlier in the US than in the rest of the world and, therefore, force the Marxists who are serious about theory to attempt to deal with those issues *before* their comrades in other countries do. Finally, the absence of a hegemonic party on the left, while representing a terrible weakness for the organized left as a whole, frees the theoretical debate from an all-but-inevitable subordination to the practical and tactical needs of party policies. It is thus a freer and less structured, and perhaps more pioneering, debate, as well as unfortunately being less focused on immediate organizational priorities of a mass socialist labor movement. Nevertheless, as America nears the end of its brief century, we may be approaching the end of American exceptionalism as well. Mass democratic egalitarian political mobilization will catch up with this richest of all capitalist societies. Its form and language will probably be quite specific, but my guess is that it will neither be the familiar language of European socialist movements, even with the Canadian accent of the New Democratic party of Canada, nor yet the left-populist Rainbow rhetoric of the Jackson campaign. It will necessarily borrow from both as well as from the feminist and other social movements and will have to include the bulk of the forces now found in organized labor and the left-wing of the Democratic party.

A Brief Prescriptive Summary

1) The United States has a rich history of both class-based and more issue-oriented radicalism. While it was the site of some of the first of the workers' political parties under capitalism it today has no independent mass socialist or labor party. In that it is alone among the industrialized capitalist democracies, and that is what is generally called American exceptionalism. The greater and more general internationalization of the economies of advanced capitalist countries and the permeation of national economies by the world market make it increasingly probable that this exceptionalism is coming to an end.

2) The peculiar specificities of the political system in what is the oldest of political democracies with a continual constitution make the

present two-party system the confusing multi-class and issues arena which diffuses political issues. As a consequence there exists a so-called hole in the American electorate which represents in part those voters who in the other industrial capitalist states vote for socialist and labor parties. Racism, which has been endemic in US politics since its founding, combined with the steady and mass immigration of workers, has generated an ethnically-charged class system which makes it more difficult to develop solidaristic class politics than is the case in more homogeneous societies.

3) However, the Jackson campaign of 1988, as well as the successes in the past of militant industrial union drives, show that economic egalitarian democratic mobilization can help bridge the ethnic and race barriers to the building of movements which push universalistic, egalitarian, social and economic policies. The key is universalist demands versus so-called specially targeted social policies: national health insurance, free and universal pre-school child care, massive housing, universal and taxable child allowances on the European model and the rest, rather than the punitive and mean social welfare policies of the caricature of the welfare state which the US has had.

4) To create a mass public for an advanced and egalitarian welfare state, the measures proposed and taken must not be earmarked for the poor or the aged or women or minorities. They need to be universalist as an extension of citizenship in a modern industrial society. To work at all these measures, while emphasizing the need for greater leisure and variety in life, must be firmly based on an effective gender-sensitive egalitarian policy of deliberate creation of labor scarcity, that is decent, non-punitive full employment. Thus the social policies advocated by socialists and social movements should be seen not as an act of generosity or charity, welcome as those sentiments are, but as a civic right. Or to use the terminology of US social policy there should be an entitlement to decent work and social services in what is still the richest society in the world.

5) The end of the American century should mark the end to the empire and the hubris which has forced on to an increasingly unwilling US population the odious role of the world policeman guarding an unjust international world economic order. This role must be given up and the maintenance of the world order should be turned over to genuine international bodies. Clearly the present unjust 'order' needs to be drastically changed. Massive disarmament initiated by a set of negotiations and unilateral initiatives can permit the development of a democratic non-interventionist security and foreign policy appropriate to a democracy in the twenty-first century. Genuine security of course requires massive efforts to bridge the North–South gap and to create a

world in which want and famine are a thing of the past. That is a national and international goal which genuine American patriots who cherish and defend the genuine interests of their country will support. What is good for General Motors or the multi-nationals is not only not what is good for America, it is an economic, ecological and often political disaster for the world.

Chapter 8

The Subject is Class and/or Perhaps Social Movements

Among the unavoidable themes in contemporary discussions of the state of socialism is the relationship of the class-based, more traditional labor and socialist movements to the new social movements.[1] However one conceives of the relationship of the two, these movements are a new phenomenon of great importance, particularly to the new, better-educated and younger publics on the left.[2] A part of the problem is that some of these new social movements or issue groups which define themselves as social movements consider themselves non- or anti-political in the ordinary sense. Yet another nagging problem is simply one of definition: what exactly should be included under the label of new *social* movements?

What Comes Under the Heading of Social Movements?

Generally there is agreement that, when they do mobilize large constituencies – and that is not all that often – women's, peace, and ecology movements should be included in any definition of new social movements. Under some circumstances ethnic protest groups, immigrant groups, organized students, human rights groups, gay and lesbian activist groups and even counter-cultural groups can qualify. Direct-action, single- and multi-issue organizations and less formal groups, squatters, free schools and alternative child-rearing communes can also sometimes become types of social movements. Entire neighborhoods in major cities and college towns have been dominated by alternative communities or social movements. Much lies in the eyes of the beholder, and opinions about the movements' importance or intellectual or moral significance will therefore vary a great deal among different observers particularly when dealing with the less formal and unstructured groups. A number of the new alternative movements are quite deliberately unstructured and avoid anything which could be taken for a program or definition. That is to say, that often one is dealing with a sensibility or mood rather than political or social-issue groups or ideas, let alone movements. But, then, on the unstructured left, 'movement' is a good 'buzz' word. As a consequence there is now a generic leftist movement equivalent of 'psycho-babble'.

The very wide range covered by the term new social movements should alert us that we are probably dealing with several very different types of issues and groups here. It is also reasonably clear that, whatever else, a number of these 'new' social movements are neither new nor social nor movements. This does not make them necessarily less important to understand as allies of the left. It is also not at all clear that more new social movements are found on the left or progressive end of the spectrum than on the right. After all, the huge revival of participatory fundamentalist grass-roots Christianity, the revivals of both orthodox grass-roots Judaism and Islam surely are of at least as much significance as some of the leftist social movements, not to speak of the very wide revival of massive, grass-roots populist nationalism. These conservative grass-roots groups often reflect the same alienation from an impersonal, cold, non-communitarian social order which comes with modernity and an individualistic and competitive capitalism.[3]

But the scene among right-wing social movements is a good bit more lively and complex than among the fundamentalist religious groups. For that matter many neighborhood, 'backyard' activists in the smaller cities and suburbs are often motivated by that same alienation towards a protective and ugly racism. An excellent example of that was the recent confrontation in the city of Yonkers, in the US, over the court order to build integrated and low-income housing which was massively resisted by an increasingly articulate and self-organized majority of the community. Similar cases can be pointed to in Britain, France and West Germany. There is a huge network of anti-abortion activists, right-wing anti-feminist women's organizations, not to mention the grass-roots vigilantes focusing on combating the menace of non-religious 'secular humanism' and the teaching of the 'dogma of evolution' in the schools. To this should be added the various armed groups of paranoids and 'survivalists' who often batten on to the crisis of the American farmers in the mid-west and the west. One could call some of these movements right-wing Emersonians, that is they have the same very American quality of believing themselves and their 'thing' to be in the very center of the universe. For the left the problem with American political culture is that it never genuinely accepted the notion of a polis and the common good as a valid moral aim for its citizens. The survivalist right-wingers 'doing their own thing' are only the flip side of the new leftist communards doing theirs. They even share the same paranoia about all government functions and agencies and love of conspiracy theories.

And if movement esoterica is of interest, there are numerous racist anti-immigrant groups like the National Front in Britain and its equivalent in France and neo-Nazi cults in Belgium and Holland and such fringe neo-fascist groups as Ordine Nuovo in Italy and the 'Mao-Nazis', who combined terrorism with opposition to the superpowers but in the name of the organic far right rather than the left. It is only worth pointing out that many such groups mobilize more people and are, if anything, in more ferocious opposition to the existing capitalist social and economic order of the West than a number of groups which are generally accepted as being a part of the new social movements.

On the more counter-cultural front, there are always the Hell's Angels and the horrendous number of mostly minority murderous youth gangs in places like Los Angeles, some of which are very large and have begun to have a more than local organization. All of these have some attributes of social movements, or what were called the post-political movements. These last probably outnumber the active feminists, ecologists and peace-activists put together, at least in Los Angeles. They certainly outnumber the organized socialist and Communist left of all varieties there.

These groups should provide a caution to all those who get too enthusiastic about communities, small affinity groups and community control. One person's community is another one's vigilante mob.[4] But they are also a signal that modern impersonal capitalist, or perhaps just industrial societies, have frayed the bonds of community beyond tolerance for too many. Something has to fill this vacuum, since humans are supremely social animals. The death of God or at least his organization on earth, the Church, has for many left a huge void.

The crisis, or at the very least the routinization, of socialism, the most universal and wide-spread secular faith of our century, also leaves an empty space which needs to be filled. That is the space occupied sometimes by the new social movements of the left and of the right. Until the new round of detente, apocalyptical fears of nuclear holocaust fueled this hunger for commitment and these movements could fill a need for many persons which neither traditional organized religion nor the mass parties of the left could.[5]

A substantial number of autonomous institutions and groups which can be treated as social movements have been around for a very long time. For example, a number of alternative institutions and groups are a part of the libertarian and anarchist milieu which has existed on the left as long as the socialist movement has. The pre-First World War East Side in New

York, and certain neighborhoods in Paris, Barcelona, and London had dense networks of alternative free schools, communes, cultural centers, free theaters, printing shops and non-institutional and anti-parliamentary direct-action movements.

The dominance of the Communist parties and the popular front 'classic' authoritarian popular unitary left culture on the left, from the 1930s through the 1950s, followed by the Maoist and Leninist sects through the 1960s and 1970s, had pushed this forgotten dimension of the non-institutional left into obscurity. The collapse of Communism as a world movement and as an attractive focus for the loyalties and imagination of young nonconformists and radicals has permitted this aspect of the past broad socialist radical sub-culture to re-emerge. The pity is that the collapse of the old left institutions and culture was so complete that a valuable part of the past history was also lost. But then the present generation of young American radicals has adopted that most American of ideologies, a vulgarized version of post-modernism, which essentially says, together with Henry Ford, 'History is bunk'. The attraction of that ideology is that ignorance of history or classical culture is not treated as a loss but as an asset.

There is a direct line of descent between some alternative movements and the old libertarians and anarchists. One should also point out that the peace groups and feminism and free cultural and educational groups are old friends on the left. They have always been there. A minimal reading of Shaw, Wilde, and of course Rebecca West or Emma Goldman not to speak of Margaret Sanger and Elizabeth Gurley Flynn, should quickly prove the point. Now it is interesting to consider why the women's and feminist themes and energies surfaced again after a period of quiescence and at the specific time they did. And, of course, that lost dimension is a precious part of the common history and should be a part of the common present of the left, but it is not new. A cursory reading of Engels's works on the origin of the family, Bebel's *The Woman Question*, or Shaw and Wilde, for all their flaws and flawed anthropology, should prove that it is simply not true that the old official socialist movement paid no attention to either gender oppression or the social construction of the nuclear family.[6]

But then, yes, official Communism and social-democracy have permitted their concerns with issues of sexism and gender oppression to become routinized and over-economistic until the revival of the women's movement. In fairness it should also be said that it was the sexist practices in the student new left and the Blacks in the civil rights movement and not the old left which provoked the rage out of which the new wave of radical feminism was born.[7] This was certainly the case in the United States, where the new wave of feminisms was born in the late 1960s.[8] The autobiographies of the activists are quite clear on this, but then unfortunately, many of the young, including young leftists, tend to ignore history.

If the peace and women's movements are not new, but sometimes social, movements, their re-emergence has been of great importance in helping to recreate a broad new left not restricted to electoralism or economic demands. The old mainline socialist left, before the instrumentalism of 'responsible' electoralist welfare state 'reformism' of the social-democrats and the organizational power fetishism of the Leninists, was a much richer, more pluralistic, culturally flexible and radical movement. That part of the past must be restored.

On the other hand, one of the new social movements *is* new, and while it has some old roots in the turn-of-century, nature-loving, youth nationalist movements of central Europe, in its current form it is essentially new. The movement in question is the new ecological movement which has taken organizational form as the Green parties or movements.

The Greens: Between a Ginger Group and an Alternative

Many younger leftist intellectuals today seem to think of the Greens as simply a new, more exciting and modern, or even post-modern form of the socialist movement.[9] Certainly this is a more generally acceptable form of that movement. The Greens are more fashionable intellectually, a softer option politically, and somehow more generationally with it. One can imagine Greens being featured on television, even in a nice health food commercial, directed at the young. This is a way to be a radical without the tiresome old economistic talk, the unfashionable hang-ups about, of all things, workers, and it is reasonably clear to most college-educated young progressives how backward, sexist, racist and fundamentally uninteresting workers are. They just do not get the press which funky ethnic movements do. Although feminism is less fashionable nowadays than it used to be in its heyday of the late 1970s it still beats by miles the labor movements, domestic and foreign, which can never be mentioned without automatically adding the modifiers old-fashioned, productivistic and sexist.

Clearly what I am trying to get at here is something hard to quantify, a question of sensibilities and intellectual styles on the left today in the US and the western world, and especially among the young and college-educated. Guevara and Castro do not make it any more; the

Greens do. But in general the softer political options do seem to get more resonance today. Thus for example, the Sandinistas, and they are certainly as soft as you can get in Marxist-Leninism, the lord be thanked, are all right.

Support for the boycott of South Africa – now that is a radical issue which seperates men and women from . . . well, at least from Jesse Helm, perhaps. Some of the more daring young seem even opposed to racism in France in that attractive but hardly earth-shaking movement *SOS-Racisme*. In contrast with the hard-edged old Communist, Marxist-Leninist and class-confrontational anti-imperialist themes, the present fashions are more communitarian and clean-cut and nice. Somehow I never thought of the radical left even in advanced capitalist countries in my own youth as being, well, nice. In a way this is a reflection of the fact that the broad democratic left is far less marginal both politically and culturally than it used to be in the United States in the 1940s and 1950s. Ironically, but significantly, that was a time when the Communist party and its various front and allied groups were incomparably organizationally stronger than the left is today.

The broad democratic left owes its present, less-ghettoized state to the positive heritage from the student, civil rights and anti-war movements of the 1960s and the social movements of the 1970s which have made it more, well, American, to be engaged and active. There are whole large parts of towns, in New York, Chicago, San Francisco, Minneapolis, Seattle, Portland and Berkeley, not to mention university towns, which are hospitable to a broadly defined progressive movement. The price paid has been a certain blandness and lack of intellectual sharpness. But that may be an inevitable trade-off, which ended with the Jesse Jackson campaign inside the Democratic party as the best that can be produced in mass social-democratic politics in the US today.

The Greens in Western Europe in many ways exemplify the present mood of fairly moderate politics where engagement over issues and politics is broadly acceptable to a whole new better-educated generation. Although we must remember that, while the Greens represent a quite broad and popular mainly generational sensibility and sentiment, at the same time they develop quite small organized political parties when they do try to enter into political competition. That is why I believe that their most constructive role today is that of being ginger groups which shake up the stodgy old massive socialist and labor movement.

The Greens in France have outpolled the Communist reformers and the other independent leftist candidates and should have a very salutary role to play vis-à-vis a socialist party with a pronounced tendency towards technocracy and insufficient nervousness about nuclear power. They can also play similar roles in Sweden and Austria. In West Germany a more flexible and left-wing social-democratic party leadership will have to move towards accepting coalitions with the Greens. In that specific case the move will probably split the Greens into their natural components: the *fundi* (fundamentalist) and *realo* (realist) wings.

But then the role of a ginger group, while most useful and constructive, is limited, and always poses the tactical question of: is it better to animate the mass left from inside the mass social-democratic and labor parties, or from the outside, in separate Green parties? That proposition is a good bit more complicated than it might appear to be, for a number of reasons. First, many activists in the Green parties are not, as I understand them, saying that we need a more modern or advanced socialist project which gives more centrality and attention to ecology, feminist, and social protest groups. What they are saying basically is that the socialist project insofar as it is a worthwhile thing *is* ecology, feminism, and those other good things and nothing else. Shades of Bernstein, with his proposition that the movement, and by implication the immediate struggles, is everything and the final goal nothing!

Fundamentalist Greens: An Anti-Industrial Alternative Vision

To be fair the more fundamentalist Greens do have a vision of an alternative, a very much alternative, social order and economy from either the existing capitalist or state socialist one. It is quite distinct from the democratic socialist vision and programs and, I do believe, quite disastrously wrong where it is not irrelevant. The fundamentalist Greens are anti-industrial and anti-modern. There are statements from Rudolph Bahro, for example, at the time when he spoke for that wing of the Greens, publicly stating that he was for the complete de-industrialization and de-urbanization of Germany and, for that matter, the whole industrial world. He proposed the massive exodus of people from the cities into the countryside. While it is true that Bahro resigned from the Greens in 1985 and went on to seek ever more spiritual salvation, this sentiment is not far from the present sensibility of the *fundi* wing of that movement. And it was significant that he had been chosen as the spokesman for that wing at the last national convention.

When listening to Rudolph Bahro speak about his vision of a natural order without cities, industries or 'artificial needs', it was almost like listening to a more modern, more humane, Pol Pot.

Surely the Stalinist experience, combined with the horrors of Cambodia, should make leftist and radical democrats at least extra-cautious about the nature of utopian notions of rapid fundamental transformation of the society, and the propositions about drastic social engineering and attempts to restructure human nature (whatever that socially formed construct should be) which necessarily find themselves at home within such views. The rhetoric backing those earlier horrors was every bit as apocalyptical and idealist and enthusiastically intolerant of differences as the rhetoric of the present generation of true believers. Bahro was in many ways an archetypal Green.

What is particularly frightening about this dangerous earth-worshipping nonsense, is that it is deliberately non- if not anti-rational. This is the sense in which the *fundi* Greens are a part of a broad generational post-modernist current of irrationality with its roots deep in the seductively brilliant thought of Nietzsche and Heidegger, which is at its core so elitist and anti-democratic, even although that thought is often only absorbed in flattened simplified versions popular among today's students and younger intellectuals. This is the cloven hoof of earth-mother communitarianism – the need for the organic, the authentic, feeling and passion, as against the cool 'patriarchal' logic of the broad left. This trend includes the rejection of science as well as scientistic fetishism. And of course it is permeated by utter contempt for the warp and woof of genuine democracy, for discussion, give and take, compromise and elected, responsible representative bodies.

The 'fundi' Greens are thus genuine heirs of parts of the American student new left of the 1960s. But that part of the student left was driven mad, in the words of one of its leaders, by the endless imperialist war in Vietnam and the racism in their society in the United States. Let us for the moment not explore how authentic this *post-factum* explanation was for the US. What drove the German new left mad? Or the Dutch one? Or the counter-cultural alternative types in Denmark? What were the monstrous crimes in *their societies* which they revolted against? Take this just a little further into the realm of the anti-parliamentary and armed struggle *engagés*, who in so many ways resemble the sentiments, though not the actions, of the Green activists. How 'authentic' were their feelings about oppression? How much of it was cultural style, impatience with a mass working-class movement which would not adopt the brand new insights of the left activists overnight, and a sense of general generational alienation? How much did these sentiments have in common with those of some of my students in the United States who over the years have stated that they had given two or three years to the working class, or the democratic left, and have left feeling disappointed, let down, even betrayed?

Petra Kelly and the other members of the fundamentalist wing of the Green movement still make my hair stand on end on the issue of de-industrialization, if only because, when I think of the consequences of those programs, I see as a consequence starvation and desperate need throughout the South. Both of those are of course unimaginable in the prosperous post-industrial societies in which the Greens function. But there is another world, too, and it would face starvation. Decent societies will not and should not be able to exist in a world which has desperate and achievable material needs and starvation – starvation for the Third World, which can be prevented by human agency, if nothing else. But then that is an essential point of difference between socialists and Greens, since if there is to be a world which is decent and liveable, a world in which socialists have some political power, the socialists in advanced industrial countries will have major political and moral responsibilities to help the Third World. They cannot do so by becoming rural arcadias.

To talk about de-industrializing the industrial world today is to doom the Third World to starvation for at least several generations. And of course *starving societies are not the seedbeds for egalitarian, participatory and democratic political communities, and therefore even less for socialism.* Thus all the Green rhetoric about solidarity with the peoples of the Third World remains just that, rhetoric. The programmatic consequences of the Greens having real political power would be a disaster for the south. Of course, having the Greens have some *influence* on the social democrats would, on the contrary, be quite constructive since it would make them more ecologically sensitive without making them subordinate everything to that one, albeit major, consideration. The problem is that within the Green movement there are those who do not acknowledge that there are any other major considerations but those of ecology. This is most obvious in the reactionary elitist version of radical ecological ideology, so-called 'deep ecology' which quite explicitly accepts that the world, especially the Third World, needs to find again a balance with nature through mass starvation if necessary.

The old mechanistic notion that every country in the world has to duplicate the path of the industrial revolution is something that has to be got rid of. Crude brutal attempts to industrialize and develop have devastated parts of the world as well as that socialism which identified with the forced march into modernity. There are *appropriate* technologies, and it is true that most energy-intensive technologies are, at present, harmful in the Third World. For that matter they are harmful to the world as a whole. But, the central question is: do we accept the idea that the problem with the poor, the problem with the working class, the problem with the unemployed, is that they consume too much, or that they do not have enough? Yes, not enough of even crass material goods, housing, decent food, good societal infra-structure (which also costs money, which is a product of material goods and services).

Do we really accept the proposition that it is a desirable if not a utopian proposition that the urban civilizations, even what Manuel Castel defines as the 'totalitarian' metropolis, be destroyed? I for one do not accept that. I think that the democratic socialist project is infinitely more difficult and complex, and therefore exciting, than the romanticist dreams of the 'purer' greens. Whatever settlements between the superpowers and Europe do emerge out of the present Cold War, peace and stability cannot and should not last if much of the world is doomed to desperate need and starvation, while the industrial North remains an island of prosperity. For genuine aid to be sent, the North must remain industrial for a long time.

Then, of course, there are left-wing Greens. They include people who think of themselves as Marxists, democratic Marxist-Leninists or even libertarians. A very good example can found in the alternative movement in West Berlin. But I think that, just like small single-issue groups and post-Leninist groups in the US, these groups are basically hackneyed. It is true that they are involved in endless, and mostly very worthy, campaigns, but I consider them essentially uninteresting for two reasons. First, I do not think that political consciousness develops simply through activating people in endless, very worthy, single-issue campaigns and confrontations. I do not think that activity and activism *per se* develop alternative conceptions of the social order. Secondly, worthwhile as activism is, it is just as sterile without theory and intellectual work as theories and programs are without activism. I think that solving this dilemma requires stable political parties of the left to try to deal with all of the complexities and consequences of modern technology, rather than devoted chiliastic activists who often reject modernity as such. However, these parties will become reduced to dull electoralism as an end unless they are surrounded by a milieu full of social movements and issue groups partially overlapping with and partially competing with the mass socialist party. In short, the mass socialist parties need the greenish social movements to retain their own identities.

The Greens in the State Socialist Societies

Ecological movements and 'green' sentiments are beginning to have an increasing impact in Eastern Europe. This is above all among the young, the quasi-oppositional and counter-cultural milieux. In a way it is a reflection of the growing unity in Europe of at least a common counter-culture. For example, today there is increasing sensitivity towards ecology in Yugoslavia, Czechoslovakia, Poland and Hungary. This is because the kind of intensive development which has occurred in Eastern Europe has been brutally harsh on the environment.

The kind of pollution which goes on in Hungary, Czechoslovakia, Poland, Romania and East Germany today is just as anti-ecological as anything that the capitalist west has done in the past. Forests are massively dying in the Czech, Polish and East German mountains. Of course, the problem has been exacerbated by the fact that until very recently it has been all but impossible to organize any non-official group in these societies, and that included ecologists or groups to protest about pollution. I have avoided loading this book down with tables, but cannot resist at least one here.[10] It is a simple comparison between selected industrial countries in sulphur dioxide emission for 1982.

The table almost speaks for itself. The problem is that when you decide

Country	Emissions (kg per $1000 GNP)
'Market-oriented'	
Japan	1
Sweden	4
France	5
West Germany	5
United States	7
United Kingdom	8
'Centrally planned'	
Soviet Union	19
Romania	28
Hungary	31
East Germany	35
Czechoslovakia	40

that 'socialism' is mass production plus heavy industry, it is going to be rough on the environment. And when, further, you have a society which permits no autonomous protest movements, then obviously there is going to be no effective obstacle to industrial waste and pollution. In the Soviet Union some scientists and intellectuals have objected to the assault on the ecology of the Soviet Union. They began with small groups and low-pitched voices, but this form of autonomous organization and protest has been permitted to grow. It even fits in with some of the nationalist and Great Russian patriotic moods, as well as with the small youth counter-culture which is emerging in the Soviet Union. Ecology is like a philosopher's stone – a movement and issue for all seasons and for almost all ideologies. This appears to be one area where Gorbachev's campaign for more public openness has some effect. It is the most unthreatening of the public spaces to open up today in state socialist politocracies.

The nuclear catastrophe at Chernobyl in the Ukraine has shaken up scientistic dogmas about the supposed safety of nuclear plants. Safety in nuclear plants depends to an enormous extent on the conscientiousness of the personnel and independent and incorruptible inspection rather than on technology. Therefore the safety problems in state socialist societies, with their surly, unmotivated workers and self-protective managerial bureaucracies, is worse than in the West where there are at least *some* independent public bodies and citizen groups with power to affect the behavior of the plant managers. Even under those circumstances there have been numerous nuclear safety scandals in the United States. The prospects in Eastern Europe and the Soviet Union are even more frightening. The political effect of Chernobyl was strongest in Sweden and Yugoslavia. In Yugoslavia massive protests have already stopped the building of new nuclear plants.

There is an open and sharp debate in Yugoslavia about completely abolishing nuclear plants as such, and the increasingly vocal and organized opponents of nuclear energy seem to be winning the battle for both the elite and public opinions, and they have won in Parliament against the pro-nuclear lobby and the cabinet. There is a growing awareness of the fact that the earth cannot be raped forever and that concern with ecology and the dangers from nuclear pollution and waste are not merely a trendy fashion in the decadent West.

On the other hand, one only has to spend some brief time in Eastern Europe and the Soviet Union to experience and see genuine avid hunger for the 'manufactured' needs and products among all strata of the population for commodities, cultural styles and even ideas from the capitalist West.

Therefore, while greater sensitivity to ecology will continue to grow and while there will be a rising and more effective opposition to the use of nuclear power, anti-industrial and anti-urban values will remain on the fringes of the oppositions in those societies.

Asceticism is not by and large the cultural style of the young and the new middle classes in Eastern European societies today. It is far more likely to be found as a style among the children of the relatively privileged intellectuals in the most advanced industrial countries of the West. It is certainly not the dominant lifestyle even there. But then I have never found the proposition that revolutionary asceticism was the appropriate cultural style for the socialist movement, and above all for a socialist society, particularly convincing.

The Greens Have a Conservative and a Radical Side

But there is also a right-wing aspect to ecology and the defense of traditional communities, particularly in Germany and Austria. That sort of mystification of blood and soil, and the worship of forests, has associations in my mind with the early Romantic and nationalist youth movements before the First World War, which were quite clearly right-wing, populist *and* anti-democratic. That is a sensitivity which is essentially anti-modern and not post-modern. I may be being subjective and archaic, but I still get nervous when young Germans get too enthusiastic about oak trees . . . those atavistic sentiments have very nasty historical associations.

The right-wing side is also the notion that, once I have my cottage by the clean and unpolluted lake, I am going to pull the ladder up after me and we cannot have the masses using and polluting my beach. Read for beach all the other goods in terms of space, which the haves have and will protect against the immigrants, the poor and the unwashed. The right-wing ecological position is saying: we have to keep East Hampton the way it is for the privileged middle class and intellectuals and therefore we cannot have buses bringing out the kids from the slums.

The right-wing ecologists say that we can create a rural arcadia for ourselves in the advanced world and forget about the rest of the world. The fact of the matter is that the world economy is now interdependent and if the socialists ever do take power in Western Europe, they are going to have to assume major responsibilities for helping the Third World countries develop. That will not be done by de-industrializing, or zero growth or by anything even resembling the potentially murderous 'deep ecology' proposals. This is not a question of charity or simple human solidarity, although it is not a bad thing for the labor and socialist movements to begin thinking more in terms of simple human solidarity; it is a question of survival.

This discussion about ecological movements in turn raises an interesting question about the possible or even necessary conjuncture between contemporary socialism, particularly democratic socialism, and modernity. I believe that there is such a conjuncture. For example, when Rudolph Bahro says, speaking as a Green, that we cannot stop producing tanks in Germany until we stop producing cars, he is saying something worth exploring a little bit. The cars that most ecologists object to when they object to cars are not the cute little Volkswagens with which they go to the East Hamptons and to the woods. They object to the cars that the smelly, styleless proletarians use for less uplifting endeavours like going to work and getting their kids and families out to picnics. There is a real elitist strand here which needs to be openly faced and understood.

A socialist society is certainly going to have to know about computers and know about advanced technology, and know about mass production. It will reorganize work drastically. It will surely reorganize leisure time drastically and with love and imagination. But it will not move towards intentional communes and new rural utopias. It will above all be a system where ordinary mortals, not full-time activists and *engagés*, feel comfortable and at home. And, feeling comfortable in a society made for humans and not in fulfilment of some abstractions born in the heads of some self-selected radical elites, ordinary human beings, not saints, will also feel empowered, rather than inadequate for not measuring up to some abstractly and arbitrarily defined model of a new socialist person.

The British Labour party, for example, is increasingly sensitive to ecological, gender and other social movement issues today. One of their more popular journals, *New Socialist*, is exceedingly responsive to these issues and there are both local and national organizations of socialist ecologists. The most significant popular journal of the socialist left in Britain, *New Statesman and Society*, pays a great deal of intelligent attention to the issues raised by the progressive social movements, sometimes even to the neglect of the themes of class and exploitation, which is probably a mistake. The Swedes, the Dutch, the Belgians and smaller parts of the French and Italian socialist movements are increasingly turning more attention to questions of gender, ecology and protection of traditional communities and cultures. The notion is spreading that democratic socialists should work to preserve certain aspects of traditional society and communities, qualified by their firm defense of individual rights, cultural differences and personal life choices in an increasingly industrialized and homogeneous world, particularly in the European Community which is becoming more economically, politically and culturally unified. This means defending the rights of cultural minorities, like gays and lesbians, like submerged national groups, like alternative communities in a society which threatens to become ever duller and more homogeneously bureaucratic and conformist.

Opposition to Full Employment: The Right to Support and Work

Linked in part with left Green, or rather social movement sensitivity, although a good deal broader and more subtle than what the Greens themselves usually say, has been the new massive attack on proposals for full employment which is usually proposed by the social-democratic labor movements. There are many strange things about this attack, which is also joined by major left-wing socialists and feminists, like Barbara Ehrenreich, Fred Block and Frances Piven in the United States, Claus Offe in West Germany, Alain Touraine and André Gorz in France and others. The passion and energy devoted to this issue by non-traditional leftists is quite strange. Essentially the argument appears to be that it is important at this stage in history to separate the right to an income from the obligation to work. This is either banal, since in practice it is accepted by the most orthodox of European social-democrats who reject 'workfare' and the concept that people have to be driven to work by fear, or a distortion of what the call for full employment, or its closest equivalent under capitalism, has historically meant in the labor movement.

It has always meant the creation of decent, well-paid jobs, socially useful jobs. And it has never within the socialist labor movement even vaguely resembled the workhouse-like caricature which opponents of the full employment strategy have claimed it to be. It is another question to raise whether the labor movement should have fought far more energetically for a radical reduction of work hours and work years, for all kinds of imaginative ways of reorganizing the way work and life fit together, all of which are reasonable criticisms which can just as easily come up within a so-called full employment strategy. Why was it not posed that way? One reason can be that something else was being got at, and it is there that the link with the Greens can be found.

The underlying issue centers on industrialism itself and the production of 'false needs'. This is an issue thinly hidden under the surface in much of the critique of consumerist society, since all too often it is the 'false needs' of the underclasses and the workers which are objectionable and not the apparently quite appropriate and objective needs of the intellectual elite and the younger counter-cultural groups. Of course the problem is complicated by the fact that modern consumer capitalism does indeed manufacture 'needs'. But it is evident that those artificial needs are even more virulently developed among the fashionable leftist post-modernist intellectuals than among the productionist blue- and white-collar workers who form the bulk of supporters of the mass democratic workers' parties. They are different, but the consumer goods expansion and urban gentrification are not primarily the products of blue-collar workers' greed for material things. The huge expansion of tourist travel, with its vast consumption of energy and degradation of nature, are not the exclusive preserve of the proletariat either.

The relation of social spending in a contemporary welfare state, given the present situation in the world economy, to full employment is quite direct and brutal. If you have near full employment (the historic figure in Sweden is under 2 per cent unemployment), you can afford to be very generous with both unemployment benefits and egalitarian and universal welfare measures (universal entitlements), since the numbers involved are small. If unemployment is at a more common Western European 8 per cent, your unemployment compensation alone costs four times as much without considering the utter waste of human lives implied. Further, if you have near full employment you can be generous about those who may want to march to a different drummer and be outside of the labor market for longer or shorter periods, for after all, only small sums are involved. If, on the other hand, hard-core youth unemployment seems to be creating a permanently unemployable lower caste of some 20 to 30 per cent of the population, as is the case in some countries with immigrant workers, and with the Blacks and Hispanics in the United States, the bounds of the social contract are strained to the utmost, since the support of this group will depend on a large degree of social generosity which is rare in complex and impersonal, non-communal societies.

A major argument is that essentially today the state, that is the state in advanced capitalist societies, is in a fiscal crisis for a number of reasons – the major one being that the world economy has been in prolonged doldrums. Further, the structural changes in the world economy, and therefore in the increasingly interdependent advanced capitalist economies, make full employment, even the limited version of full employment which had been possible under welfare-state capitalism, impossible. Some would argue that it is undesirable even if achievable. Therefore, the argument goes, a classic social-democratic strategy is economically and politically impossible and illusory. For one thing the capitalist classes are today much more confrontational, above all in the United States; for another, the working class, old and new, is more atomized and therefore all but impossible to organize.

Movements Against Oppression Based on Gender

A point made with great poignancy and effectiveness by Foucault and, following him, the more sophisticated advocates of the centrality of the new social movements' striving for the rebirth of an effective and new left stress is the equality of oppression in modern society. This is an enormously important insight into the fact that socialism was born as a movement and most of its activists, thinkers and writers joined the movement, through struggles against many different oppressions, not just through opposition to class exploitation.

What that means is that the oppression of individuals and groups as a consequence of race, gender, sexual preference, ethnic prejudice, lifestyle or political viewpoint is as urgent and as painful as the oppression based on class and the individual's position in the process of production. Or to put it simply, perhaps oversimply, that no oppression is 'privileged' compared to others as a basis for organizing a socialist movement. To operationalize this would mean that organizing ethnic minorities, gays and lesbians, Blacks and Hispanics, persons choosing alternative lifestyles, the young identifying themselves either as students or as counter-cultural groups, is as relevant as the traditional left focus on unions and workers has been. It would also mean that women in their workplace roles as mothers engaging in the biological reproduction of the society, women choosing to assert a separate feminist sensibility, are as, if not more, relevant for the organization of a socialist movement as industrial and other workers.[11]

Note that I write 'workers', always a gender-neutral term since, of course, workers can be and are increasingly male and female in all advanced industrial societies. In point of fact the elimination of gender stereotyping in employment must be one of the major goals of modern progressive and socialist politics. This should immediately alert one to the fact that what are in question are often overlapping categories, sometimes with multiple overlaps. Thus we can have a Black, female, gay, politically radical, poor, worker. All those separate identities are the subject of different, very painful, oppressions and exploitations in both modern and traditional societies. This is so not only in industrial societies; some of the worst oppression is in traditional societies and communities, which is one more reason to fight to radically change those societies.

This is not being Euro-centric or suffering from an excess of Western cultural arrogance: burning widows was and is oppressive even though it could be a cultural norm in some societies; child labor is super-exploitative even if custom justifies it; stoning homosexuals may be a custom in some traditional societies but it is certainly brutal, not to speak of clitoridectomy practiced in some African and Muslim societies. No passionate references to and denunciations of slavery, imperialism and Hiroshima and various crimes of western capitalism make these oppressions less real.[12]

To treat the concerns raised by women's movements and feminists in the west as a form of cultural imperialism is wrong, since even the theories and often the practices of the national independence and Marxist movements of the societies of the south are also 'imports' from the imperialist heartlands. So are both the ideology of anti-imperialism and the theories of imperialism. What is at stake are rights of human beings, which are no less basic for being sometimes stated with an American or Western European feminist or leftist culturo-centric insensitivity.

This is an area where 'Third Worldist' rhetoric and demagoguery are particularly self-damaging since the status of women in most societies of the Third World is a very major factor in their continued backwardness and slowness in moving ahead economically and socially. One of the more reliable indicators of a genuine social revolution, and this was true of all the great historic ones, is that a mass of women at least temporarily shake off the yoke of patriarchal oppression and assume their role in the struggle as equals. This phenomenon occurs in mass struggles for independence and mass working-class struggles as well. One of the signs of how socially progressive and advanced Solidarity in Poland was in 1980 was its remarkable set of demands for women's rights. Women played heroic roles in the Chinese and Yugoslav revolutions and in a number of Third World revolutionary liberation struggles.

To be sure, after the revolution, the pendulum on women's rights, and above all participation, has often swung back, although never as far back as where it began. The new regime then has to work hard to try to change the socially created norms and values which keep women classified as second-class human beings. This must be done, since it is the status of women which is the first target of the conservative and backward forces in these societies. There are also very practical reasons for placing women's rights and entry into the economy at the center of the tasks of the Third World modernizers. Without that taking place women will not be able to, or want to, control population growth which in so many countries is a ticking demographic time-bomb absorbing all of the results of growth and development.

Empowering women, which means as a first step political and economic equality, so that social equality is not so much verbiage, is a primary task of the democratic left wherever it finds itself. This is even though in many countries nationalists, even nationalists who are radical critics of capitalism, reject full equality for women as a cultural artifact of a white culture they hate, as is the case with some Black nationalists in the United States. This has to be fought by the left, the women's movement and the progressive Blacks. They must counter the reactionary talk among many nationalists, all too often with some support from Black women activists, about a high birth-rate being a weapon in the struggle against the white controlled West.

Equality, full equality and the ability to develop the way one wants to without the socially constructed restraints of the traditional society, are the aims of socialists and socialist-feminists. This should be an oxymoron, a term which is internally contradictory, since, just as genuine socialists cannot be anything but democratic, they should not be anything but feminists.

That means that after the struggles for equality in the economy and political society are won we will have to begin imagining different types of arrangements which can replace the present nuclear families as alternative options for those who desire them. The egalitarian societies will be far more varied and pluralistic than any current definition of 'normal' nuclear family can project. But people should obviously also be able to pick that option too, without being financially and socially locked into dependence and inequality. This is an area where current demands can project images of the future in areas such as extensive and fully paid child care and parental (not maternity) leave.

The debate with cultural feminists is a different one, and one which goes beyond the scope of this work. But it deserves at least a few brief comments. There are obvious parallels between the cultural feminists and cultural nationalists. In both cases the response to historical and current oppression has been to claim that the oppressed group is not only equal but is superior to the oppressing group. This can either be formulated by claiming that the oppressed group or gender are somehow more authentic representatives of genuine human values and their adoption should be universal for the society as a whole, or that the oppressor group (whites, males or, even better, white males) is so fundamentally flawed that complete separation is required.

Thus a not unnatural outgrowth of this type of reaction is feminist or lesbian separatism; lesbian because male culture is defined as so oppressive that the only way for a woman to maintain her identity is to reject totally all attributes of the male-dominated, necessarily sexist, culture, and orient herself politically, socially and sexually solely to women. Another 'natural' outgrowth of cultural feminism has been the development of a virulent active movement for state-imposed censorship of pornography which is loosely enough defined to include all but the dullest of 'nice' erotica defined as 'politically and culturally' correct. Shades of the Victorian era! This current in American cultural feminism is now in a violent confrontation with those sectors of the women's and feminist movement and the civil liberties organizations which are hostile to censorship and suspicious of the sexual puritanical themes in American life.

That sexual puritanism is, of course, much more at home on the right, and the result is that some prominent feminists like Andrea Dworkin found themselves arguing on the same side as the Reagan administration in favor of censorship of sexually explicit films, and journals. They also joined in popular right-wing mobilization campaigns in cities like Minneapolis and Indiana to enforce censorship. The argument is that pornography encourages rape. It is hardly documented and one could add that in a society as highly charged with implicit and explicit sexual symbolism for everything, including the sale of cigarettes and cars, one hardly needs pornography to be encouraged to think of de-personalized sex. More troubling is the failure to distinguish between fantasy and actual desire in some of the more lurid pornography, and the assumption that fantasy can overwhelm all other childhood and adult socialization and education. There has always been an element of fantasy and play in erotic imagination. In effect a good part of this cultural feminist thought is profoundly suspicious of sexuality itself in all but the rigidly prescribed 'correct' form, in act or in imagination. This is hardly the cutting edge of a movement to liberate humankind from the yoke of socially constructed gender roles.[13]

The equivalent among Blacks in the US and the UK are the Black separatist, back-to-Africa, groups, which insist on changing their names (getting rid of the slave name) and religion (getting rid of white man's religion), changing to forms of ahistorical race-exclusivist Islam, since Islam was *par excellence* a universal religion and not a 'Black man's religion'. Whatever sympathies one may have for the oppressions which have caused these archaic, separatist fantasies, they can clearly have no place in any universalist movement struggling to democratize society and establish socialism. A great deal of charlatanism and historical fiction is involved in these theories and world views.

The left intellectuals have been reluctant to engage in any discussion or debate with Black nationalists or cultural feminists over the fictive histories on which much of the narrowly political views of the past of slavery and imperialism or gender oppression and definition have been based. For that matter, African history or ethnography, as well as totally imagined histories and anthropologies of Amazons or matriarchal societies in the historical era, have been spared critical examination by the Marxists and the left. This is a form of patronizing which will have to be overcome if any genuine unified action between Black and white leftists, and mutual respect between male and female feminists, is to develop. But, then, myth-building has been essential to both nations and movements before. The question is how to strike a balance between the useful myth and a rational movement which appeals to the emotions and the intellect of its followers.

Socialists not only defend democracy, which is essentially a collective category, but they also defend liberty, which is the right of people to live different lives no matter how 'weird' or unreasonable these may seem, so long as they harm no one and interfere with no one else's rights. The problem for a society and a community is that the someone else whose rights are being interfered with may be under-age children. Here one must walk with great caution indeed. Clearly children also have rights and society, especially a socialist society, is going to have to defend those rights even sometimes from the biological parents. But that is a horrible culturo-centric trap. After all, I, for example, personally believe that children of superconformist fanatical religious sects are often in more need of protection from their sexually repressive legal custodians than children of those who live bohemian or nonconformist lifestyles. This cannot be left to bureaucrats and social workers to decide on, but then again it cannot remain the property of that most secretive and sometimes oppressive of human institutions, the nuclear family.

Therefore there are areas where strong affirmative laws with social sanctions are needed, there are others where social pressures and sanctions are more appropriate and people can simply move to more congenial surroundings and settings, and then of course *there are those vast areas of personal life which must never be permitted to become the subject of the will and decisions of the political community*. This is above all true in most cases of voluntary associations where power, money or institutional domination are not involved, like what consenting adults do sexually to please each other, for example.

Any civilized democratic or socialist society should obviously reject legal or social sanctions against consensual adult sexuality or sexual self-identity. Repressive measures and social and economic discrimination against gays in many societies calling themselves progressive or socialist is yet another intolerable identification of socialism with oppression and backwardness. No statements about threats to the cultural identities or traditions of nations, or about the supposed 'un-naturalness' of a practice which has existed at least as long as recorded human history, can change the ugly repressive record of Cuba and the Soviet-type societies on this question. They are joined in this dishonorable role by many, if not most, of the Third World 'socialist' societies, although there repression has been somewhat leavened with hypocrisy and inefficiency. It was certainly not imperialism and the United States that the Cuban Communists were fighting in Cuba when they repressed gays.

However, it must be acknowledged that for most gay activists in advanced capitalist democracies a civil-libertarian attitude is not really enough. Questions of accepting gay pride and identity are raised, as well as the gay contribution towards a more gender-flexible future for humanity. Personally, I am not at all sure that androgyny is the wave of the future or that it should be. In a decent tolerant society a plurality of views and practices would be accepted on this as well as on other questions. But, again personally, other than struggling for equal rights and a right to social space and equality, I do not quite see what makes gays, or lesbians a *social movement*, at least not in most cases. All oppressions do not create social movements, all forms of struggle for rights do not generate movements, social or otherwise.

Thus, for example, civil liberties are an issue socialists should clearly support everywhere, though, except sometimes under authoritarian regimes, it is almost never a social movement, but that does not make it less worthy. Equally, one can conclude that gay rights should be defended with the utmost firmness by socialists, and at the same time conclude that they are not a social movement. While clearly gays who are socially progressive are obviously welcome in any leftist coalition, gayness itself, however socially defined, does not necessarily make for progressive politics. One could almost argue for the opposite in the case of the gay subculture as distinct from most gays as individuals.

Any sub-culture which places such a major emphasis on youth, sexuality and physical beauty is oppressive in exactly the way in which feminists describe the mainstream patriarchal culture as being oppressive, to both women and men. It makes an objectified, stylized impersonal young male symbol the target of one's sexual fantasies and desires – a sexual hunk with nothing but youth and good looks. This is as objectionable as the *Playboy* cover girl is as a metaphor for a woman. Not to speak of those gay fashions in black leather with the obvious, although only symbolic one would hope, association with Nazi and Hell's Angels' uniforms. Just so that I am understood clearly, while I find both forms of objectification of sexual symbols offensive, neither should be subject to social or legal sanctions, but merely criticism and debate. And perhaps after debate, rejection as an appropriate practice, on the left.

Instead of a Brief Summary: A Note on Class and Social Movements

Much of the debate about the relationship of social movements to class seems to miss the point that the question is not moral but analytical and strategic. Morally it is impossible to choose between the pains caused by the different forms of oppression as targets for the left to attack. Sexual, gender, ethnic, racial, religious, national, generational, cultural and class oppression and repression are all urgent and must be attacked. None is necessarily more 'privileged' as being more important than others in terms of the personal impact, or even in terms of how much consciousness of injustice it may arouse in the individual or group directly affected. That is not the issue. All these oppressions cause pain and that pain can vary from individual to individual, but *not all oppression is of equal cross-cutting strategic unifying utility for a social transformational party or movement to address.*

Some categories are broader and more inclusive, others of great and passionate importance in asserting identity (national and religious groups often do that), still other categories set the group against other groups in that fulfilling its demands does not necessarily do anything for the others oppressed. Yet again, some others have an unusually important strategic place in society for the given moment. An example of the last category would have been the railway and telephone and telegraph workers during some historical revolutions and counter-revolutions. At other times students and young people have been of central importance, as in the civil rights movement in the southern US in the 1960s. Today class, if by that we mean both the traditional blue-collar unionized workers and the new working-class employed in the huge new institutions and bureaucracies of the welfare states and most of the mass of new underpaid, super-exploited, un-unionized workers in the expanding service sector, includes the largest number, which is the key to building the mass base for a broad left in the United States and other industrial societies. It pulls in the largest number of persons at the bottom of these societies, and in the United States these are the Blacks, the Hispanics, the young and the women, to which one adds the workers in the traditional sector whose security and living standards have been subjected to continual assault for a decade. That is the new public of the traditional left.

To raise the issue of class is to raise the issue of power in its sharpest and most uncompromising form! The old endless abstract argument of who is or is not in the working class may be of great interest to Marxologists or sociologists. I prefer to simplify a bit at this point. As the union organizers at Harvard University in their recent successful organizing drive put it, *You Can't Eat Prestige*. When the majority of technical and secretarial personnel at Harvard voted for a union despite a bitter and highly organized anti-union campaign by Harvard, they became a part of the working class, for practical and strategic purposes. That is, when they organized, they became a part of the organized working class.

They will probably never express it that way, since that is not a part of the popular vocabulary in the US, but they will act that way and this will be over issues which are not normally viewed as union issues but which will increasingly have to become union, that is class, issues. Those are the classic issues of the women's movement and of the social welfare movements: child care at work to make it possible for single mothers to work, respect and dignity which one gets through a minimum of job security and a re-classification of jobs so that the historic wage discrimination against jobs defined as mostly women's is stopped. Not a revolution exactly but it illustrates my point that the class (in this case union) strategy will probably do more for a larger group of women, Blacks and underpaid workers that any 'social movement' or gender-specific strategy would have. On the other hand, to organize a union today one needs the spirit and techniques of social movements, of causes. That is where they converge. At other points it may well be that gender will have that role or even ethnic identity, since all of these cut across a number of roles which people play in real life. While we all have a multiplicity of roles the strategically relevant question is: which situations bring to the surface which role as the salient one, *as the one which will predict the behavior and attitudes of the greatest number of people one is trying to move?* My view is that increasingly it will be class, defined to include the insecure, heavily female, currently re-composing working class in modern industrial societies. I simply cannot visualize it being gayness, or generational grievances, although those identities may well lead to major militant struggles for expanding democratic and citizen rights. But my view clearly rejects the notion that the issues of class are counterposed to a focus on social movements and the struggles for empowerment and widening democratic entitlement. On the contrary, they must go hand in hand if a sense of movement is to be re-created for the broad labor and socialist left as well as for their new generational and class allies.

Conclusion: Towards a Socialist Strategy – The Present Conceptual Stalemate

A major weakness of most social-democratic programs today is that they have all too often accepted the model and logic of industrialism inherited from capitalism as the only one that is possible or even imaginable. To be fair, the times have not been very promising for extensive experimentation with new radical programs. The social-democratic parties were if anything less imaginative during the good times, between the late 1940s and the early 1970s. But if a different type of industrial civilization is *unimaginable*, then the only realistic strategy for a labor or social-democratic government is to administer capitalism in as humane, socially just and egalitarian a way as possible. No advance beyond a socially sensitive welfare state, egalitarian full employment and some form of partnership between labor and capital, mediated by a democratic state, is possible, that is to say, a form of neo-corporatism mediated by a state which 'tilts' in favor of unions and the majority of working people. That in effect was the sum total of the programs of most social-democratic and labor parties, at their best, over the past four decades. To be sure, the degree of 'tilt' in favor of labor and egalitarianism could vary greatly from country to country and from strategic opportunity seized or missed as the case might be. The parameters of social policy initiatives of the social-democrats, however, remained within welfare *capitalism.*[1]

The current debate inside the largest and most significant social-democratic party in the world, the German SPD, represents a promising departure from this stalemate. It points to a major historical, theoretical and strategic shift which will be as significant as the Keynesian reformist program adopted in 1959 at Bad Godesberg. The new direction has been heavily influenced by three relatively new political and social factors: the collapse of the belief in and possibility of maintaining the post-war productivistic Keynesian economic management providing full employment and an expanding welfare state; the major openings towards reforms in Eastern Europe and the Soviet Union which posit the possibility of ending the Cold War consensus and the consequent political and military dependence on the United States; and the growing impact of the Greens and social movements, especially the women's and peace movements, representing significant publics which the social-democrats must reach if broad left-wing majorities are to be again possible. Summarized, the new thinking calls for an ecologically responsible, low-energy, socially sensitive strategy for full employment and greater egalitarianism. It also proposes a broadened strategy of economic opening towards the 'East' and a continued consolidation of the European Community which is to be pushed into major initiatives to deal with the growing North–South gap along the lines of the Brandt-Manley proposals. These initiatives spell out a greater Western European assertiveness in its traditional alliance with the United States. It also implies more energetic engagement around both North–South issues and with democratic reforms in Eastern Europe and the USSR.

Single countries' experiments with reflation and structural reforms of the society and economy have proved dangerous, given the interdependent and stagnant state of the European and world economy, for example in the first socialist administration in France in 1981–6. This will make the second socialist government at least more cautious. This may mean that it will do better in managing the economy. Unfortunately it will also make it more cautious in innovating social or cultural policies to make France more egalitarian and democratic. It will necessarily also make it more 'European'. While the French experiences suggest caution and the limits of what is possible for autarchic experiments with the economy, the experiences of Austria and Sweden, on the other hand, do show that single countries have a range of possible options to resist the general economic trends: to maintain full employment and an advanced welfare state in a period of world economic stagnation and in the teeth of the hostility of the international banking system. That is after all what social and economic policy of the socialist movements and social-democratic governments should be about at the very least.

The Need for Radical and Redistributive Social Policy

The point that unemployment is a socially constructed category in terms of defining who exactly is unemployed and available for work is rarely made. How many 'unemployed' would be on the rolls if there was a mandatory parental leave of eighteen months for all, as is proposed in Sweden, if every worker had a five-week vacation, as is the law in France, if the sacred cow of the 40-hour week were sharply cut to 30, if extensive adult education and re-training created a new untraditional class of students. One can add other policies which would reduce what are defined as unemployed further: what if generous and universal child allowances made parenting a socially and economically possible option for those who find that societally vital role gratifying? Why do sabbaticals only make sense for university professors? But even with less imaginative strategies, clearly, energetic social policy can reduce the numbers without doing so the way the Reagan administration has by creating poorly paid, insecure jobs.

Socialists have two powerful arguments for a radical assault on the organization of work in modern industrial society. The first is that the huge increases in productivity of the past two decades in the countries of advanced capitalism have simply not been fairly distributed. The wealthy got wealthier and the workers got unemployed, which would seem on the unfair side. Instead, a radical cut in the working day, week and life of people should be financed by a frankly redistributionist wealth tax, rather than increases in income tax which generally hit the middle and lower income groups. So the first argument for redistributive policies is that huge technological increases in productivity now make the traditional organization of work irrational and anti-social, since it forces millions on the scrap heap of unemployment while the economic capacities exist to redistribute work and income more justly.

For a radical assault on the hours, days and years of work to be anything but economic suicide, the socialist parties and the trade union movement have to make that push internationally, beginning in the unified European Common Market which is around the corner, in 1992, and pushing similar changes at least in the advanced industrial countries for a start. Such a policy would also set up new standards for the struggling labor movements in the Newly Industrialized Countries (the NICs), and of course would require more direct aid for those struggles from the labor movements in the advanced industrial world. The reasons for the internationalization of labor strategy in this regard are even more obvious than in the others, given the ability of multi-nationals to shift funds and production around the world. That is one more reason why even moderate reformist labor-based parties must put the question of control over the export of capital and jobs on the political agenda. Without such controls they are open to continual economic blackmail.

A second argument for a redistributive strategy which is gender-sensitive is that an economy has to have a *societal* purpose and, one could add, a moral justification. Surely a set of arrangements which doom an increasing proportion of the population to marginal and insecure employment so that a small minority can get wealthy in what is increasingly a 'casino economy' cannot be it. Classical capitalism worked morally with the assumption that the massive pursuit of individually rationally selfish economic goals would produce social good, and an advanced technology and economy, which in turn improves the lives of all. In short, that a rising tide would lift all boats. That is increasingly made a mockery of by an economy where billions are not made by manufacturing or inventing new processes but by moving speculative paper and gambling on real estate.

The further point is that, in this moral critique of capitalism and the market fetishism, socialists are joined by the arguments made by the Catholic Church in most of its recent statements on the economy and the dignity of labor. Fulfilling, decent, well-paid and respected work is a human right and it is a right superior to that of the right of capital to make larger profits. Clearly, when a society cannot for whatever reason provide such work, it is obliged to at least provide decent, non-humiliating, support for however long it takes to restructure the economy so that it can provide the closest equivalent of full employment that is feasible.[2]

The preoccupation with the market and productivity must also be assaulted if the increasingly urgent ecological problems are to be dealt with – the standard argument against cleaning up the environment and switching to less wasteful systems of production is cost. For that cost to be more tolerable it should not be a part of competitive advantage for one industrial country over the others. In other words, an environmental strategy cannot be autarchic any more than a radical restructuring of the work-time can be. New strategies towards work and the increased sensitivity to the overwhelming problems of environment on the only planet we inhabit require a new internationalism for the labor and socialist movement. Pollution is almost a classic example of a problem which requires a trans-national solution, as the recent ecological crises in the North Sea, the Adriatic, with acid rain, and of course the Chernobyl nuclear disaster, show. The greenhouse effect which is raising the *world's* temperature surely requires an international solution. Here one should, however, add a note of caution. Yes, an international solution, but the lion's share of pollution comes from the most industrialized countries of the world and they have a special responsibility.[3] A whole pandora's box of questions lies here – for an international solution to be at all effective would require the ability to enforce decisions. In today's world that would mean an open domination of the Third World by the more industrially advanced countries, East and West. A more modest approach could be something like the present nuclear non-proliferation agreements, which, let us note, have slowed up but not prevented determined states from obtaining the capacity to make nuclear weapons. Either way a nasty dilemma.

New Alliances Against Social and Economic Injustice

Social and economic policies are so obvious a point of convergence between the socialist movement and the Catholic Church as well as some of the major Protestant denominations that it is a strategic opening crying to be used by both sides. What is needed are not more rounds of Marxist–Christian dialogues, interesting and fruitful as those might be to some. Instead what would be of immediate use would be joint commissions and task groups directly addressing the problems of the modern economy and social policy! Anti-clerical and anti-'papist' historical biases of the classic left have prevented this from being done with the seriousness that it deserves, up to now. It is curious that some of this convergence is taking place in solidarity work in the Third World and around peace issues and the general North–South questions.

What I propose is that a major thrust be made to develop joint socialist–Christian (and other faiths when possible) social and economic programs and policies for the advanced industrial world. That is where the power is and that is where new alliances are most urgently needed. Even the moderate *official* line of the Church today is that there is a social mortgage on property and wealth, and that society and humanity are the holders of that mortgage. Therefore, in so far as the owners and administrators of property and wealth do not use their rights in a way consistent with societal rights and welfare of the workers, the mortgage should be presumably called in, that is, it should be placed under social control. That should not have to imply bureaucratic state ownership. After all, social control may take many forms. The central point is that there is no *moral* point at dispute over private property in industry and banking between social Catholicism and socialists any more.

In addition to the natural alliance between democratic socialists and the Church over major issues of social policy and the economy, clearly there are also a great many points of convergence not only on North–South issues of social justice but also on the whole question of nuclear weapons and the need to end the political and military dominance by the superpowers in the contemporary world. These are alliances waiting to be made.

While socialists are sometimes oblivious to what has been happening to the Church and the churches in terms of social and economic policy, right-wing Catholic and Protestant laypersons are up in arms against what they see as the sharp shift of the religious institutions to the left and to support for unions and social change. While the Catholic Church is most systematic in its shift on macro-economic and social questions, the larger

Protestant denominations and the more progressive sections of the other world faiths are all increasingly drawn to social and economic issues.

The larger socialist parties have always had a religious-socialist tradition and sometimes an organized religious-socialist wing within them. Clearly a great deal of consistent attention is needed to make the socialist movement hospitable to religious people with socialist views, not as useful cannon fodder but as partners in trying to reshape the language and reach of socialist politics. Human beings are not merely economic animals. There is a dimension of need and identity and a moral vision which the religions at their best do provide and to which the socialist movement is sometimes tone deaf.[4]

This is tricky terrain since, if the socialist parties are not to be totalizing parties, they can never and should never try to be the substitute for religious commitment. But the socialist movement, which is or should be a much broader category than the socialist electoral party, desperately needs those dimensions of fellowship, concern and moral thrust which the religions at their best provide.

The Narrow Utopianism of Contemporary Social-Democracy

Socialist and labor parties have by and large accepted as a day-to-day proposition that administering the capitalist state, an essentially capitalist although perhaps somewhat mixed economy with all of the necessary although unloved bureaucratic structures which accompany such a state, suitably mediated, represents the only achievable goal at this time. This mediation would include an egalitarian welfare state and the protective measures for the living standards of working people, won over the years by the labor movement.

Such a society would also have large, powerful, socially responsible and egalitarian trade unions to protect the interests of the workers. In practice this means both the classic blue-collar workers and the *new working class*, mostly concentrated in the human services sector vastly expanded during the post-war decades and which would and should continue to expand under a social-democratic welfare state.[5] Through an ever-widening set of universal entitlement and measures which also attack gender and ethnic discrimination, this society would move gradually but surely towards a more egalitarian and humane social order. A social-democratic government would also help, more or less along the lines proposed by the Brandt plan, to alleviate the North–South gap and press for a general lowering of the military tensions and armaments around the world.

In this imaginary best of all possible social-democratic worlds, the flight of capital would be made impossible through legal restrictions on the free movement of capital. Thus the use of customary and effective normal crude blackmail against unions and socialist governments would be made much more difficult. This limitation on the free movement of capital would also be reinforced through the writing into collective bargaining agreements normal rights for the unions to inspect the corporate books and records at any time and thus to be informed of any major proposed investments or other movement of larger sums of capital.

Further, presumably this would not be merely a veiled form of protectionism and autarchy but would somehow be quite consistent in ways not as yet specified, with the aim of also helping the less developed countries in the Third World. And, oh wonder of wonders, all this would be accomplished without mass mobilization *which requires a movement which is a good deal more than an electoral party* by the peaceful and solely electoral road, without great social tensions and conflict. This would be accomplished without the forces of capital stepping out of the framework of decent democratic parliamentarianism and legality. Now, in my opinion, all of this is a most touching form of utopianism, although a somewhat pedestrian utopianism, and represents an analytic error which could well become a fatal error. It represents reasonable, decent and in good part achievable aims with one enormous, 'however'. That is, that this also requires a stable, growing economy without excessive international competition which in turn permits a basically trickle-down system of income distribution. This means steady income and benefit increases for the working population without fundamentally endangering private ownership of capital and profits, and above all not touching that most sacred of all sacred cows, the basic unequal income and property distribution. That distribution has been essentially untouched in any of the advanced welfare states over decades of labor and progressive governments. That trickle-down distribution of welfare benefits and steady income growth is increasingly unachievable in contemporary economies, and it is therefore not the sudden increased beastliness of the individual capitalists within the industrial nation-states, but the greater cruelty of the international economic environment and the increased cohesion of the world economy, which make those 'soft' option less possible today.

Under conditions of sharp class confrontation the ruling classes have historically been known, alas, to be less than absolutely devoted to the democratic rules of the game and to be willing to dispense with inessential institutions like parliamentarianism, freedoms of press, speech and assembly. The labor and socialist parties are not only the firmest and most consistent defenders of the democratic state and legal and social order in bourgeois societies, which is a good and logical thing since they are the ones most responsible for those aspects of those states and societies which make them democratic, but also, unfortunately, seem quite incapable of understanding that their love and respect for democracy is not necessarily shared by their class opponents.

That set of beliefs also forms some of the reasons why the socialist parties have succeeded in boring so much of their potential publics and have allowed those past, present and potential future activists to lapse into the apathy which is so characteristic of the growing Americanization of the political and social scene in advanced industrial societies. Now, it should be clear that I, for one, have no doubt that even a limited social-democratic view is superior to the present practices in the US and Britain. It remains superior to the very modest improvements in social policies which we could expect from any future Democratic administration in the US. *The problem is that it is an exhausted policy for the socialist and labor movements in Western Europe where much more is possible, and needed.*

However, it is clear that the defense, and imaginative and intelligent expansion, of the welfare state are not minor issues. For one thing it is clearly the most broadly popular and acceptable of the current immediate socialist programs and it is where their public support is widest. It directly affects the lives of the millions who live today and sets the parameters within which one can develop policies and strategies for going further. That is, it is in only a few countries that the welfare state is secure in the same sense that, let us say, parliamentary democracy itself is secure. And therefore the first strategic point should be clear: socialists must insist that the social welfare state as a principle of organization of modern industrial capitalist democracies is a part of the democratic social contract: it is a civic right not a field for political bargaining. An attack on the welfare state is an attack on the legitimacy of the social order itself in a modern democracy. The second point, and one which is less clear, is that a socialist society, even a society moving towards socialism, must be egalitarian.

That means that socialists must favor wealth taxes which are frankly redistributionist. While not necessarily favoring equal incomes, socialists certainly want radically to reduce the range of economic and social differences and keep reducing those differences mostly through a combination of steeply progressive income taxes and massive investments in the universally available and distributed social goods – schools, child care, health, culture, housing, leisure, pensions, and the rest – thus sharply reducing the part of income which is made up by salaries. Socialists will also favor large inheritance taxes as a matter of social principle and equity so that all individuals have a right to make their own lives according to their talents, efforts and choices. Within such parameters, however, democratic socialists favor diversity and the minimum of societal interference with personal choice and liberty. Production of goods is, of course, not a personal thing but a supremely social task. Therefore, in a socialist society production will remain basically socially owned and democratically controlled and organized with whatever plurality of forms of social and private property and combinations of market, allocation by plan and indicative and macro-planning that turns out to be most consistently effective. The socialist society will assume those forms of property ownership and control which are most comfortable for the varied traditions and societies on the road to their own variants of socialism at their different paces.

This, of course, implies that a socialist society is one which is continually changing and evolving. There are two firm foundations of democratic socialist strategy for moving beyond the welfare state: genuine democracy; and popular power which in turn implies, no matter how unfashionable it may now be, the massive transfer of private control over the economic and financial system from the capitalist minorities to democratic social control. Despite all the negative experiences with centrally run and bureaucratically planned economies in state socialist politocracies, democratic social control over the economy and the financial system must unavoidably also include the use of a democratically controlled state, with a popularly controlled and responsible administration. No amount of insistence on workers' control and self-management, which will be introduced widely in any socialist-run society, can eliminate the role of democratic planning through a state.

Socialists and the Problem of Merging Vision and Strategy

There are probably many more peace activists, and many more people active in anti-racist, anti-imperialist and solidarity campaigns within the Third World liberation movements and in feminist and women's organizations struggling for basic democratic and popular rights in, for example, the left wing of the social-democratic party than in the Green party in West Germany today. This is equally true of most of the socialist parties in the rest of Western Europe. In discussing the Green challenge to the existing socialist and labor parties, we have often lost sight of the fact that there is a left wing and a right side to ecology. It can represent the struggle for popular rights and be a sign of a desirable increasing awareness that humankind cannot rape nature forever without drastic consequences for the future and life itself, or it can be the assertion of elitist and romantic nostalgia. It has both of these sides, sometimes at the same time. It is true that ecological movements and activists raise a major truth which has been ignored by the cultists of progress within the left and that is that earth is the common heritage of humankind, and that reckless exploitation of nature can endanger humanity itself.

It is a problem. Let me put it this way. I do not think a socialist society is a society that will solve all problems and in which history will stop because 'contradictions no longer exist.' On the contrary, I think that a socialist society is an unending project. I think that one can move towards a more decent social order and a more democratic order, but I do not think that history comes to a stop upon the achievement of a goal or group of goals set by a political movement. Secondly, *I think that one has to think of a society made by men and women as they are and not as they can or should become*. The problem with most of the past, explicitly self-defined, socialist projects is that they were either intentional communities built by people who wanted to live that way, authoritarian grim state socialisms or were placed in such a distant future that they became far too abstract.

As the bitter East European joke goes, 'Socialism is still on the horizon! And what is the horizon? It is the imaginary line set in the distance which retreats as you approach it.' In any case the state 'socialist' societies seem unfit for ordinary working people or even the non-political elites to live in. Damn it, socialism is supposed to be a society which would be lively, adventurous and fun for normal people, not just political activists!

The socialism which I am trying to imagine is quite simply a society in which the vast majority of the people in practice control their economic, social, and political existence. And I acknowledge that such a society would be fraught with contradictions. It would be extremely difficult democratically to convince the broad majority and the working classes that they have to share, that they have to help the Third World. On the other hand, it is not as hopeless a task as it may seem, since even today Sweden, Holland and Norway give a great deal more of their GNP towards the development of the Third World than the rest of the world does and this has happened because a mass social-democratic workers' movement decided that this was a priority and convinced its members and voters.

Therefore, it is not impossible but is merely very, very difficult, and one needs movements willing to spend considerable time and energy to do this. And these are movements which do so in societies which are still capitalist, parties and movements which do see it as a major moral and political responsibility of theirs. What I am really arguing, and what was the unstated assumption behind this, is that you cannot have socialist consciousness and politics without an organized socialist movement, without a socialist party or a conscious socialist movement. That is a major problem with Solidarity in Poland. I think it is a movement struggling for gains, most of which are socialist. The struggle for democratic rights and representation was the essential presupposition of any advance towards socialism. There are, however, goals beyond democratic rights and a civil society which need to be spelled out and consciously put forward by a movement which takes political responsibility for what it advocates.

The demand for workers' control which was raised in Poland in 1982, and earlier in 1956 and in 1951, and which emerged in all the upheavals in Eastern Europe, in East Berlin, in Pozdan in the Hungarian Revolt of 1956, was clearly socialist. Those demands which would have fleshed out the abstraction called 'workers' power' were clearly socialist and egalitarian. Most of the activists confronting the state socialist authorities were not conscious that their demands were socialist and they certainly did not use socialist terminology, since that had been profaned by the party and the politocratic state and intelligentsia. They also could not and did not think through the international implications of their demands. Mass movements are often unsophisticated about questions which are not matters of immediate strategy. After all, the workers' movement invented socialist parties a century or so ago to deal with that problem.

Many of the Solidarity activists and East European and Soviet oppositionists have been passionately pro-US and pro-Reagan because they thought that Reagan was going to be tough with the Russians and their own political bosses. Of course, the toughness was all verbal. The capitalist West and the US are and were more concerned with saving the investments of Poland's creditors than with a mass democratic trade union run by workers and therefore prone to economic 'irresponsibility'. But the East European and Soviet democratic activists were focused on their immediate oppressors and often believed, as do so many US leftists and Third World revolutionaries, that the enemy of my enemy is necessarily my friend. That is not strange, after all. Clearly, if your immediate problem is to get your own bureaucracy's Soviet-sanctioned boot off your back, you are not going to be very worried about South Korea and Chile initially. But the question is, what happens to mass popular and workers' movements when the boot is off their back?

There is no way to answer such a question with any certainty. The more sectarian as well as the more academic left in the United States, Western Europe and of course, the Third World, have tended to argue that a high degree of prosperity and security made workers in the US selfish and therefore consciously or unconsciously complicit with the policies of US imperialism. This is a very complicated issue. It has not been the most skilled workers and best-paid workers who have the most conservative unions. On the contrary, the Machinists' Union (IAM) and the Auto Workers' Union (UAW) are among the most progressive unions in the US on both domestic and international questions. However this is additionally complicated in the United States by deep-seated and ingrained racism. And unions and their members are very much a part and product of this society, despite the repeated support of the unions' leadership for civil rights struggles and progressive social policies.

On the other hand, I find it both inspiring and cheering that it is the best-paid and most unionized and most secure working classes in Europe, that is the Swedish, Norwegian and Dutch workers, who have been consistently the most willing to give the largest percentage of GNP that any country gives towards Third World governments and towards Third World development. Their parties and trade unions have been exemplary in solidarity campaigns on behalf of liberation movements and trade unions in the Third World. They are the movements which have been most receptive to measures increasing equality of the sexes and have been the most responsive to ecological demands. They have also pursued solidaristic wage pattern-bargaining, which has lowered the pay differentials between the skilled and unskilled workers. This has also tended to equalize the wages between men and women. So, one need not be all that pessimistic about the possibility of a decent socialist labor movement being able to convince people that they should act on the basis of solidarity and not only economic egotism, provided that it is taken on as a task by the movement. But that is a conscious task and policy and not something which comes naturally out of one's class location, as primitive Marxists used to sometimes think and argue.

This is why I think that one cannot have democratic socialism without a socialist movement. *There are no socialists who are not organized socialists.* The socialist project is not a question of saving one's individual soul, it is a supremely collective endeavor. Thus, one can have scholars of Marxism, but not independent Marxists; one can have scholars of socialism, but not independent, that is unorganised, socialists.

Moving Towards Some Tentative Conclusions

When dealing with something as difficult to describe in firm and coherent, let alone quantifiable, terms as the moral or spiritual crisis of an idea or a movement, one must try to be imaginative, tentative and sometimes even intuitive. This is difficult for socialist leaders and theorists to do, since the entire training and culture of the Marxist and socialist movement since its foundation has militated against that type of mental exercise. *One of the problems with contemporary socialism is that it has lost the essential dimension of imagination and subjectivity*. It is the sort of thing which was so evident and attractive in, for example, Oscar Wilde's *The Soul of Man Under Socialism* and which has been pushed aside through mechanistic and scientistic Marxism and late Fabianism.

That lost dimension is now being reintroduced into the socialist movement by contemporary socialist feminism and the social movement activists. This broader and humane side was always a part of the socialist and labor movement but, from the beginning of the century, this side of the movement has been increasingly marginalized, given the movement's preoccupation with electoralism and political power, until the 1960s when it re-emerged mostly around the student and new social movements.

Today it is painfully obvious to all informed observers that the mass socialist movements and organizations are going through a profound intellectual and moral, although not as yet organizational, crisis both because of a *radical decentering of the focus of the subject of socialist strategy and a blurring of the image of what is the goal, or, better, what should be the goals of the socialist movement*. That last has in turn been made increasingly vague because the notion of what socialism should be has not been seriously addressed, given the traditional bias in the socialist movements and Marxism itself against anything which even smacks of utopianism.[6]

To put it bluntly, the goals of socialism had to be taken on faith. The trouble is that the performance of the living, existing socialist and Communist movements and parties has made it *impossible* to demand that anything be taken on faith any more. Perhaps the loss of innocence is a sign of maturity, but that also means that it is now necessary to create a socialism for political adults. The trouble is that there is a great deal of debris which must first be removed for this process to begin.

Existing movements, trade unions and parties represent at the same time both the absolutely indispensable building blocks for the new projects in terms of the human resources and traditions of the movements and, *as they are now constituted*, a major obstacle to beginning the painful task of recreating a socialism for the twenty-first century. Whatever else it may or may not do, such a project, if taken on seriously, must perforce interfere with business as usual and the day-to-day preoccupations of maintaining a party.

Mass parties, even mass workers' parties (or, one should probably add, *especially mass workers' parties*), have little patience with efforts which do not have an obvious and clear instrumental utility. This is, of course, why the trade unions and mass workers' parties of Western Europe were caught so flat-footed by the onset of the economic crisis of the early 1970s which made it impossible to ignore any longer the fact that, as far as programmatic initiatives were concerned, the emperor was naked. The socialist and labor movement was simply unwilling to waste time on future-oriented and speculative discussions and thinking. The movement will remain in a crisis until it begins to realize that this type of a discussion is an urgent, even life-and-death priority, for any survival beyond the most immediate future.

Without a systematic effort to deal with the longer-range problems, the socialist and workers' movements will remain frozen in the present class and political stalemate in the advanced industrial societies. The entire class and political landscape of these societies is fluid and changing and, for the labor and socialist movements to do more than merely survive and follow the trends, they have to begin doing again what they used to do. They have to engage in fundamental analysis of where these societies are going, to understand the new class boundaries and formation, and address the new forms of oppression of modern urban civilizations. Socialists have to have something to say about what should be a desirable society and develop a convincing strategy about how to get there.

That is a tall order for democratic mass movements which reject the leadership of vanguards of self-selected intellectuals and professional revolutionaries. At the same time it is reasonably clear that these vanguards did not do all that well, and that, warts and all, the democratic socialist movement's sins of omission and commission left the idea of socialism far less injured than the record of the revolutionary vanguards.

At the same time, I obviously think that it is premature to bury the idea of a feasible democratic socialist movement and an imaginable democratic socialist project. Why this is so seems intuitively clear to me and it is, I firmly believe, more than hope. That is, I think there are visible contemporary political and social trends which give reasons to look forward to a revival of socialism in the advanced industrial countries of the world.

This revival will necessarily affect North America as well. Even that last bastion of the world capitalist system, the United States, will be at least indirectly affected. After all, we do live in an increasingly interdependent world. There is nothing at all inevitable about this, as there is no inevitability about human history which is ultimately made by human beings and not by any blind forces of history. It is merely a possible and more probable outcome of currently existing trends.

It is the capitalism which continues to fetishize a mythical market rationality and archaically continues to put property rights ahead of human rights which would seem to have a poor prognosis for the future. In particular, a capitalism which, in the United States, increasingly favors banking and financial manipulation over creating goods and services, would not only seem to have a poor prognosis for long-range survival but is increasingly open to fundamental moral criticism as being essentially parasitic and destructive not only from the traditional left but the Catholic Church and other great religious institutions. That the authoritarian state socialist politocracies hardly seem to have a glowing future today is taken for granted even by many of the leaders of those societies. Whatever the states ruled by Communist parties represent today, it is not the wave of the future, even a negative future of anti-utopia.

The prophetic vision, or rather nightmare, of George Orwell's *1984*, whose negative hero O'Brien foresaw a future with a boot smashing a human face forever, also seems much more improbable today than it did in the decades immediately after the war. Nothing about this is in any way inevitable, but if the great historically probable options for industrial societies still remain as I think they do, socialism or barbarism, with both the images of socialism and barbarism evolving and becoming more rounded out, it seems today that the odds are at least slightly better on a socialism which is in its essence democratic.

It is difficult today, for all the reasons which have originally blocked the founders of the modern socialist movements in the past from so doing, to imagine a socialist society. In addition to all their reasons – and they were not an absence of imagination – there are ones which they could not have imagined. We live in an era which has included the Holocaust, the rise of fascism and Nazism, and the development of a threat to the continued existence of humanity itself through nuclear weapons. In the meantime the socialist movement and vocabulary have been ravaged through the rise of Stalinism and its derivatives. Whatever else it lost, the movement certainly lost its innocence. Those who would talk about socialism today must deal with that loss.

We have no moral right to use a language which has become the instrument of political repression in much of the world without specifying how we propose to deal with that reality. It is not possible to use that vocabulary and pretend that the words and concepts have not *themselves* become slippery and ambiguous through their use by real movements and governments. We cannot pretend that Communist repression does not exist, even though that repression certainly has a more human face than it did in the days of high Stalinism. As a consequence, we have to specify, and specify very clearly indeed, how the socialism we choose to speak about differs from the varying 'currently existing socialisms'. That difference cannot be based simply on the claim that we, the democratic socialists in the advanced industrial societies, value political democracy and individual liberties and that our motives are decent and pure. The continual struggles in Eastern Europe and the Soviet Union for democratic rights are standing evidence that democracy is not a culturally specific 'western' peculiarity and hang-up.

I, for one, do not think that it is useful or even proper to question the moral stature and commitment of the individual Communist leaders and activists before they came to power. They were heroic and devoted and for the most part fought for what they understood to be socialism and democracy. As personalities, the ones whom I knew were usually less fanatical and dogmatic as individuals than the members of smaller and 'purer' Trotksyist and left socialist groups. It is precisely that which makes the subsequent evolution and fate of these people, who began as devoted and self-sacrificing militants of what they joined as a great liberating and egalitarian movement, one of the tragedies of our time.

This is merely a speculation at this point, though one which is worth raising given the sterility of theoretical innovations coming from mass organized workers' movements facing the present economic crisis. If socialism as a historical alternative is long overdue in advanced industrial western countries, this cannot be, given the almost universal 'ripeness' of advanced industrial societies, a matter explicable only by specific national conditions in each individual country. Some of the basic paradigms of Marxist theory and praxis need to be re-examined in order to explain the static class stalemate which characterizes the late capitalist countries today.

While there were good reasons not to work out detailed descriptions of an imagined socialist or Communist economic and social order in what Marx called the cloud cuckoo land, the movement and the idea have paid a heavy price for that self-denial. Not only has the absence of a utopian imagination limited the appeal of socialism all too often to 'politicals' but it has encouraged the trend in both social-democracy and Communism towards instrumental hacks as the party activists and leaders.

Those people might be as personal types a slightly better lot than the chiliastic dreamers demanding instant gratification or revolution as the case may be, but this anti-utopianism has encouraged a crackpot 'practicality' which has all but destroyed the movement. This instrumental practicality has encouraged an amoral or at best a morally indifferent preoccupation with strategy, tactics and maneuvers and has stressed discipline and organizational loyalty. In that sense the Leninists were the best Bernsteinians; it is they who made flesh his revisionist slogan of the beginning of this century, 'the final goal is nothing, the movement is everything.'

But, of course, mass social-democracy has not been much less devoted to discipline and party 'responsibility'. After all, factions are prohibited in the Austrian socialist party, while they are, and have been for quite a while, permitted in the Italian Communist party. Of course the predilection to conformity, responsibility and discipline mean one thing in a ruling party within a one-party regime and quite another in a non-ruling party in a politically competitive, pluralist environment. Granted all the limitations of that pluralism, genuine issues of social and economic power are concerned. This stress on instrumentality has done the movement great harm. It has made it unresponsive to new cultural and social stirrings, especially among the young. It has made it appear hackneyed and, yes, boring. A sense of adventure or a set of ideas and ideals worthy of devoting a lifetime to are essential for a movement. They are unnecessary for an electoral party or ruling coalition. But, if socialism is to revive and move forward, it must regain the sense that it is a movement.

Being a serious socialist in the contemporary United States has always involved carrying a double burden, sectarianism and opportunism. A weak movement has encouraged both extreme fragmentation and extreme opportunism. Thus, on one hand, the political landscape is strewn with true believing, super-Leninist, Maoisant and Trotskyist sects. The American Communist party is one of the most dogmatic and slavishly servile to everything the Soviets have done, or proposed to do, in the world. The only reservations they have shown about Soviet policies have been towards the decent initiatives by Gorbachev to dismantle the stifling Stalinist heritage and to open up debate in the Soviet Union. On the other hand, the minimal tasks which desperately need accomplishing in American society are so obvious.

That there is massive backing for advanced welfare state measures and a more democratic foreign policy in the US has been repeatedly confirmed by poll after poll. The remarkable campaign by Jesse Jackson in the 1988 presidential Democratic primaries was a spectacular demonstration of wide-scale discontent with the present social, economic and foreign policies of both major parties in the United States. Although it was many other things as well, the Jesse Jackson campaign is economically and socially clearly a social-democratic campaign which uses the language of radical populism and ethnic empowerment more familiar on the US political landscape. While the need for social-democratic politics in the

United States has existed for a very long time, a whole set of events may be making those politics more relevant for the last decade of this century. They are at the outset not even terribly complicated. Just catching up with the more advanced Western European welfare states would do for starters. The scandalous US domestic social policies have been accompanied by the most blatant state intervention into the economy for a radical redistribution of income in favor of the rich that has been recently seen in the western world. The costs of a worldwide empire have included a paranoid style of politics, where much of the defense and foreign policy was determined in terms of what would play for the most Yahoo-like public through the mass media. Merely listing the dreadful 'accomplishments' of the United States for the past decade in foreign and military policy should give pause to those who write so blithely about our era being characterized by a crisis of the welfare state or even of socialism.

A Brief Summary

For the first time since the late 1920s there are prospects, fragile and tentative to be sure, of changes in the authoritarian Soviet society which would make it more open to change and less repressive. A thorough-going crisis of the state 'socialist' systems in Eastern Europe makes them not the wave of the future but the holdovers representing increasingly unloved and unlovable regimes ruling over squalid and inefficient economies. That in itself removes an enormous burden from the modern socialist movements in the advanced capitalist countries. They are increasingly freed from the necessity to have to differentiate what they consider to be socialism from the 'currently existing socialisms'. No reasonable person is assumed to be really for setting up those systems in the West anymore – that is something to be thankful for. Surely, those two phenomena alone are grounds for at least modest cheerfulness on the part of democrats and democratic socialists. The cheer, of course, is based on two facts. The first and obvious one is the rapidly diminishing attractiveness of those authoritarian models of state socialism which made socialism such a political and moral burden in the rest of the world. Secondly, it must be a matter of no small cheer that life may get more tolerable in those societies and space may be developing for the growth of civil societies in which the struggle for democracy and socialism becomes possible.

It is also a matter of great import for the prospects for moving towards a more egalitarian and just world order that as vast an institution as the Catholic Church has shifted from being the stern anti-Communist supporter of *status quo* to a critic of the present world order. This should certainly have a major impact on both North–South relations and on the prospects of internally mobilized social and economic change in large parts of the Third World.

The emergence of greater Western European self-confidence and autonomy creates a terrain for the labor and social-democratic parties, reinvigorated by the challenge from the social movements and the Greens, to resume their development towards a more egalitarian advanced welfare state as the battlefield on which to fight for the advance towards an egalitarian, self-managed and pluralist society which, of course, is what socialism represents.

And finally, a chastened United States less wracked with the preoccupations of maintaining, by force if necessary, a world order which dooms much of humankind to poverty, exploitation and tyranny, removes one of the major if not the major barriers towards change in the Third World and hopefully, opens the terrain for political contestation in the United States about foreign and defense policy. There are many reasons why American exceptionalism, that is the fact that the United States alone among advanced industrial societies has no mass labor or socialist party, may be coming to an end. Not that, unfortunately, the growth of such a party is imminent. But at least the welfare state programs of the advanced industrial societies in Europe and Canada are becoming more evidently and urgently needed in the United States.

After all, one of the bases for the continuation of American exceptionalism was what seemed to be a uniquely prosperous and mobile American society. It is clearly no longer so and, more to the point, more and more Americans are aware of the fact that it is no longer so. The growth of a large and influential social democratic party in Canada (the New Democratic party) creates an ever-present example to the American trade unions and progressives of what can happen in the society which is most like that of the United States. The increasing interdependence of the Canadian union and the NDP make the NDP more typical of a social-democratic party. Not only is Canada in many ways more similar to the US than any other society, but of course Canadian trade unions are often sections of US trade unions, both of which will make the discussion of the Canadian experience and example difficult to avoid. Surely, some of the trade union leaders, such as they are in the United States at this time, might want to know why it is that Canadian unions are increasing in size when theirs are decreasing. They might even develop a little curiosity about a relationship between organized labor and the political party which it supports that is not treated by that party as a backdoor, illicit affair to be kept from the sight of all decent people and above all voters.

Of course, one of the problems is that much of what passes for the left in the United States has been all but completely indifferent, not only to the Canadian example, but to all examples of any conceivable, feasible and relevant contemporary socialist movements, that is, socialist movements appropriate to mass industrial democracies not facing revolutionary change. This means all present advanced industrial societies, since none faces the prospect of revolutionary change. The commitment to a more 'revolutionary' socialism, or to the various Third World romantic images of socialism, has been and remains a major obstacle to moving to that which may be actually possible in the United States. Surely, Canada is a more relevant experience for US leftists to understand and study as a possible 'model' for political activity than the many Third World countries and revolutions which have served as examples in their turn. I insist on this despite the fact that it has always been morally imperative and politically perfectly valid to attack US intervention in Nicaragua and other Third World countries and to extend solidarity and sympathy to the victims of US interventionism and aggression. There is a distinction, however, between this solidarity with victims of US imperialism and the analysis of what are appropriate programmatic and organizational forms for this society. The trouble is that mobilization in opposition to immediate crimes of interventionism and imperialism is urgent, immediate and exciting and the second represents a very long march of institution-building and the development of a program which speaks in an authentic American idiom to the universal problems which socialism tries to address. Romantic self-indulgence and revolutionary posturing simply delay getting on with what is both essential and possible: the development of a politics of a democratic and feasible socialism for advanced industrial societies. Only such a vision and politics of socialism can make a socialist movement in the advanced industrial countries work.

The many decades of long separation of democracy and socialism in both practice and theory in the Soviet Union and the Eastern European countries has been of huge and continued service to the enemies of socialism. It has created obvious moral and political absurdities, such as the present Polish situation, in which the large majority of the industrial working class is in conflict with a supposed workers' government which has turned to military repression to maintain its rule and which is trying to ram market criteria down the workers' throats, without accepting those other aspects of market-type societies in the west – free, worker-run trade unions and political pluralism. This *reality* does enormous damage to the liberating image of Marxism and socialism within the working class and democratic publics of the industrial west. As a consequence, it cannot be ignored in the name of some imaginary unity of Marxists or the left. There is no common democratic or socialist project shared by those seeking to build a mass democratic socialist movement and those who defend 'the presently existing socialist societies'.

One of the most important grounds for at least a guarded optimism in the otherwise bleak end of the 1980s is the increasing prospect of an end to the Cold War as we have known it. The Cold War has been the essential prop for the entire post-war Atlanticism and has kept the labor movements of Western Europe first divided and then subservient to the needs of a 'security' depending on maintaining close ties with the United States. However, the US has been increasingly obviously locked in confrontation and combat, not with Soviet expansionism, but with the whole idea of radical social change throughout the world. The alliance is therefore increasingly difficult to justify even for quite moderate labor movements and social-democratic parties. The growing prospect that the two superpowers are moving towards winding down the present stage of the arms race will make that alliance increasingly unnecessary in addition to being unloved.

But the cutting back of military expenditures, desirable as it is for the United States and Western Europe, urgently needed as it is by the Soviet Union and desperately overdue as it is for the Third World, is not merely an economic boon to all concerned. *It puts into question the very basis for continuing the Cold War in its present form* and thus makes it both possible and relevant to attempt to conceptualize what the political, social and economic terrain will look like in a post Cold-War era. For one thing it makes possible the removal of one of the major obstacles to a restructuring of the political policies of the more advanced industrial societies towards more just and egalitarian policies nationally and, above all, internationally. It is the Cold War which has underpinned the continuation of the present world order which dooms most of the world to poverty and squalor. It did so by treating all of the revolts against the world *status quo* within the framework of the Cold-War superpower confrontation.

This is a *world order* which is imperialist, in the classic sense of the word. It is a system no longer maintained, if it ever was, primarily through direct colonial overlordship but through the continued existence of a world market and economy which is inherently exploitative and unjust. The United States has been the mainstay of that world system since the Second World War and the instrument for legitimating that role at home and abroad has been the Cold War and the Soviet threat.

Thirdly, and we should all be grateful for this, both superpowers are increasingly less able to 'manage' their own alliances. We are moving towards a far more multi-polar world and one in which a frozen confrontation between two blocs becomes increasingly obsolete. The world becoming more multi-polar does not, of course, mean that there will not be miserable and murderous nasty local wars – the present one in the Persian Gulf representing a particularly bloody example – it merely means that a major direct confrontation of the two nuclear superpowers is less likely. *And it is useful to remember that it was the shadow of that potential superpower conflict which terrified most of humankind, since it was that war which posed the threat of total annihilation.*

The end of the Cold War is still in the future, to be sure, but it is a more obviously possible future today than that of a nuclear confrontation between the two superpowers. That is a great and important change. Surely, the memory of those years when the apocalyptic prospect of nuclear holocaust was ever-present as an imminent possibility has not been forgotten. But, if the prospect of real military confrontation recedes, the basis for a continued Western European subordination to the United States becomes far less obvious. The natural economic interests and political predilections of the two parts of the Atlantic alliance have not converged for decades.

Fear of nuclear blackmail or war kept them together, despite increasing differences. It was military muscle, not political economic or moral leadership, which gave the US its pre-eminent role within the alliance in the last two decades. It used to be said among experts on the Soviet Union that the Soviet Union was a superpower only in its military strength and potential. In all other respects it was very much a second-class economy and society. The same paradigm can increasingly now be applied to the United States.

The United States lives in what, in comparison with the advanced European industrial societies, is a fetid slum in terms of racism, social policies, housing, health, education, care for the aged, child care, crime, drugs, and all other features of social life which should be expected to accompany a high living standard in the richest country in the world. It is high time, long overdue time, to begin the long and exciting adventure to create a decent and humane egalitarian society, that has conquered racism and sexism, that will accept its responsibility to help build a just and peaceful world, to take at least the first steps towards democratic socialism. Not by any means an inevitable future, but a possible and attractive future worth living for and working for today.

Appendix 1

The Socialist Left in the US: The Varieties of Marxism and Socialism

Before delving into some of the debates and issues of American Marxism and socialism, it would be useful briefly to describe the organizations and parties which have some relationship to Marxist theory. I use the term 'relationship,' although it should be clear that, for some of these parties, the claim is that they are nothing more nor less than the living embodiment of Marxist theory in day-to-day practice. The less significant the sect, the more ferocious its claims to Marxist orthodoxy. Roughly, one can divide the organization and party scene into the following groupings: Maoists and post-Maoists; the Communist party USA (CP-USA) and a few relatively orthodox split-offs; the Trotskyist groupings and parties; the post-Leninist groups; and the democratic socialists, of whom at least a substantial part claim to be in the tradition and spirit of contemporary Marxism.

The Maoists and post-Maoists present a bewildering range of fissioning sects at this point, some of which do manage to publish substantial journals for given periods of time. The realities of the reforms in China seem to doom most of these to become a colorful part of the history of American Marxist sects. One of their contributions to the American left scene is the banal, and historically wrong, slogan which they have introduced into countless demonstrations, 'The people united shall never be defeated.' Alas, would that it were true. There has always been a link between Maoism in the US with the more anti-theoretical and anti-intellectual forms of populism and Third Worldism. Several of the groups which existed vaguely a decade ago have evolved towards a reformist strategy in the US combined with a more sympathetic view of the Soviet Union and East European states. A good example would be the old Communist Workers' party. They are now working within the Jackson wing of the Democratic party.

The Communist party USA has been remarkable in its pro-Moscow orthodoxy, almost unique among parties in the advanced industrial world in that respect, and has retained a number of mostly ageing theorists who, although not particularly original, have contributed some substantial historical work on American labor and Black history. Only the liberalization and moves towards democratization of the Soviet Union have provoked the CP-USA to show some reservations about Soviet policies. They show deep reservations about Gorbachev's political and economic reforms, and find the old Stalinist heritage more congenial. The journal most open to them, though not at all a party journal, is *Science and Society*. The most fruitful developments in American Communist theories about the society in which the party sought to act have, however, been consigned to the memory-hole and are unmentionable. I refer there to the works of Earl Browder, who was by far the most original thinker the American Communist party produced and who ran the party during its years of greatest success from the early 1930s to the end of the Second World War. He was certainly the most interesting theorist of 'American exceptionalism' who has worked within the Communist movement.

Most American Communists in the early and mid-1920s belonged to what were called the foreign language organizations of the party, and the English speakers – a concept defined most generously – were a only small minority, roughly 15 per cent of the membership. Given that fact, and the enormous respect which the Bolshevik revolution inspired among Communists the world over, it is not strange that the American Communist party unquestioningly accepted the leadership of the Communist International. On its instructions, the party adopted, as a guide to its tactical and strategic work, the theory of the existence of a repressed Black nation which should be allowed and encouraged to secede and form a separate Black state in the south. This theory, which has reappeared from time to time as the party line changed, and is still current among some Afro-American nationalists, did an enormous amount of damage to the practical work of the party, while adding nothing to its understanding of the American political scene. Therefore it is not necessarily a bad thing that Marxism and socialist theories have a distinct fate independent from the Marxist and socialist parties and organizations in the US today.

The Trotskyists have had a disproportionate influence on leftist intellectuals in the US, in part because of the relative weakness of Communist theorists. However, although Trotsky himself had written intelligently, if wrong-headedly, about the US in the late 1930s, most of the Trotskyist theoretical energies were focused for years on the so-called Russian question, or the class character of the Soviet Union and the societies within its orbit. The two major theories were the orthodox Trotskyist theory that the Soviet Union was a degenerated workers' state where a gangster-like bureaucracy rules over a society based on the gains of the socialist revolution in October 1917. In consequence, a *political change* is necessary, but not a *social revolution*. The second major Trotskyist theory is that the Soviet Union is a new, exploitative class society best defined as bureaucratic collectivist, where the bureaucracy has evolved into a new class which exploits the working class through its monopoly of both state and economic power. While the debates may seem arcane today, the consequences for the left were, of course, not. In any case, while the Trotskyist groups have their party journals, the influence of Trotskyism now somewhat diluted is felt far more through broader journals of Marxist opinion including the *New Left Review*, published in England, and a number of independent journals such as *Against the Current*, etc.

The post-Leninist groups cover a catch-all category for groupings which have come through the new left and defined themselves as Marxist or Marxist-Leninists. They are generally of no intellectual or theoretical interest whatsoever. The main theoretical point (if one can call it that) of these groupings seems to be a relentless call for immediate armed revolutionary struggle in the United States in the name of the oppressed of the world and, most specifically, such marginal groups as the Black Liberation Army, the Puerto Rican FLAN, and others. What is perhaps interesting about those entirely middle-class groupings for a future anthropologist of Marxist movements is the coarsening of language and theory which they seem to have gone through in developing what can best be described as machine translations of slogans from obscure languages. They also serve to confirm the stereotypes which more primitive members of police forces have of what leftists should be like.

Democratic socialists have a unified if small national organization, the Democratic Socialists of America (DSA), which probably unites the large majority of those democratic socialists and neo-Marxists who still work in the living tradition of Marx. The organization itself has no theoretical journal, deliberately, since it encourages groups of members to produce independent publications which deal with matters of socialist theory and practice. Since a range of views are found within the DSA, its members and theorists write for a range of publications. The most important ones are: *Dissent*, which originated in the early 1950s from a group of former 'Trotskyisant' intellectuals, which today publishes a wide range of views; the *Socialist Review*, which is a publication of a younger grouping of democratic socialists on the West Coast; on matters of social policy, journals such as *Social Policy* have a heavy input from DSA members, as does the weekly paper, *In These Times*. Others theoretically inclined write for *New Politics*.

A number of prominent publicists, political journalists and social scientists with a national if not international reputation are members of this organization, which is in consequence somewhat top heavy. There are several other publications which deal substantively with matters of Marxist or socialist theory, such as *Politics & Society* and *Kapital State*, which are more distant from any organization. Two very serious publications, *Social Texts* and *Telos*, which deal with matters of Marxist theory, are influenced by the democratic socialists. In addition to all of the above, the *Monthly Review* is probably the widest-read Marxist journal in the country and well known abroad, and it keeps a firm independence from all Marxist organizations. The *Monthly Review* is not only a vehicle for very serious discussion of the economy and of the international scene, but also has what is in many ways the best independent Marxist publishing house in the English-speaking world.

Clearly this thumbnail sketch is not meant to be exhaustive, because the sheer number of journals and organizations can be both bewildering and depressing. It might, therefore, be as well to mention several other groupings which do not neatly fall into the above pattern. There is a small, predominantly Black Communist organization, the Communist Labor party, which combines considerable originality in its discussions of the contemporary American scene with an unfortunate nostalgia for Joseph Stalin. Another grouping of some interest, at the moment fragmented, is Solidarity, who represent a rather attractive younger group of revolutionary democratic socialists. This group, for all its attractiveness, is not particularly theoretically distinct from the more left-wing members of the DSA. Its members write for *Against the Current* and are active in solidarity work with Central America and support work with rank-and-file groups of unionists stuggling against their bureaucracies. The rise of Jesse Jackson and his 'Rainbow Coalition' as a force within the Democratic party poses a major problem for Solidarity, since they are adamant in their opposition to working within the Democratic party. That is a serious problem, since almost all the forces they seek to influence express themselves electorally through that party and participate in the internal battles in that party's primaries.

That has always been the problem for the left in the United States, how to relate to the two-party system which seems built into the US political structure. There are only a few possible reactions to that reality: either you work within the structure of a major party, presumably to realign it towards a labor or social-democratic type formation, you try to build an independent third party, or you reject electoral politics and rely on mobilizing mass movements outside the formal political system. The mass mobilization can also be a part of strategy of working within the Democratic party *or* of working for an independent third party or of rejecting electoral politics entirely. Those have been the alternatives with which generations of American leftists have wrestled for over a hundred years.

Appendix 2

A Historical Note on the Yugoslav Revolution

Given the present uniqueness of Yugoslavia among countries run by Communist parties, it is useful to examine how it evolved to where it is today. The Yugoslav Communist party developed into a mass party with a substantial membership of over 150,000 members during the bitter civil war and revolutionary struggle against the Axis occupiers and their satellites, as well as against their class enemies, during the Second World War.[1] The Yugoslav party took power essentially though its own efforts and armed struggle. It owed relatively little to direct Soviet aid which came very late in the war. To be sure, the victory of the Yugoslav Communists would not have been possible without the immense contribution that the Soviet Union had made on the main front against Nazi Germany, which was without a doubt the Russian front. The Soviets also helped in the liberation of Belgrade.

However, it remains a fact that the Yugoslav Communists regarded the liberation of Yugoslavia as primarily the result of their own enormous and costly efforts. One consequence was that the party cadres had a great deal of self-confidence, having defeated both the internal class enemy and the foreign occupier, more or less on their own. Immediately after the Second World War, the Yugoslav Communist leadership regarded themselves as the most orthodox, authentic and 'hard' of the East European Communist organizations. They made nuisances of themselves at international Communist gatherings by attacking the French and Italian Communist parties for their 'softness' in not having taken power at the close of the war.[2]

This specific character of the Yugoslav Communists guaranteed that there would be trouble in their relationships with both the Soviet Union and the Soviet East European allies and dependencies. The Yugoslavs viewed themselves as *allies* of the Soviet Union and a valuable and important part of the world Communist movement. Since the Soviets, in those years of high Stalinism, had no room in their alliance for a partner, even a junior partner, the break was inevitable. But it was the 'hardness' of the Yugoslav party and its leadership which made that break *possible*.

The fact that they did survive an excommunication from the world Communist movement is mainly thanks to the ruthlessness of the Yugoslav political police and the Yugoslav party in dealing with massive and natural pro-Soviet and pro-Stalin sentiment among the older cadres of the party, the army and the police. Reliable statistics on persons who were purged as 'Cominformists', or pro-Stalinists, real and imagined, are still a subject of acrimonious debate in Yugoslavia. However, those who did time in the notorious Goli Otok concentration camp in the early 1950s do not number more than 10,000. A number of these had been very high functionaries in the army, police and government.

The subject of the camps and the purge of the Cominformists, however, remains a trauma because it is often assumed, with some grounds, that many 'Cominformists' were mistaken idealists, and in any case were deserving party cadres. Some were jailed completely by mistake. It is undisputable that the regime in the camps was brutal, molded on the model of the Stalinist camps, and that the prisoners were forced to 'admit their errors' while in the camps.

The whole episode was characteristic of the deep Stalinist heritage of the party and police at the time of the break with the Cominform. That makes the later political and cultural developments of the Yugoslav system all the more remarkable. It also explains several troubling anomalies about the Yugoslav League of Communists and the special role of Marshal Tito during his lifetime. Throughout Tito's life, and to a lesser extent after his death, there has been a deep ambivalence about the Soviet bloc and the heritage of the Communist International. This was less visible during the days of sharp confrontation between the Cominform and Yugoslavia, in the early 1950s, when the official Yugoslav line continued describing the Soviet Union as 'state capitalist', that is, a non-socialist exploitative society, and when the Yugoslavs entered into a defensive military alliance with Greece and Turkey, both of which were NATO members. However, after Khruschev's fence-building trip to Yugoslavia, despite zigs and zags in Yugoslav-Soviet relations, both the Balkan Pact and the insistence on the non-socialist character of Soviet society were quietly dropped. Tito even made several speeches which seemed to tilt towards the Soviet side in the Cold War. For example, when the Soviets began nuclear tests again, while negotiating a nuclear agreement with the United States in 1961, Tito, in a speech in Algiers, said that one had to 'understand' the Soviets. However, this was not a consistent policy and the Yugoslavs maintained an independent policy, particularly within the non-aligned movement. The

Comintern inheritance was seen more clearly in the great reluctance even to consider models which were anything but variations of a one-party model and to resist any formal democratization of internal party life, such as the legalizations of tendencies or factions based on political programs rather than local republic leaderships. That part of the heritage cost the Yugoslavs dearly by guaranteeing the development of the present situation of a League of Communists divided along lines of nationalism and regional loyalties, rather than by cross-cutting political alignments which would bind the country together.

Notes and References

Chapter 1

1. An embarrassment of riches exists for any bibliography on socialism. I will not overload this book but will suggest works which deal with the *crisis*, or what I understand to be the crisis of socialism. Each chapter will have its own brief bibliographic footnote.

A very good collection of classic and contemporary texts on socialism, with a fine introduction, is in Irving Howe, *The Essential Works of Socialism*, New Haven, Yale University Press, 1986. More theoretically substantial is Lezek Kolakowski, *The Main Currents of Marxism*, vols 1, 2 and 3, New York, Oxford University Press, 1981.

Important books on the crises of socialism include: Paul Sweezy, *Post-Revolutionary Society*, New York, Monthly Review Press, 1980; Michael Harrington, *The Twilight of Capitalism*, New York, Simon & Schuster, 1976; also his *Socialism*, New York, Bantam, 1986; and his *The Next Left*, Henry Holt, 1986; Michael Rustin, *For a Pluralist Socialism*, London, Verso, 1985; Gavin Kitching, *Rethinking Socialism*, London, Methuen, 1983; Christine Buci Gluckman, *Gramsci and the State* (English edition) London, Lawrence & Wishart, 1980; Michel Beaud, *Le Socialisme a l'epreuve de l'histoire*, Paris, Seuil, 1982. *Democracy and Civil Society* by John Keane, London, Verso, 1988, and the collection edited by John Keane, *The Civil Society and the State*, London, Verso, 1988; plus the round table edited by Erik Hobsbawm, *The Forward March of Labour Halted?* London, Verso, 1981 center in on the questions of the crisis of the socialist movements and ideas. To these distinguished works add my *Democratic Socialism: the Mass Left in Advanced Industrial Societies*, Bogdan Denitch (ed.), Montclair, Allenheld & Osmun, 1981. More works will be cited in the following chapters. These are only the more recent and general works dealing with the crisis of socialism, mostly in advanced industrial societies. The works on the Third World, the social movements and race and gender issues appear in the appropriate chapters, as do the more detailed references to West European socialist, Communist and social-democratic parties and movements.

2. Lost innocence is a recurrent phenomenon and theme in the histories of the socialist movement. Even more it is a theme in the personal histories of radicals and ex-radicals as well as of socialists and ex-socialists. Above all, it is characteristic of the Communist movement which has left untold debris in the form of bitter ex-leftists behind. My own loss of innocence took place in the mid-1940s, when I first joined the socialist movement and began reading novels and memoirs. If I had to guess I would say it was the novels of Arthur Koestler, George Orwell and Manes Sperber that gave a touch of human authenticity to the polemical and documentary books by Leon Trotsky, Borkenau and Ruth Fischer.

What has never ceased to astonish me is how often the wheel has had to be rediscovered. That is, how wave after wave of young activists and intellectuals would come to the reluctant conclusion that there is no 'land of genuine socialism' and that talk of Gulags and political repression are not anti-Soviet, or anti-Cuban or anti-Mao or anti-socialist slander. The 'New Philosophers' who emerged out of the French new left and Maoism used the already somewhat worn-out truths about Soviet repression and authoritarianism to justify their move to the political right.

3. For a more detailed discussion of 'politocracy' see Chapters 2 and 3. The term was first popularized by Yugoslav socialist theorists like Svetozar Stojanovic in trying to describe the post-revolutionary societies of Eastern Europe and the Soviet Union.

4. The Yugoslav Communist party, re-named the League of Communists of Yugoslavia, or the LCY, in 1952 is important in discussions about the crises of socialism, since it has been independent of the Soviet Union longer than any other ruling, or non-ruling, Communist party. It has also been more open to fundamental debates about the nature of socialism, workers' self-management,the role of the party, decentralization and multi-ethnicity than any other Communist and most socialist parties. It is therefore important out of all proportion to its size and certainly does not deserve its present relative obscurity which is the result of its current grim economic, political and ethnic problems. I will use the term party or LCY more or less interchangeably throughout the book, as it is used in Yugoslavia. See Chapter 3 for a detailed discussion.

5. These are excerpts from a very long poem which *30 years ago* described a mood which was amazingly like the current mood in Poland and Eastern Europe. The only difference is that far fewer intellectuals and workers will agree even sarcastically that 'socialism is a good thing' today.

6. One has to watch out for jargon, but praxis is a term sufficiently specific and central to Marxism to need to be used. It basically means the constant interaction of theory and practice and the mutual self-correction and criticism of theory and practice. The problem is that Marx was not only German but did write in a philosophical Hegelian language which often translates with considerable difficulty into more sensible languages like English and French. Unlike the present generation of academic Marxists, I will try to avoid Hegelianizing English.

7. Whenever I feel pessimistic about the role and importance of the left in the United States, and that is all too often, I do remind myself and others that the weak American left did far more to confront its own government's imperialist adventures in the cases of Vietnam and Central America than the far more massive, orthodox and organized Communist left in France did during the wars in Indo-China and Algeria. There *is* something to the radical tradition of the United States that is too often forgotten.

8. The POUM, the Workers' Party of Marxist Unity in Catalonia, was an independent Marxist organization fighting on the side of the Spanish Republic against Franco's fascist revolt. Since they were critical of the blood purges which were going on at that time in the Soviet Union, the Communists and their sympathizers denounced them as Trotskyites, wreckers and 'objective' agents of fascism. They were, of course, none of those things. They were decent, independent, somewhat sectarian, left-socialists and as such they had all our retroactive sympathies. They were made familiar to a wider public in

George Orwell's wonderful personal memoir of the Spanish Civil War, *Homage to Catalonia* (many editions).

Chapter 2

1. This is a minimal bibliography on the crisis of the East European and Soviet systems and does not pretend to be a general description. A reasonable start would be with Leon Trotsky, *The Revolution Betrayed,* New York, Pioneer Publishers 1945; Isaac Deutscher's biography of Trotsky, or at least its first two volumes, *The Prophet Armed* and *The Prophet Disarmed,* New York, Oxford University Press, 1954. This could be followed by *The Great Purge Trial,* edited by Robert C. Tucker and Stephen F. Cohen, New York, Grosset & Dunlap, 1965. I would also recommend Paul Sweezy, *Post-Revolutionary Society*, New York, Monthly Review Press, 1976.

A general coverage of the world Communist movement is found in Fernando Claudin, *The Communist Movement: From the Comintern to the Cominform* (2 vols.), New York, Monthly Review Press, 1975. Max Schactman *The Bureaucratic Revolution: the Rise of the Stalinist State*, New York, Donald Press, 1962, is an important, hard-to-find, work.

For international affairs two books are good starting points, George Kennan, *Russia and the West under Lenin and Stalin*, Boston, Little Brown, 1960, and *The Domestic Context of Soviet Foreign Policy,* edited by Seweryn Bialer, Boulder, Westview Press, 1981.

To this should be added: *Blue Collar Workers in Eastern Europe*, edited by Charles Gati and Jan Triska, London, George Allen & Unwin, 1981; *Socialism, Politics and Equality*, by Walter D. Connor, New York, Columbia University Press, 1979; *Social Structures of Eastern Europe*, edited by Bernard Lewis Faber, New York, Praeger Publishers, 1976; and Mark Rakovski (pseudonym), *Towards an East European Marxism,* New York, St Martin's Press, 1978. There are, of course, a large number of other deserving books.

2. This is not because I regard these regimes as any variant of socialism, but because they have become for the vast majority of people the paradigm of what is wrong with socialism. All basic economic reforms of these systems must have as their essential precondition the destruction of the present stubbornly entrenched privileges which are primarily those of the politocracy and their families and allies.

Any discussion of the crisis of the East European, Soviet and other variants of state socialism must necessarily begin with the question of their political and economic similarities, in other words, their common character, if there is one. I believe that the best way to describe these systems is as *politocracies*, that is *systems in which the political elites, ruling through the single Communist party, control the state and the economy and through those society*.

This is not the place to develop an extensive rationale for my present preference for the term 'politocracy' to describe societies diversely known as state socialist or currently existing socialisms or authoritarian socialism. I borrow the term with considerable gratitude from the well-known Yugoslav political theorist, Svetozar Stojanovic. I think it is superior in explanatory power to the other independent Marxist (generally Trotskyist-influenced) attempts to describe the societies which emerged after the isolation of the Bolshevik revolution and the counter-revolution led by Stalin in 1929/30 created an unprecedented new social and political order.

The terms used among independent Marxists had ranged from degenerated workers' state (early Leon Trotsky) to state capitalism, bureaucratic collectivism, etc. My own early preference was for those terms which indicate that these were new social formations, radically different from either the previous authoritarian capitalist states or from workers' states. To put it as directly as possible, whoever ruled, whatever class was in power, it seemed clear to me that it was not the working class. The new political elites, having emerged out of the revolutionary socialist tradition, continue to use and manipulate, albeit ever more routinely, the language and symbols of a common socialist tradition.

Both the realities and fantasies about these systems, which defined themselves and were accepted widely as some variants of socialism, were something for which some kind of intellectual and above all moral responsibility was laid at the door of socialism itself, as a project and a world view. This is in no small part because a number of western Marxists or socialists do continue to refer, to this very day, to these societies as socialist, although usually with a modifier such as the euphemism 'currently existing socialism' or simply as 'state socialism'. What I am implying is that these societies have similar class structures and an essentially similar class in power. However, I now believe that politocracies have a wide range of possible political forms with more or less autonomy for independent organizations and trade unions and more or less political rights and individual liberty. Just like bourgeois societies!

3. The gap is even more depressing if comparisons are made with the Asian rim 'tigers'. Even if one argues that, all things considered, including the state of the world economy, the economic performance of these regimes is not all that terrible, but merely humdrum, that will not do. The whole point of these regimes was that they provided very high growth at a certain political price. The price has long been paid.

4. And of course the Communist parties are held responsible for the horrible economic and cultural mess of these societies. As Walesa said on 6 February 1989, at the opening of the negotiations for the recognition of Solidarity by the Polish government. '. . . the country is ruined, but it was not some elves that ruined it, but a system of exercising authority, that detaches citizens from their rights and wastes the fruits of their labor' (quoted in the *New York Times*, 7 February 1989).

5. While I do not believe that this claim is taken seriously by either the workers or the elite, it may be taken seriously by younger officers and above all by the conscript soldiers who are themselves most likely blue-collar workers. Therefore massive clashes between workers and the forces of order are devoutly to be avoided.

6. The discrimination against the children of the old educated and middle classes in admission to the universities, which was quite severe in the first years of Communist rule, dwindled over the years in most of the East European states.

7. That was how Egypt, Serbia, Bulgaria and Romania gradually gained their independence from the Turkish empire. The problem with this image is that those states gained their full independence gradually. However, at key moments they *also fought* their Turkish masters, usually with foreign military and diplomatic support. That makes Ottomanization at best a very clumsy metaphor.

8. For that matter, the current Soviet advice to their friends throughout the Third World is to make whatever terms with the world market possible, that is, with

the 'currently existing' world market, controlled by capitalist powers and norms. This is an obvious massive ideological retreat in the face of the stubborn reality of the failure of the Third World models which had adopted features of the Soviet economic or political model.

9. For that matter, non-working-class autonomous social movements are most powerful and effective in those societies which have powerful working-class socialist parties and movements and traditions.

Chapter 3

1. An earlier version of this chapter appeared in *Praxis International*, Summer 1989; a shorter version appeared in *Dissent*, Winter 1989. A more extensive work including some of the material enclosed here is *The Crisis of Yugoslav Socialism* (forthcoming). For general background consult: Barbara Jelavich, *A History of the Balkans*, vol. 2, Cambridge, Cambridge University Press, 1983; Vladimir Dedijer et al., *History of Yugoslavia*, New York, 1974; George Hoffman and Fred Warner Neal, *Yugoslavia: and the New Communism*, New York, Twentieth Century Fund, 1962; and Jozo Tomasevic, *War and Revolution in Yugoslavia*, vol. 1 and 2, Stanford, Stanford University Press, 1975. For a description of post-revolutionary Yugoslavia, see Branko Horvat, *An Essay on Yugoslav Society*, Armonk N.Y. Sharpe, 1969; Bogdan Denitch, *The Legitimation of a Revolution: The Yugoslav Case*, New Haven, Yale University Press, 1976; Ellen Turkish Comisso, *Workers' Control Under Plan and Market*, New Haven, Yale University Press, 1979. Other relevant works are *Yugoslavia in the 80s*, edited by Pedro Ramet, Boulder, Westview Press, 1985, and Stephen Burg, *Conflict and Cohesion in Socialist Yugoslavia*, Princeton, Princeton University Press, 1983.

2. Svetozar Stojanovic is a former editor of the original Yugoslav edition of *Praxis*, the most influential humanist Marxist journal in Yugoslavia in the late 1960s and early 1970s. It sponsored the Korcula Summer School, an amazing gathering of socialist, Communist and dissident Marxist theorists from around the world. It included major future dissident figures from Eastern Europe and theorists of the revival of a new left in the west like Marcuse and Serge Mallet. The journal was effectively prevented from publishing in 1973, but its former editors remained a major intellectual force in Yugoslavia particularly in philosophy and sociology. Stojanovic is author of several books which have been translated into English, for example, *Between Ideals and Reality: A Critique of Socialism and its Future*, New York, Oxford University Press, 1973. The best English language reference to *Praxis* and the Praxis school is in *Praxis: Marxist Criticism and Dissent in Socialist Yugoslavia*, by Gerson Sher, Bloomington, Indiana University Press, 1977.

3. In addition to the scarce and hard-to-obtain foreign language editions of *Praxis*, the best sources on this important group are: *Praxis*, by Gerson S. Sher, Bloomington, Indiana University Press, 1977; *The Rise and Fall of Socialist Humanism*, by Mihailo Markovic and R.S. Cohen, Nottingham, Spokesman Books, 1975; and *Marxist Humanism and Praxis*, edited by Gerson S. Sher, Buffalo, Prometheus Books, 1978.

4. Yugoslav census statistics are reasonably accurate. In 1981 (the last census) the national breakdown of the population was as follows:

	Population (1000)	percentage
Serbs	8,140	36.3
Croats	4,428	19.8
Moslems*	2,000	8.9 (mostly Bosnian slavs)
Slovenes	1,754	7.8
Albanians	1,730	7.7
Macedonians	1,340	6.0
'Yugoslavs'	1,219	5.4
Montenegrins	579	2.6
Hungarians	427	1.9

*Muslims in this case are 'Muslim as an ethnic group' which means slavs who are Muslim and speak Serbo-Croatian, the category as used in the census excluded Muslims who are Albanian, Turkish or Gypsy. No other group came to more than 1% of the population

5. There is a wide interest in civil society and the 'legal' state. John Keane's collection, *Civil Society and the State,* London, Verso, 1988, has been cited in current political debates by, among others, Dr Stipe Suvar, the President of the Collective Presidency of the LCY. The basic contribution of John Keane is in his *Democracy and Civil Society,* London, Verso, 1988. Also see *Class and Civil Society: the Limits of Marxian Critical Theory,* Jean Cohen, Amherst, University of Massachusetts Press, 1982.

6. *Nomenklatura* is a shorthand for the official (formal or informal) lists of approved candidates for important posts and jobs in the society. This is the concrete way that the party exercises its authority and has been responsible for the career paths of thousands of incompetent but loyal League activists who keep rotating from job to job in an ever-ascending spiral. Cultural life, professional associations, many faculties, a few journals and of course the informal cooperative and the small private sector are outside the *nomenklatura.* These areas are therefore suspect to those party cadres who have learned nothing and forgotten nothing in the decades since the break with the Soviet bloc.

7. For that matter *both* the 'market' and the 'plan' were political inventions, myths within politocratic regimes. The dominant myth of the last decades of this century in Eastern Europe and the Soviet Union is not that of the plan, which was a fiction, since commands are not a plan, but that of the supposedly objective and impartial market. The 'market' under conditions of one-party monopoly of power and without independent unions is also a myth, since the decisions on allocation of resources will continue to be made politically as will, of course, the distribution of the results of improved production.

8. This represents a problem for many radical governments in the Third World. For example, the revolutionary Nicaraguan government had difficulty in accepting the separate ethnic identity of their Caribbean coast, or the Ethiopian government's bitter war on the Eriterean national independence movement. The fate of the Kurds remains a moral scandal. Multi-ethnicity is not a Euro-centric problem, nor will it go away with the abolition of capitalism and/or imperialism. See my essay 'The

Dilemma of the Dominant Ethnic Group', in *Socialism in the World*, vol. 65, 1988, Belgrade.

9. The republics and provinces are uneven in size and not at all homogeneous in national make-up. Census figures from 1981 are indicative:

Country	Pop. (1000)	Nationality. (in percentages rounded out)
Bosnia-Hercegovina	3,941	Moslem, 40; Serb, 37; Croat, 20; Other, 3
Montenegro	565	Montenegrin, 67; Moslem, 13; Serb, 8; Albanian, 7; Other, 6
Croatia	4,391	Croat, 79; Serb, 14; Other, 7
Macedonia	1,808	Macedonian, 69; Albanian, 18; Turk, 6; Other, 7
Slovenia	1,838	Slovene, 92: Croat, 3; Other, 5
Serbia (+ provinces)	9,005	
Serbia, alone	5,491	Serb, 89; Moslem, 3; Albanian, 3; Other, 6
Vojvodina province	1,969	Serb, 56; Hungarian, 22; Croat, 7; Other, 14
Kosovo province	1,545	Albanian, 85; Serb, 9; Montenegrin, 2; Other, 4

The ethnic breakdown shows just how hard it is to achieve any 'fair' distribution of federal posts by national criteria. In practice *two* criteria are used: that of the federal unit irrespective of size, and within the units, that of nationality.

10. There is a general consensus among Yugoslav political scientists and theorists that the political system had become almost impossibly complicated in an attempt to create an open society which at the same time assured the continued party monopoly. Kardel, the major theorist and author of the present Constitution, had turned to Proudhon and his ideas about the free association of communes and associated labor. The idea was at all cost to avoid even the hint of multi-party pluralism, which was seen as an archaic and more backward form of democracy than the Yugoslav form which supposedly has broad elements of direct democracy and is evolving to a non-party system. For more detailed discussion see, April Carter, *Democratic Reform in Yugoslavia*, London, 1983; Stephen Burg, *Conflict and Cohesion in Socialist Yugoslavia,* Princeton, Princeton University Press, 1983; and 'Party Monopoly and Political Change,' by Wolfgang Hopken, in *Yugoslavia in the 80s*, edited by Pedro Ramet, Boulder, Westview Press, 1985.

11. Intolerable pressure includes assaults and rape, more often threats of assault and rape, against what is an increasingly small and aged minority. A general breakdown of law and order in Kosovo seems to have been a permanent feature of that province's life. That breakdown affects the Albanians in Kosovo, and there has been a massive migration of Albanians from that underdeveloped province as well.

12. Albanians are a majority in Kosovo but a minority in 'Serbia as a whole', that is a Serbia including the provinces. Thus a solution to Kosovo's nationalist

confrontation will either offend the minority within Kosovo, that is the Serbs and Montenegrins, or, as seems the direction of the present policy, alienate the Albanians. Serbian national populists consider the Albanians as a minority within a newly 'united' Serbia including the provinces.

13. That is one of the reasons why so many work as unskilled manual workers or run small pastry shops outside of Kosovo, and why such a high ratio of administrative workers to others is found in Kosovo. Work *had* to be found for at least some of the graduates of the vast Pristina University. Unemployment in Kosovo is catastrophic – the rate of employment in Kosovo is 42 per cent of the national average!

14. When the official Serbian political establishment and press speak of the 'will of the people' expressed by mass demonstrations and meetings, they clearly mean the Serbian and Montenegrin people. Albanian demonstrations are simply prohibited. Half a million Albanians had some contact with the police during the last eight years, that is, were arrested, had their identities checked, etc.!

15. Corporatism and neo-corporatism are concepts which have been in vogue for the last two decades, that is, during the period when hopes in socialist transformations have declined among both western and eastern political theorists. Probably the most influential works on neo-corporatism are, Phillipe Schmitter, 'Still the Century of Corporatism?', *Review of Politics*, January 1974, and Schmitter and Gerhard Lehmbruch (eds), *Trends Towards Corporatist Intermediation*, Beverly Hills, Sage, 1979.

16. Schmitter and Lehmbruch (eds), *Trends Toward Corporatist Intermediation*, Beverly Hills, Sage, 1979, p. 119.

Chapter 4

1. A brief list of essential readings on this topic is difficult to propose. For one thing it would have to exclude many of the classic works by Marx, Lenin, Trotsky, Bukharin and Luxemburg. However, with all the caveats, I believe the following works to be both accessible and essential: George Lichteim, *Imperialism*, New York, Praeger, 1971; Michael Harrington, *The Vast Majority*, New York, Simon & Schuster, 1977; a collection edited by Richard Fagen, Carmen Diana Deere and Jose Luis Coraggio, *Transition and Development: The Problems of Third World Socialism*, New York, Monthly Review Press 1986; Wolfgang Mommsen, *Theories of Imperialism*, New York, Random House (English edition, 1980). James H. Mittleman, *Out from Underdevelopment*, New York, St Martin's Press, 1988, is an excellent polemical intervention into the whole issue.

For more specialized readers three background volumes are heavy but necessary going: Immanuel Wallerstein, *The Modern World System*, New York, Academic Press, 1974; Arghiri Emmanuel, *Unequal Exchange*, New York, Monthly Review Press, 1972; Marina and David Ottaway, *Afro-Communism*, New York, Holmes & Meier (particularly the second edition, 1986).

2. A good example of this is in the collection *Class, State and Power in the Third World*, edited by James Petras, Montclair, N. J., Allenheld & Osmun, 1981. This volume is in my terms 'Third Worldist', whereas the equally anti-imperialist work by Noam Chomsky, *Turning the Tide: U.S. Intervention in Latin America and the Struggle for Peace*, Boston, South End Press, and London, Pluto Press, 1985, is

free of that taint, that is, Chomsky does not gild the lily of Third World regimes or activists in order to attack the US.

3. Let it be noted that many 'non-aligned' countries are very aligned indeed, if not allied, with one of the two superpowers. Cuba is only the most obvious example.

4. See Seweryn Bialer (ed.), *The Domestic Content of Soviet Foreign Policy*, New York, Praeger, 1971; Anatoly Yanov, *Detente after Brezhnev*, Berkeley, Institute of International Studies, University of California, 1977; 'Soviet Global Power and the Correlation of Forces', by Vernon Aspaturian, in *Problems of Communism*, May/June 1980, vol. XXIX; 'The Other Superpower: The USSR and Latin America 1917–1987', by Marc Edelman, in *The NACLA Report*, Jan./Feb., 1967, vol. XXI.

5. A very sensitive discussion of this attitude towards the Soviet models of party and mass organizations is found in Marina and David Ottaway's *Afro-Communism*, New York, Holmes & Meier, 1986, in which they contrast Benin, Angola, Ethiopia and Mozambique with the 'African Socialist' countries like Tanzania, Algeria and Tunisia. My own estimation is that *both* 'models' are in serious trouble.

6. Peter Clement's in 'Moscow and Southern Africa', in *Problems of Communism*, March/April, 1985, vol. XXXIV, stresses that Moscow's aims seemed to be guided more by considerations of prestige than those of security. The growing distancing of the countries in Southern Africa from the USSR and their attempts to build economic and political bridges to Western Europe and the US will increase as the end of the high state of tensions between the US and USSR sink in. It becomes clear that the USSR will have *less and not more* resources available for its friends in the Third World.

7. I have always had a problem with the promiscuous use of the term 'freedom fighter'. While there is massive support for removing the Soviet troops from Kabul, it is not at all clear that 'freedom', in any sense of that word, is the aim of the Afghan Muslim fundamentalists. The victims of the victory of these 'freedom fighters' will be all secular elements and, above all, women. That is one more reason why the Soviet role in Afghanistan was pernicious and that of their clients criminal. They help provoke the kind of polarization in which the victims will be the chances for democracy and women's rights.

8. An extensive bibliography exists on the Communist International, or the Comintern. A good start is: Merle Fainsod, *International Socialism and the World War*, Cambridge, Harvard University Press, 1935, and Franz Borkenau, *World Communism*, New York, Norton, 1939. A polemical volume, *The Third International After Lenin*, by Leon Trotsky, New York, Pioneer Publishers, 1936, and his two-volume, *The First Five Years of the Communist International*, New York, Pioneer Publishers, 1953, are very valuable.

More specialized and dealing with the Communist International and the Third World are: Stuart Schram and Helene Carrère d'Encausse, *Marxism in Asia*, London, Allen Lane, Penguin Press, 1965; *Comintern and the World Revolution 1928-1943*, by Kermit McKenzie, New York, Columbia University Press, 1964; and John Haithcox, *Communism and Nationalism, M. N. Roy, and Comintern Policy 1920–1939*, Princeton, Princeton University Press, 1971.

9. Franz Borkenau, *World Communism*, New York, Norton, 1939; Ruth Fischer, *Stalin and German Communism*, Cambridge, Harvard University Press, 1946; Evelyn Anderson, *Hammer or Anvil: The Story of the German Working-Class Movement*, London, Victor Gollancz, 1945; Barrington Moore, *Injustice, The Social Bases of Obedience and Revolt*, White Plains, M. E. Sharpe, 1978. The

issue of social-democratic failure to extend the revolution to the industrial heart of Western Europe remains the key debate about 'lost chances' and the historical responsibility for Nazism and Stalinism.

10. Collective farming in Bulgaria, Hungary and the GDR have not been disastrous, although they nowhere match genuinely advanced modern farming such as that in Denmark and Holland.

11. They have already moved in the direction of associate membership in the World Bank and the IMF. Hungary, Poland and the Soviet Union are the most obvious candidates for membership in the near future, as is Yugoslavia. In any case they have stopped denouncing these institutions of the world capitalist market as instruments of maintaining the exploitation of the less developed. They are *very* responsible about meeting their obligations to the financial community. This will be even more the case if major loans become the goal of the Soviet leadership. They cannot afford Fidel Castro's advice to Latin American debtor nations, to stop paying interest on international debts.

12. See my article, 'Violence and Social Change in the Yugoslav Revolution', in *Comparative Politics*, vol. 8, no. 3, April, 1976, particularly the conclusion on page 477 where I argue that Angola, Mozambique, Guinea-Bissau and Algeria have better prospects than other de-colonialized countries, because prolonged revolutionary struggle required mass mobilization.

13. Not very much material is readily available on the Spanish anarchists, which is a pity because an extraordinarily rich tradition of self-help and rural mobilization is being lost for the activists of the socialist movement. The materials are becoming very 'academicized' and are hard to obtain. Yet for the Third World there are valuable lessons and organizational models in the anarchist experiences. The best general introduction is in Murray Bookchin, *The Spanish Anarchists: The Heroic Years 1868–1936,* New York, Free Life Editions, 1977; also see Sam Dolgoff (ed.), *The Anarchist Collectives: Workers' Self-management in the Spanish Revolution,* New York, Free Life Editions, 1974; Daniel Guerin, *Anarchism,* New York, Monthly Review Press, 1970 (this edition has an excellent introduction by Noam Chomsky).

14. Very typical, one could write archetypical, are the works by Arghiri Emmanuel and Immanuel Wallerstein (Emmanuel, *Unequal Exchange,* New York, Monthly Review Press, 1972; Wallerstein, *The Modern World System,* New York, Academic Press, 1974). However, it appears that this intellectual fashion is going the same way as interest in students as the new revolutionary class and theories of the new left went. Life has its small mercies.

Chapter 5

1. A brief bibliography on this topic would begin with John Palmer, *Europe without America: The Crisis in Atlantic Relations,* New York, Oxford University Press, 1987; Kees van Pilj, *The Making of an Atlantic Ruling Class,* London, Verso Books, 1984; Ernest Mandel, *Europe versus America,* London, New Left Books, 1968; Michael Newman, *Socialism and European Unity,* London, Junction Books, 1983; Andre Gunder Frank, *The European Challenge,* Nottingham, Spokesman Books, 1983; E.P. Thompson, *The Heavy Dancers,* New York, Pantheon 1985; Stuart Holland, *Out of Crisis: A Project for European Recovery,* Nottingham,

Spokesman Books, 1983; *Global Challenge*, Michael Manley and Willy Brandt, London, Pan Books, 1985; and Regis Debray, *Les Empires contre l'europe*, Paris, Gallimard, 1985. See also note 1 of Chapter 7.

2. The US official skewed view of the balance of forces between itself and the USSR, and Warsaw and NATO during the height of the new Cold War can be found in *The United States Military Posture*, 1983. It is criticized in Congressman Ronald V. Dellums, *Defense Sense: The Search for a Rational Military Policy*, Cambridge, Ballinger, 1983, and my 'Neither Bellicose nor Helpless: A Democratic Left Proposal for Defense Policy', in *Dissent*, Spring, 1987. The US view, backed by a number of Atlanticist hawks, is based on obvious fraud. The arms balance in Europe is counted *without* the French forces since they are formally not in NATO. The Warsaw Pact troops are treated as a homogeneous mass without taking into account the dubious reliability of Polish, Romanian, Hungarian and Czechoslovakian troops. It is also usual to grossly inflate the technological efficiency of Warsaw Pact troops. Gorbachev's obvious willingness to accept deep asymmetrical cuts means that that con job cannot last into the 1990s.

3. Two or three works are a useful background: Barry Buzan, *People, States and Fear*, Chapel Hill, University of North Carolina Press, 1983; E.P. Thompson, The *Heavy Dancers*, New York, Pantheon, 1985; *Search for Sanity: The Politics of Nuclear Weapons and Disarmament*, edited by Paul Joseph and Simon Rosenblum, Boston, South End Press, 1984; and Alex Cockburn, *The Enemy*, New York, Bantam, 1985.

4. This is not because of any great victories of either common sense or pro-peace sentiments in Washington and the new Bush administration so much as budgetary considerations. In an era of no-growth military budgets, the other services and their advocates were sure to gang up against an item like the 'Star Wars', which was a bottomless pit of costs. Among the military services, the budget *is* a zero-sum game. How many planes, submarines and tanks were to be sacrifices for Reagan's science-fiction dream?

5. As the Bush administration stupidly bullies Western Europe in 1989 to accept expensive and unnecessary 'modernization' of both conventional and nuclear forces.

6. A background work is Jerry W. Sanders, *Peddlers of Crisis: The Committee on the Present Danger and the Politics of Containment*, Boston, South End Press, 1983, for a description of a key group in developing support for the second Cold War.

7. Just how hostile the populations of the Eastern European Warsaw Pact allies are to *the alliance* is a grossly neglected and underestimated factor in discussions about European security. During the incredibly malign Nazi invasion and oppressive racist occupation, *millions* of Soviet citizens, from the occupied Baltic Republics, Crimea, Ukraine, Georgia and even the Great Russian Republic itself either welcomed or actively collaborated with and fought in the Nazi armies. Why should anyone assume that the Eastern Europeans are more loyal to the Soviet alliance than were the Soviet citizens themselves?

8. To be fair, the record of the Gorbachev administration is mixed and improving in this area. There *have* been major advances in human rights and liberalization in the USSR. The desire of the Soviets to hold a human rights conference in Moscow is a good sign of the increased acceptance of the legitimacy of the issue. On the other hand, the Soviets often sound as if they consider human rights to be purely

an internal issue, and that detente implies non-interference in internal affairs of other states.

9. No condition should require the Soviet Union to cut off aid to its friends in the Third World as a precondition for arms reduction agreements. Economic reasons and the increasing turn of Soviet policy towards cooperation with the West and the US will have that effect anyhow. This may be a genuine misfortune for the liberation movements and radical governments in the Third World.

10. See John Mason, 'Nuclear Politics in France' and Pierre Hassner, 'The French Right and Foreign Policy', both in *Telos*, no. 67, Spring, 1986. Also see Paul Bracken, *The Command and Control of Nuclear Forces*, New Haven, Yale University Press, 1983; and Diane Johnstone, *The Politics of Euromissiles*, New York, Schocken Books, 1985. Also of interest is Samy Cohen, *La Monarchie nucleaire*, Paris, Hachette, 1986. John Mason's research on French nuclear policy has been very useful to me in formulating my own opinions about this subject.

11. An interesting socialist version of the left-Gaullist politics is in Regis Debray's, *Les Empires contre l'europe*, Paris, Gallimard, 1985. Versions of that view are becoming more common among the left wing of the German social-democrats. This is a far more activist version of previous neutralism. For one thing it is far more skeptical about both superpowers, and more oriented to a special European role in regards to the Third World.

Chapter 6

1. Background: G.D.H. Cole, *A History of Socialist Thought*, vols 2 and 3, London, George Allen & Unwin, 1954: James Joll, *The Second International*, New York, Praeger, 1956; Milorad Drashkovitch (ed.), *The Revolutionary Internationals 1964–1943*, Stanford, Stanford University Press, 1966; Michael Harrington, *Socialism*, New York, Bantam, 1986; Carl Schorske, *German Social-Democracy, 1905–1917: The Development of the Great Schism*, Cambridge, Harvard University Press, 1955; Richard Hunt, *German Social-Democracy 1918–1933*, Chicago, Quadrangle Books, 1964; Leszek Kolakowski, *Main Currents of Marxism*, vols 2 and 3, New York, Oxford University Press, 1981; Wolfgang Abendroth, *A History of the European Working Class Movements*, New York, Monthly Review Press, 1966; Anton Pelinka, *Social Democratic Parties in Europe*, New York, Praeger, 1983; William Paterson and Alistair Thomas, *Social Democratic Parties in Western Europe*, New York, St Martin's Press, 1977; Colin Crouch and Alessandro Pizzorno (eds), *The Resurgence of Class Conflict in Western Europe Since 1968*, London, Macmillan, 1978; Walter Korpi, *The Working Class in Welfare Capitalism*, London, Routledge and Kegan Paul, 1978; *The Socialist Register 1985/86: Social Democracy and After*, edited by Ralph Miliband, John Sayville, Marcel Liebman and Leo Panitch, London, Merlin Press, 1986; Ernesto Laclau and Chantal Mouffe, *Hegemony and Socialist Strategy*, London, Verso Books, 1985; Gosta Esping-Andersen, *Politics against Markets: the Social Democratic Road to Power*, Princeton, Princeton University Press, 1985; John Pontusson, 'Behind and Beyond Social Democracy in Sweden', *New Left Review*, vol. 143, Jan./Feb., 1984.

2. I use the terms social-democratic and socialist more or less interchangeably when referring to the parties and movements, and the parties are those of the Socialist and Labor International or the Second International. This is what remained of the

united world socialist workers' movement after the split following the Bolshevik revolution in 1917, and the formation of the Third Communist International.

3. There has been a revival of interest in anarchism in France, the United States, and West Germany. Some background books: *The Essential Works of Anarchism*, edited by Marshall Shatz, New York, Quadrangle Books, 1972; the excellent work by Murray Bookchin, *The Spanish Anarchists: the Heroic Years 1986–1936*, New York, Free Life Editions, 1977; on Anarcho-Syndicalism also consult Peter Stearns, *Revolutionary Syndicalism and French Labor*, New Brunswick, Rutgers University Press, 1971.

4. See the issue on Trotsky and Trotskyism in *Studies in Comparative Communism*, Spring–Summer, 1977. A friendly work is Ernest Mandel (ed.), *50 Years of World Revolution 1917–1967*, New York, Merit Publishers, 1968; and James Cannon, *The History of American Trotskyism*, New York, Pathfinder Press, 1972.

5. An important work on the influence of the major theorist of pre-war social-democracy, Karl Kautsky, on the Communist–socialism split is Massimo Salvadori, *Karl Kautsky and Socialist Revolution 1880–1938*, London, New Left Books, 1979.

6. Nathanael Greene, *Crisis and Decline: French Socialist Party in the Popular Front Era*, Ithaca, Cornell University Press, 1969.

7. Among the many works on the Spanish Civil war, Gabriel Jackson, *The Spanish Republic and the Civil War 1931–1939*, Princeton, Princeton University Press, 1965, seems to me to be the least partisan.

8. See the already cited McKenzie, *Comintern and the World Revolution 1928–1943*, New York, Columbia University Press, 1964.

9. If one is to read only one work on the international Communist movement, with a fairly heavy emphasis on Europe, I recommend Fernando Claudin, *The Communist Movement: from the Comintern to the Cominform*, New York, Monthly Review Press, 1975, for the period from 1943 to the 1960s. For the earlier period, use note 1 in Chapter 2.

10. An interesting personal testimony from the major leaders is in Philip Kramer, *Socialism in Western Europe: The Experience of a Generation*, Boulder, Westview Press, 1984.

11. See the discussion of the German SPD in Chapter 9. Several works are a useful background: Ralf Dahrendorf, *Society and Democracy in Germany*, London, Weidenfeld & Nicolson 1960; John Carr, *Helmuth Schmidt: Helmsman of Germany*, London, Weidenfeld & Nicolson, 1985; William Graf, *The German Left since 1945: Socialism and Social Democracy in the German Federal Republic*, New York, Cambridge University Press, 1976. All general works on European socialism have major sections on West Germany and the SPD.

12. The Swedish movement organizes a much larger proportion of the workforce but West Germany is the industrial giant of Western Europe and the economic leader of the European Community. That is why the West German social-democratic movement is dominant in the Socialist International and is the pace-setter in Europe.

13. See, for example, Richard Tilford (ed.), *The Ostpolitik and Political Change in Germany*, London, Saxon House, 1975.

14. A comparison of social policies is in Hugh Heclo, *Modern Social Politics in Britain and Sweden*, New Haven, Yale University Press, 1974. On Sweden see Richard Scase (ed.), *Readings in the Swedish Class Structure*, New York,

Pergamon Press, 1976; also see John D. Stephens, 'The Ideological Development of Swedish Social Democracy', and Ulf Himmelstrand, 'Sweden: Paradise in Trouble' in Denitch (ed.), *Democratic Socialism*, Montclair, N.J., Allenheld & Osman, 1981.

15. Euro-Communism was an intellectual rage during the 1970s. Several things killed it, the most important being the success of the socialist parties in France and Spain in taking over the hegemony on the left. A further problem was that it became hard to maintain a clear identity for a non-revolutionary socialist working-class-oriented organization *distinct* from social-democracy. The only successful Communist parties are either (a) the substitutes for social-democracy in their own country, in the case of Italy, or (b) classic authoritarian Stalinist parties which remain more pro-Soviet than Moscow, as in the cases of Portugal and Cyprus. Sources on Euro-Communism: Neil McInnes, *The Communist Parties of Western Europe*, London, Oxford University Press, 1975; *The Politics of Euro-Communism*, edited by Carl Boggs and David Plotke, Boston, South End Press, 1980; Ernest Mandel, *From Stalinism to Eurocommunism*, London, New Left Books, 1979.

16. The best short and balanced description of Euro-Communism is in Neil McInnes, *Euro-Communism*, Beverly Hills, Sage Publications, 1976.

17. The social-democrats did not do all that poorly during the doldrums either. Their performance during the post-1973 recession shows that their policies did make a difference and that they did expand their votes in their strongholds. The stubborn exception to this rule seems to be the British Labour party, although, to be fair, it should be clear that if Britain did not keep its undemocratic 'first past the post' electoral rules and introduced the type of proportional representation which is used in civilized European countries, the Labour party would be heading an anti-Tory coalition government. *Socialists in the Recession* by Giles and Lisane Radice, London, Macmillan Press, 1986, is a nice review of socialist performance during the recession.

18. Two works on Sweden and the Swedish social-democrats are minimal reading: Marquis Childs, *Sweden: the Middle Way on Trial*, New Haven, Yale University Press, 1980; and John Stevens, *The Transition from Capitalism and Socialism*, London, Macmillan, 1979. More substantial and up-to-date is Gosta Esping-Andersen, *Politics Against Markets: The Social Democratic Road to Power*, Princeton, Princeton University Press, 1985. For a Swedish social-democrat's view see Sven Johansson, 'When is the Time Ripe?', *Political Power and Social Theory*, vol. 3. Also see: Robert Dahl (ed.), *Political Oppositions in Western Democracies*, New Haven, Yale University Press, 1966.

19. This is argued with much passion by John Stevens in *The Transition from Capitalism to Socialism*, London, Macmillan, 1979.

20. For a full description see R. Meidner, *Employee Investment Funds*, London, Allen & Unwin, 1978. Also see John Stevens, *The Transition from Capitalism to Socialism*, London, Macmillan, 1979.

21. A sharp critique of post-war social-democracy is: Leo Panitch, *Social Democracy and Industrial Militancy: The Labour Party, the Trade Unions and Income Policy 1945–74*, Cambridge, Cambridge University Press 1976. It is questionable just how typical the British Labour party ever was of 'social-democracy' in theory; it certainly was never that in organizational structure.

22. Alas, that is one of the very few things in which the small democratic socialist organization in the United States, the Democratic Socialists of America (DSA), has

been ahead of its sister parties in the Socialist International. It has had a half of the leadership posts reserved for women for almost a decade. That made it the first, at least in something, among the world socialist organizations.

Chapter 7

1. Somber reassessment of the role of the United States in an ever more integrated world economy became more common during the Reagan administration. As the US debts began to get ever higher and it began to slide back in both world trade and aspects of high technology, a pessimistic view became a new consensus among the more sophisticated modern historians and political analysts. The inability to project military power, one field where the US remained effectively pre-eminent for policy goals had a good deal to do with pessimism, or realism. The most substantial works of the new realists are: Paul Kennedy, *Rise and Fall of the Great Power: Economic Change and Military Conflicts 1500–2000*, New York, Random House, 1987, and David Calleo, *America and the World Economy*, Bloomington, Indiana University Press, 1973; and his more recent, *Europe and America: The Future of the Western Alliance*, New York, Basic Books, 1987. To these should be added John Palmer, *Europe without America*, New York, Oxford University Press, 1987.

2. The unequal exchange argument has been discussed in Chapter 4. The sharpest form of that argument is Aghiri Emmanuel, *Unequal Exchange*, New York, Monthly Review Press, 1972. That point of view, that is that American *labor*, that is to say workers including Black and women workers, consciously participates in the exploitation of the Third World, fits very well with the other critiques of productivism and consumerism. This is why it is popular among people who are not necessarily Marxists and do not draw particularly radical conclusions from such an analysis. It merely confirms and legitimates the widespread anti-labor and working-class attitudes among younger intellectuals today.

3. Reverend Jesse Jackson has become the focus of both hope and acrimonious debate. A way of beginning to enter the themes of the debate could be with Sheila Collins, *The Rainbow Challenge: The Jackson Campaign and the Future of U.S. Politics*, New York, Monthly Review Press, 1986, a very optimistic view of the campaign and its potential for the future. A more critical work is Adolph L. Reed, *The Jesse Jackson Phenomenon: The Crisis of Purpose in Afro-American Politics*, New Haven, Yale University Press, 1986. Manning Marable, *Black American Politics from the Washington Marches to Jesse Jackson*, London, Verso Books, 1985, provides useful background. The argument about the progressive if not social-democratic potential of the 'hole in the American electorate' has been forcefully put forward by Frances Piven and Richard Cloward in their *Why Americans Don't Vote*, New York, Pantheon Books, 1988.

4. See Appendix 1 for a very brief outline on the history of socialism in the United States and its varied organizations, parties and sects. Daniel Bell, 'The History of Marxian Socialism in the United States', in *Socialism and American Life*, Drew Egbert and Stow Person, Princeton, Princeton University Press, 1952, is still very sound. Irving Howe, *Socialism and America*, San Diego, Harcourt, Brace, Jovanovich, 1985; and Paul Buhle, *Marxism in the United States: Remapping the History of the American Left*, are more recent sound general works on American socialism.

5. The best summary of the discussion on American exceptionalism is in Seymour Martin Lipset, 'Why No Socialism in the United States?' in *Radicalism in the Contemporary Age,* edited by Seweryn Bialer, New York, Westview Press, 1977. That volume also has a useful extensive bibliography, 'Sources of Radicalism and Revolution, a Survey of the Literature,' by William Overholt. The entire issue is treated at greater length in *The Failure of a Dream? Essays in the History of American Socialism*, edited by John Lasslett and Seymour Martin Lipset, New York, Doubleday Anchor Books, 1974. The two important books for the exceptionalism of American labor unions are: Selig Perlman, *A Theory of the Labor Movement,* New York, Macmillan, 1928, and *History and Labor in the United States*, edited by John Commons et al., New York, Macmillan, 1926.

6. While there are more contemporary monographs on details of American Communist history I still consider Theodore Draper, *The Roots of American Communism*, New York, Viking, 1957; and his *American Communism and Soviet Russia: the Formative Period,* New York, Viking, 1960, to be the soundest overall work. To this could be added the one-volume *The American Communist Party: A Critical History 1919–1957* by Irving Howe and Louis Coser, Boston, Beacon Press, 1957.

7. The American Communists achieved their greatest successes under Earl Browder during the Second World War. An interesting history of the party during that period when it began to approach the role of a mass working-class party is Maurice Isserman, *Which Side Were You On? The American Communist Party During the Second World War,* Middletown, Wesleyan University Press, 1982.

8. There are, after all, two open 'card-carrying' socialists in the US Congress, members of the Democratic Socialists of America, both elected and re-elected as Democrats. Interestingly, both are Black. There are certainly many more who would be open, i.e. 'card carrying', members if red-baiting was not a well-developed political ploy in US politics. After all, if as pallid a figure as Dukakis could be baited for being a member of the American Civil Liberties Union, membership in the American affiliate of the Socialist International does not promise many extra votes today.

9. David Halle, *America's Working Man,* Chicago, University of Chicago Press, 1984; Pat Walker (ed.), *Between Labor and Capital,* Boston, South End Press, 1979; and Stanley Aronowitz, *Working-Class Hero: A New Strategy for Labor,* New York, Adama Press, 1983, discuss the changes in the structure of the American working class and the strategic consequences which probably follow.

10. A fairly broad traditional statement is: John McDermott, *The Crisis in the Working Class and Some Arguments for a New Labor Movement,* Boston, South End Press, 1980.

Chapter 8

1. The problem with a bibliography here is arbitrarily to decide how far back to begin. Again, in the interest of brevity, I would propose a short list: Seweryn Bialer (ed.), *Sources of Contemporary Radicalism,* vols 1 and 2, Boulder, Westview, 1977; Richard Cloward and Frances Fox Piven, *The Politics of Turmoil*, New York, Pantheon, 1972, as well as their *Regulating the Poor,* New York, Pantheon, 1970; Lawrence Lader, *Power on the Left: The American Radical Movements Since 1946,*

New York, Norton, 1979; George Lipsitz, *Class and Culture in Cold War America*, New York, Praeger, 1981; Maurice Isserman, *If I Had a Hammer: The Death of the Old Left and the Birth of the New Left*, New York, Basic Books, 1987; Richard Lowenthal, *Social Change and Cultural Change*, New York, Columbia University Press, 1984; Donald Hodges, *The Bureaucratization of Socialism*, Boston, University of Massachusetts Press, 1981; Chaim Waxman (ed.), *The End of Ideology Debate*, New York, Simon & Schuster, 1968, deals with the general development of the new left and social movements.

On class and social movements: Ellen Meiksins Wood, *The Retreat from Class*, London, Verso Books, 1986. A shorter version is in 'Marxism Without Class Struggle' in *Socialist Register*, 1983. The same issue of the *Register* has three important articles, 'Women, Class and Family,' by Dorothy Smith; 'Masculine Dominance and the State', by Varda Burstyn, and 'André Gorz and his Disappearing Proletariat,' by Ralf Miliband, 'The New Revisionism in Britain' in *New Left Review*, vol. 150, March/April 1985; André Gorz, *Farewell to the Working Class: An Essay on Post Industrial Socialism*, Boston, South End Press, 1982. Also see Nicos Poulantzas, *Political Power and Social Classes*, London, New Left Books, 1973; Ernesto Laclau, *Politics and Ideology in Marxist Theory*, London, Verso, 1979.

The debate moved on to the intersection of class, gender and social policy in Frances Fox Piven and Richard Cloward, *The New Class War*, New York, Pantheon, 1982; articles in the *Socialist Review*, no. 81, 1985, 'The Economics and Politics of Full Employment' by Juliet Schor, and no. 82, 'Full Employment: False Necessity or Justice,' by Fred Block.

A useful collection on class and the new working-class is in Pat Walker (ed.), *Between Labor and Capital*, Boston, South End Press, 1979; and one can also turn to Michael Harrington, *The Next Left*, New York, Henry Holt, 1986, for a discussion of the issues of class and full employment. Also see the wheel rediscovered in 'S(He) Who Does not Work Shall Eat All the Same: Tomorrow's Economy and Proposals From the Left', by André Gorz in *Dissent*, Spring, 1987. The issues of strategy and tactics are contemporary. A bibliography is therefore very controversial.

2. The first form in which the challenge to the 'old' left of the mass working-class parties and unions took place was around the issue of the role, significance and eventual class location of the *student movements* of the 1960s. The phenomenon was world-wide but it can be said to have had three major centers, the United States, France and West Germany. See: Alain Touraine, *The May Movement: Revolt and Reform*, New York, Random House, 1971; Bernard Crick (ed.), *Protest and Discontent*, London, Pelican, 1970; a reconstructed 'Maoisant' new leftist, *The Imagination of the New Left: A Global Analysis of 1988*, by George Katsiaficas, Boston, South End Press, 1987; on a soberer note see Erik Hobsbawm, '1968 – A Retrospect', in *Marxism Today*, May, 1978. Also see Maurice Isserman, *If I had a Hammer*, New York, Basic Books, 1987.

3. A short article 'Social Movements in the Reagan Era,' by Bogdan Denitch, in *Telos*, no. 53, Fall, 1982, raises in some detail the question of right-wing social movements.

4. The whole issue of what exactly is a community and a social movement is therefore a battleground for rival views on strategy, tactics and aims of democratic struggles and socialist movements, that is, of course, the weakness of much of the concern with civil society and single-issue social movements. Chantal Mouffe

makes a very good point when she argues that without an idea of the common good one cannot talk about individual liberty. See 'The Return of the Citizen', *New Statesman*, 7 October 1988.

5. How else can one explain the intense zeal of the protestors against the nuclear rockets and US bases in West Germany and Britain in the early 1980s? No serious person expected a war in Europe or a world war. An entire movement sub-culture and faith developed with a powerful language and symbolism of its own and these things were not there to be an analysed but, on the contrary, to be believed.

In point of fact no small emphasis by radical feminist peace activist ecologists was made of the difference between the 'old' left 'masculine' insistence on logic and argument as against the 'new' social movement and feminist emphasis on intuition and faith. To attempt to understand and analyse, at least in my case here, is not necessarily to reject much of what these activists were trying to do. That intuitive and committed side of socialism has to be reintroduced into the movement if it is to survive. This cannot be done at the expense of analytical sharpness and honesty.

6. An interesting example of the interaction of the classical socialist movement is described in *The Emancipation of Women: the Rise and Decline of the Women's Movement in German Social Democracy 1863–1933*, London, Pluto Press, 1976. Also see section 8 in Joanne Barkan, *Visions of Emancipation: The Italian Workers' Movement Since 1945*, New York, Praeger, 1984. This was obviously not only a feature of the European socialist movement, as can be seen in Mary Jo Buhle, *Women and American Socialism, 1870–1920*, Urbana, University of Illinois Press, 1981.

7. Lest it also be forgotten it was Stokely Carmichael, the leader of SNCC (the Southern Non-Violent Coordinating Committee), who gave the infamous statement 'The position of women in the movement is prone' in reply to a question about the position of the women in the civil rights movement in struggle. I know of no old left organization, Communist, Trotskyist or socialist, which would not have repudiated such a remark and censured or disciplined any leader that made it.

8. A solid introduction to modern feminism in the US is in Lynn Chancer, 'The Current State of the Feminist Movement,' in *Socialist Perspectives*, edited by Phyllis Jacobson and Julius Jacobson, New York, Katz-Cohl Publishing, 1983. Also see: Sheila Rowbotham et al., *Beyond the Fragments: Feminism and the Making of Socialism*, London, Merlin Press, 1979; Lydia Sargent (ed.), *Women and Revolution: The Unhappy Marriage of Marxism and Feminism*, Boston, South End Press, 1981; and a cultural slant in Ann Snitow et al. (eds), *The Powers of Desire*, New York, Monthly Review Press, 1983.

9. A very good summary of the present-day politics of the Greens in West Germany, where they are most vital, is: Werner Hulsberg, 'The Greens at the Cross Roads,' in *New Left Review*, vol. 152, July/August, 1985. A good general source of ecological information is in the publications of the Worldwatch Institute.

10. Source: Worldwatch Institute, based on data in OECD Environmental Data, Compendium, 1985 (Paris, 1985); Paul Marer, *Dollar GNPs of the USSR and Eastern Europe* (Baltimore, Md., Johns Hopkins University Press, 1985, p. 187; *State of the World*, 1987, Worldwatch Institute, Norton, 1988.

11. There is recognition of this problem that is very clear in the round-table, *The Impasse of Socialist Feminism* with Deidre English, Barbara Epstein, Barbara Haber and Judy McLean in the *Socialist Review*, no. 79 Jan./Feb., 1985.

12. There is an insightful review-article by Val Moghadam, 'Feminism and Islam' in *Socialist Review*, no. 74, Jan./Feb., 1985. The book is *In the Shadow of Islam: The Women's Movement in Iran*, compiled by Azar Tarabi and Nanid Yeganeh, London, Zed Press, 1984.

13. On the social construction of gender and the implication of that for the social order see: Cynthia Fuchs Epstein, *Deceptive Distinctions: Sex, Gender and the Social Order*, New Haven, Yale University Press, 1988.

Conclusion

1. Within these parameters, however, a wide range of failure or success is possible. See: Leland G. Stauber, *A New Program for Democratic Socialists: Lessons from Market-Planning Experience in Austria*, Carbondale, Four Willows Press, 1987; Hugh Helco, *Modern Social Politics in Britain and Sweden*, New Haven, Yale University Press 1974; a neo-liberal argument in Steve Kelman, *Regulating America, Regulating Sweden*, Cambridge, MIT Press, 1981. The central question in this as in many other debates is what room is there for *conscious political intervention?* The question is anything but theoretical.

2. I am aware of the 'modern' argument against full employment and can only make two points about it. One that it is not so new, it was very present indeed in the old classical socialist movement. Marx's son-in-law, Lafargue, even wrote a longish pamphlet entitled 'Why Work?'. For a more modern argument see: John Keane, 'Work and the Civilizing Process,' in his *Democracy and Civil Society*, London, Verso, 1988. The second point is that I believe the argument to be profoundly wrong since a new socialist civilization will not be based on new ways of distributing goods but *also and centrally* on reorganization and democratization of production.

3. Again this is complex. While industrial countries do create most of the pollution, NICs like Brazil can be enormously destructive of the environment to a point where they threaten the earth as a whole. The best example is the massive destruction of the forests in Brazil. But there are other examples; the destruction of forests in India and Africa may well bring about ecological catastrophes.

4. A refreshing exception to this is in the special edition of *Monthly Review* July/August 1984, 'Religion and the Left.' Also see: Cornel West, *Prophesy Deliverance: Afro-American Revolutionary Christianity*, New York, Westminster Press, 1982. The principal publisher of books on radical theology in the US is Orbis Books, the publishing division of Catholic Maryknoll Missionaries. Also see Michael Harrington, *The Politics at God's Funeral*, New York, Henry Holt, 1979.

5. The term 'the new working class' was popularized by a brilliant French socialist theorist, Serge Mallet. For sources in English see: *The Worker in 'Post-Industrial' Capitalism's Liberal and Radical Responses*, edited by Bertram Silberman and Murray Janowitch, especially the section 'The New Worker: A New Revolutionary Vanguard?'. Note articles by Alain Touraine, Bogdan Denitch and Stanley Aronowitz. Also see *Between Capital and Labor*.

6. A nice short work on this topic is Vincent Geoghegan, *Utopianism and Marxism*, London, Methuen, 1987.

Appendix 2

1. The fact that the partisans led by the Communist party of Yugoslavia immediately entered into the struggle for power and a new social order in 1941 is what differentiates the Yugoslav Resistance from the others in Europe during the Second World War.

2. They were also very confrontational towards the United States and Great Britain over the new frontiers which were being drawn towards Italy, to the point where the Soviets had repeatedly to restrain their younger, smaller and more ferocious partner.

Bibliography

Abendroth, Wolfgang, *A History of the European Working Class Movements*. New York: Monthly Review Press, 1966.

Allworth, Edward (ed.), *Ethnic Russia: The Dilemma of Dominance*. New York: Pergamon Press, 1980.

Anderson, Evelyn, *Hammer or Anvil: The Story of the German Working-Class Movement*. London: Victor Gollancz, 1945.

Aronowitz, Stanley, *Working Class Hero: A New Strategy for Labor*. New York: Adams Press, 1983.

Aspaturian, Vernon, 'SovietGlobal Power and the Correlation ofForces,' *Problems of Communism*, vol. XXIX, May/June, 1980.

Barkan, Joanne, *Visions of Emancipation: The Italian Worker's Movement Since 1945*. New York: Praeger Press, 1984.

Beaud, Michel, *Le Socialisme a l'epreuve de l'histoire*. Paris: Seuil, 1982.

Bialer, Seweryn (ed.), *The Domestic Content of Soviet Foreign Policy*. New York: Praeger Press, 1971.

Bialer, Seweryn (ed.), *The Domestic Content of Soviet Foreign Policy*. Boulder: Westview Press, 1981.

Bialer, Seweryn (ed.), *Radicalism in the Contemporary Age*. New York: Westview Press, 1977.

Bialer, Seweryn (ed.), *Sources of Contemporary Radicalism*, vols 1 and 2. Boulder: Westview Press, 1977.

Boggs, Carl and David Poltke (eds), *The Politics of Euro-Communism*. Boston: South End Press, 1980.

Bookchin, Murray, *The Spanish Anarchists: The Heroic Years 1868–1936*. New York: Free Life Editions, 1977.

Borkenau, Franz, *World Communism*. New York: Norton, 1939.

Bozic, Ivan, et al., *History of Yugoslavia*. New York: McGraw-Hill, 1974.

Bracken, Paul, *The Command and Control of Nuclear Forces*. New Haven: Yale University Press, 1983.

Brandt, Willy and Michael Manley, *Global Challenge*. London: Pan Books, 1985.

Brea, Juan and Mary Low, *The Red Spanish Notebook*. San Francisco: City Lights Books, 1979.

Burg, Steven, *Conflict and Cohesion in Socialist Yugoslavia*. Princeton: Princeton University Press, 1983.

Buhle, Mary Jo, *Women and American Socialism, 1870–1920*. Urbana: University of Illinois Press, 1981.

Buzan, Barry, *People, States and Fear*. Chapel Hill: University of North Carolina Press, 1983.

Calleo, David, *America and the World Economy*. Bloomington: Indiana University Press, 1973.

Calleo, David, *Europe and America: The Future of the Western Alliance*. New York: Basic Books, 1987.

Cannon, James, *The History of American Trotskyism*. New York: Pathfinder Press, 1972.
Carr, John, *Helmut Schmidt: Helmsman of Germany*. London: Weidenfeld & Nicolson, 1985.
Carter, April, *Democratic Reform in Yugoslavia*. Princeton: Princeton University Press, 1984.
Childs, Marquis, *Sweden: The Middle Way on Trial*. New Haven: Yale University Press, 1980.
Chomsky, Noam, *Turning the Tide: U.S. Intervention in Latin America and the Struggle for Peace*. Boston: South End Press, 1985; London: Pluto Press 1987.
Claudin, Fernando, *The Communist Movement: From the Comintern to the Cominform* (2 vols). New York: Monthly Review Press, 1975.
Clement, Peter, 'Moscow and Southern Africa,' *Problems of Communism*, vol. XXXIV, March/April, 1985.
Cloward, Richard and Frances Fox Piven, *The New Class War*. New York: Pantheon, 1982.
Cloward, Richard and Frances Fox Piven, *The Politics of Turmoil*. New York: Pantheon, 1972.
Cloward, Richard and Frances Fox Piven, *Regulating the Poor*. New York: Pantheon, 1970.
Cloward, Richard and Frances Fox Piven, *Why Americans Don't Vote*. New York: Pantheon Books, 1988.
Cockburn, Alex, *The Enemy*. New York: Bantam, 1985.
Cohen, Jean, *Class and Civil Society: The Limits of Marxian Critical Theory*. Amherst: University of Massachusetts Press, 1982.
Cohen, R.S. and Mihailo Markovic, *The Rise and Fall of Socialist Humanism*. Nottingham: Spokesman Books, 1975.
Cohen, Samy, *La Monarchie nucleaire*. Paris: Hachette, 1986.
Cohen, Stephen and Robert Tucker (eds), *The Great Purge Trial*. New York: Grosset & Dunlap, 1965.
Cohen, Stephen (ed.), *An End to Silence: Uncensored Opinion in the Soviet Union*. New York: Norton, 1982.
Cole, G.D.H., *A History of Socialist Thought*. vols 2 and 3. London: George, Allen & Unwin, 1954.
Collins, Sheila, *The Rainbow Challenge: The Jackson Campaign and the Future of U.S. Politics*. New York: Monthly Review Press, 1986.
Comisso, Ellen Turkish, *Workers' Control Under Plan and Market*. New Haven: Yale University Press, 1979.
Commons, John (ed.), *History and Labor in the United States*. New York: Macmillan, 1926.
Connor, Walter, *Socialism, Politics and Equality*. New York: Columbia University Press, 1979.
Coraggio, Jose Luis, Carmen Diana Deere, et al., *Transition and Development: The Problems of Third World Socialism*. New York: Monthly Review Press, 1986.
Coser, Louis and Irving Howe, *The American Communist Party: A Critical History 1919–1957*. Boston: Beacon Press, 1957.
Crick, Bernard, *Protest and Discontent*. London: Pelican, 1970.
Crouch, Colin, and Allesandro Pizzorno (eds), *The Resurgence of Class Conflict in Western Europe Since 1969*. London: Macmillan, 1978.

Dahl, Robert (ed.), *Political Oppositions in Western Democracies*. New Haven: Yale University Press, 1966.
Dahrendorf, Ralf, *Society and Democracy in Germany*. London: Weidenfeld & Nicolson, 1960.
Debray, Regis, *Les Empires contre l'Europe*. Paris: Gallimard, 1985.
Dellums, Ronald, *Defense Sense: The Search for a Rational Military Policy*. Cambridge: Ballinger, 1983.
Denitch, Bogdan (ed.), *Democratic Socialism: The Mass Left in Advanced Industrial Societies*. Montclair, N. J.: Allenheld & Osmun, 1981.
Denitch, Bogdan, *The Legitimation of a Revolution: The Yugoslav Case*. New Haven: Yale University Press, 1976.
Denitch, Bogdan, 'Neither Bellicose nor Helpless: A Democratic Left Proposal for Defense Policy,' *Dissent* Spring, 1987.
Deutscher, Isaac, *The Prophet Armed*. New York: Oxford University Press, 1954.
Deutscher, Isaac, *The Prophet Disarmed*. New York: Oxford University Press, 1954.
Dolgoff, Sam (ed.), *The Anarchist Collectives: Workers' Self-Management in the Spanish Revolution*. New York: Free Life Editions, 1974.
Draper, Theodore, *American Communism and Soviet Russia: The Formative Period*. New York: Viking, 1960.
Draper, Theodore, *The Roots of American Communism*. New York: Viking, 1957
Drashkovitch, Milorad (ed.), *The Revolutionary Internationals 1943–1964*. Stanford: Stanford University Press, 1966.
Edelman, Marc, 'The Other Superpower: The USSR and Latin America 1917–1987,' *The NACLA Report*, vol. XXI, Jan./Feb. 1987.
Egbert, Drew and Stow Person, *Socialism and American Life*. Princeton: Princeton University Press, 1952.
Emmanuel, Arghiri, *Unequal Exchange*. New York: Monthly Review Press, 1972.
English, Deirdre, Barbara Epstein, et al., 'The Impasse of Socialist Feminism,' *Socialist Review*, no. 79, Jan./Feb. 1985.
Epsing-Andersen, Gosta, *Politics Against Markets: The Social Democratic Road to Power*. Princeton: Princeton University Press, 1985.
Epstein, Cynthia Fuchs, *Deceptive Distinctions: Sex, Gender and the Social Order*. New Haven: Yale University Press, 1988.
Faber, Bernard Lewis (ed.), *Social Structures of Eastern Europe*. New York: Praeger, 1976.
Fainsod, Merle, *International Socialism and The World War*. Cambridge: Harvard University Press, 1935.
Feher, Ferenc and Agnes Heller, *Eastern Left, Western Left*. Atlantic Highlands, N.J.: Humanities Press, 1987.
Fischer, Ruth, *Stalin and German Communism*. Cambridge: Harvard University Press, 1946.
Frank, Andre Gunder, *The European Challenge*. Nottingham: Spokesman Books, 1983.
Gati, Charles and Jan Triska (eds), *Blue Collar Workers in Eastern Europe*. London: George Allen & Unwin, 1981.
Gaucher, Roland, *Opposition in the USSR 1917–1967*. New York: Funk & Wagnells, 1969.
Geoghegan, Vincent, *Utopianism and Marxism*. London: Methuen, 1987.

Gluckman, Christine Buci, *Gramsci and the State*. London: Lawrence & Wishart, 1980.
Gorz, André, *Farewell to the Working Class: An Essay on Post Industrial Socialism*. Boston: South End Press, 1982; London: Pluto Press, 1987.
Graf, William, *The German Left Since 1945: Socialism and Social Democracy in the German Federal Republic*. New York: Cambridge University Press, 1976.
Greene, Nathanael, *Crisis and Decline: The French Socialist Party in the Popular Front Era*. Ithaca: Cornell University Press, 1969.
Guerin, Daniel, *Anarchism*. New York: Monthly Review Press, 1970.
Haithcox, John, *Communism and Nationalism: M.N. Roy and Comintern Policy 1920–1939*. Princeton: Princeton University Press, 1971.
Halle, David, *America's Working Man*. Chicago: University of Chicago Press, 1984.
Harrington, Michael, *The Next Left*. New York: Henry Holt, 1986.
Harrington, Michael, *The Politics at God's Funeral*. New York: Henry Holt, 1979.
Harrington, Michael, *Socialism*. New York: Bantam, 1986.
Harrington, Michael, *The Twilight of Capitalism*. New York: Simon & Schuster, 1976.
Harrington, Michael, *The Vast Majority*. New York: Simon & Schuster, 1977.
Hassner, Pierre, 'The French Right and Foreign Policy,' *Telos*, no. 67, Spring, 1986.
Helco, Hugh, *Modern Social Politics in Britain and Sweden*. New Haven: Yale University Press, 1974.
Hobsbawm, Eric, '1968 – A Retrospective,' *Marxism Today*, May 1978.
Hobsbawm, Eric, *The Forward March of Labour Halted?* London: Verso, 1981.
Hodges, Donald, *The Bureaucratization of Socialism*. Boston: University of Massachusetts Press, 1981.
Hoffman, George and Fred Warner Neal, *Yugoslavia and the New Communism*. New York: Twentieth Century Fund, 1962.
Holland, Stuart, *Out of Crisis: A Project for European Recovery*. Nottingham: Spokesman Books, 1983.
Horvat, Branko, *An Essay on Yugoslav Society*. Armonk, N.Y.: M.E. Sharpe, 1969.
Horvat, Branko, *The Political Economy of Socialism*. Armonk, N.Y.: M.E. Sharpe, 1982.
Howe, Irving, *The Essential Works of Socialism*. New Haven: Yale University Press, 1986.
Howe, Irving, *Socialism and America*. San Diego: Harcourt, Brace, Jovanovich, 1985.
Hunt, Richard, *German Social-Democracy 1918–1933*. Chicago: Quadrangle Books, 1964.
Isserman, Maurice, *If I Had a Hammer: The Death of the Old Left and the Birth of the New Left*. New York: Basic Books, 1987.
Isserman, Maurice, *Which Side Were You On? The American Communist Party During the Second World War*. Middletown: Wesleyan University Press, 1982.
Jackson, Gabriel, *The Spanish Republic and the Civil War 1931–1939*. Princeton: Princeton University Press, 1965.

Jackson, Richard, *The Nonaligned: The UN and the Superpowers*. New York: Praeger, 1983.
Jacobson, Julius and Phyllis Jacobson (eds.), *Socialist Perspectives*. New York: Katz-Cohl, 1983.
Jelavich, Barbara, *A History of the Balkans*, vol. 2. Cambridge: Cambridge University Press, 1983.
Johnstone, Diane, *The Politics of Euromissiles*. New York: Schocken Books, 1985.
Joll, James, *The Second International*. New York: Praeger, 1956.
Joseph, Paul and Simon Rosenblum (eds), *Search for Sanity: The Politics of Nuclear Weapons and Disarmament*. Boston: South End Press, 1984.
Katsiaficas, George, *The Imagination of the New Left: A Global Analysis of 1968*. Boston: South End Press, 1987.
Keane, John, *Democracy and Civil Society*. London: Verso, 1988.
Keane, John, *Civil Society and the State*. London: Verso, 1988.
Kelman, Steve, *Regulating America, Regulating Sweden*. Cambridge: MIT Press, 1981.
Kennan, George, *Russia and the West under Lenin and Stalin*. Boston: Little Brown, 1960.
Kennedy, Paul, *Rise and Fall of the Great Powers: Economic Change and Military Conflicts 1500–2000*. New York: Random House, 1987.
Kitching, Gavin, *Rethinking Socialism*. London: Methuen, 1983.
Kolakowski, Lezek, *The Main Currents of Marxism*, vols 1, 2, and 3. New York: Oxford University Press, 1981.
Konrad, George and Ivan Szelenyi, *Intellectuals on the Road to Class Power*. New York: Harcourt, Brace, Jovanovich, 1979.
Korpi, Walter, *The Working Class in Welfare Capitalism*. London: Routledge & Kegan Paul, 1978.
Kramer, Philip, *Socialism in Western Europe: The Experience of a Generation*. Boulder: Westview Press, 1984.
Kusin, Vladimir, *The Intellectual Origins of the Prague Spring*. Cambridge: Cambridge University Press, 1971.
Laclau, Ernesto and Chantal Mouffe, *Hegemony and Socialist Strategy*. London: Verso Books, 1985.
Laclau, Ernesto, *Politics and Ideology in Marxist Theory*. London: Verso Books, 1979.
Lader, Lawrence, *Power on the Left: The American Radical Movements Since 1946*. New York: Norton, 1979.
Lehmbruch, Gerhard and Phillipe Schmitter (eds), *Trends Towards Corporatist Intermediation*. Beverly Hills: Sage Publications, 1979.
LeoGrande, William, 'Evolution of the Nonaligned Movement,' *Problems of Communism*, vol. 29, 1980.
Lewis, Paul, *Eastern Europe: Political Crisis and Legitimation*. New York: St Martins's Press, 1984.
Lichteim, George, *Imperialism*. New York: Praeger, 1971.
Liebman, Marcel and Ralph Miliband et al., *Socialist Register 1985/1986: Social Democracy and After*. London: Merlin Press, 1986.
Lipsitz, George, *Class and Culture in Cold War America*. New York: Praeger, 1981.

Lowenthal, Richard, *Social Change and Cultural Change*. New York: Columbia University Press, 1984.
McDermott, John, *The Crisis in the Working Class and Some Arguments for a New Labor Movement*. Boston: South End Press, 1980.
McInnes, Neil, *The Communist Parties of Western Europe*. London: Oxford University Press, 1975.
McInnes, Neil, *Eurocommunism*. Beverly Hills: Sage Publications, 1976.
McKenzie, Kermit, *Comintern and the World Revolution 1928–1943*. New York: Columbia University Press, 1964.
Mandel, Ernest, *Europe versus America*. London: New Left Books, 1968.
Mandel, Ernest (ed.), *Fifty Years of World Revolution 1917–1967*. New York: Merit Publishers, 1968.
Mandel, Ernest, *From Stalinism to Eurocommunism*. London: New Left Books, 1979.
Marable, Manning, *Black American Politics from the Washington Marches to Jesse Jackson*. London: Verso Books, 1985.
Mason, John, 'Nuclear Politics in France,' *Telos*, no. 67, Spring, 1986.
Meider, R., *Employee Investment Funds*. London: Allen & Unwin, 1978.
Micunovic, Velko, *The Moscow Diary*. New York: Doubleday, 1980.
Mittleman, James, *Out from Underdevelopment*. New York: St Martin's Press, 1988.
Moghadam, Val, 'Feminism and Islam,' *Socialist Review*, no. 74, Jan/Feb, 1985.
Mommsen, Wolfgang, *Theories of Imperialism*. New York: Random House, 1980.
Moore, Barrington, *Injustice, the Social Basis of Obedience and Revolt*. White Plains: M.E. Sharpe, 1978.
Newman, Michael, *Socialism and European Unity*. London: Junction Books, 1983.
Ottaway, David and Marina Ottaway, *Afro-Communism*. New York: Holmes & Meier, 1986.
Palmer, John, *Europe without America: The Crisis in Atlantic Relations*. New York: Oxford University Press, 1987.
Panitch, Leo, *Social Democracy and Industrial Militancy: The Labor Party, the Trade Unions and Income Policy 1945–74*. Cambridge: Cambridge University Press, 1976.
Paterson, William and Alistair Thomas, *Parties in Western Europe*. New York: St Martin's Press, 1977.
Pelinka, Anton, *Social Democratic Parties in Europe*. New York: Praeger, 1983.
Perlman, Selig, *A Theory of the Labor Movement*. New York: Macmillan, 1928.
Petras, James (ed.), *Class, State and Power in the Third World*. Montclair, N. J.: Allenheld & Osmun, 1981.
Poulantzas, Nicos, *Political Power and Social Classes*. London: New Left Books, 1973.
Radice, Lisane and Giles Radice, *Socialists in the Recession*. London: Macmillan Press, 1986.
Rakovski, Mark, *Towards an East European Marxism*. New York: St Martin's Press, 1978.
Ramet, Pedro (ed.), *Yugoslavia in the 80s*. Boulder: Westview Press, 1985.
Reed, Adolph, *The Jesse Jackson Phenomenon: The Crisis of Purpose in Afro-American Politics*. New Haven: Yale University Press, 1986.

Rowbotham, Sheila et al., *Beyond the Fragments: Feminism and the Making of Socialism*. London: Merlin Press, 1979.
Salvadori, Massimo, *Karl Kautsky and Socialist Revolution 1880–1938*. London: New Left Books, 1979.
Sanders, Jerry, *Peddlers of Crisis: The Committee on the Present Danger and the Politics of Containment*. Boston: South End Press, 1983.
Sargent, Lydia (ed.), *Women and Revolution: The Unhappy Marriage of Marxism and Feminism*. Boston: South End Press, 1981; London: Pluto Press, 1988.
Scase, Richard (ed.), *Readings in the Swedish Class Structure*. New York: Pergamon Press, 1976.
Schactman, Max, *The Bureaucratic Revolution: The Rise of the Stalinist State*. New York: Donald Press, 1962.
Schmitter, Phillipe, 'Still the Century of Corporatism?' *Review of Politics*, January, 1974.
Schorske, Carl, *German Social-Democracy, 1905–1917: The Development of the Great Schism*. Cambridge: Harvard University Press, 1955.
Schram, Stuart and Helene Carrère d'Encausse, *Marxism in Asia*. London: Allen Lane and Penguin Press, 1965.
Shatz, Marshall (ed.), *The Essential Works of Anarchism*. New York: Quadrangle Books, 1972.
Sher, Gerson, *Praxis: Marxist Criticism and Dissent in Socialist Yugoslavia*. Bloomington: Indiana University Press, 1977.
Sher, Gerson (ed.), *Marxist Humanism and Praxis*. Buffalo: Prometheus Books, 1978.
Snitow, Ann et al. (eds), *The Powers of Desire*. New York: Monthly Review Press, 1983.
Stauber, Leland, *A New Program for Democratic Socialists: Lessons from Market-Planning Experience in Austria*. Carbondale: Four Willows Press, 1987.
Stearns, Peter, *Revolutionary Syndicalism and French Labor*. New Brunswick: Rutgers University Press, 1971.
Stevens, John, *The Transition from Capitalism*. London: Macmillan, 1979.
Stojanovic, Svetozar, *Between Ideals and Reality: A Critique of Socialism and its Future*. New York: Oxford University Press, 1973.
Sweezy, Paul, *Post-Revolutionary Society*. New York: Monthly Review Press, 1980.
Tarabi, Azar and Nanid Yeganeh (eds), *In the Shadow of Islam: The Women's Movement in Iran*. London: Zed Press, 1984.
Thompson, E.P., *The Heavy Dancers*. New York: Pantheon, 1985.
Tilford, Richard (ed.), *The Ostpolitik and Political Change in Germany*. London: Saxon House, 1975.
Tomasevic, Jozo, *War and Revolution in Yugoslavia*, vol.1 *The Chetniks*, vol. 2 *The Ustashi*. Stanford: Stanford University Press, 1975.
Touraine, Alain, *The May Movement: Revolt and Reform*. New York: Random House, 1971.
Trotsky, Leon, *The First Five Years of the Communist International*. New York: Pioneer Publishers, 1953.
Trotsky, Leon, *The Third International After Lenin*. New York: Pioneer Publishers, 1936.
Trotsky, Leon, *The Revolution Betrayed*. New York: Pioneer Publishers, 1945.

Van Pilj, Kees, *The Making of an Atlantic Ruling Class*. London: Verso Books, 1984.
Walker, Pat (ed.), *Between Labor and Capital*. Boston: South End Press, 1979.
West, Cornel, *Prophesy Deliverance: Afro-American Revolutionary Christianity*. New York: Westminster Press, 1982.
Willet, Peter, *The Non-Aligned in Havana*. New York: St Martin's Press, 1981.
Wood, Ellen, *The Retreat from Class*. London: Verso Books, 1986.
Yanov, Anatoly, *Detente after Brezhnev*. Berkeley: Institute of International Studies, University of California, 1977.

Index